The Hidden Places of Withdrawn
LINCOLNSHIRE
and
NOTTINGHAMSHIRE

By
David Gerrard

ii

Published by:
Travel Publishing Ltd
7a Apollo House, Calleva Park
Aldermaston, Berks, RG7 8TN

ISBN 1-902-00766-2

© Travel Publishing Ltd

First Published:	*1989*	*Fourth Edition:*	*1996*
Second Edition:	*1993*	*Fifth Edition:*	*1999*
Third Edition:	*1994*	*Sixth Edition:*	*2001*

HIDDEN PLACES REGIONAL TITLES

Cambs & Lincolnshire	Chilterns
Cornwall	Derbyshire
Devon	Dorset, Hants & Isle of Wight
East Anglia	Gloucestershire & Wiltshire
Heart of England	Hereford, Worcs & Shropshire
Highlands & Islands	Kent
Lake District & Cumbria	Lancashire & Cheshire
Lincolnshire & Nottinghamshire	Northumberland & Durham
Somerset	Sussex
Thames Valley	Yorkshire

HIDDEN PLACES NATIONAL TITLES

England	Ireland
Scotland	Wales

Printing by: Scotprint, Haddington
Maps by: © Maps in Minutes ™ (2000)   © Crown Copyright, Ordnance Survey 2001
Editor: David Gerrard
Cover Design: Lines & Words, Aldermaston
Cover Photographs: Church of the Lord Tennyson Association, Sowerby, Lincolnshire;
Grimsthorpe Castle, Lincolnshire; Bricklands, Sherwood Forest,
Nottinghamshire © www.britainonview.com

Foreword

The Hidden Places is a collection of easy to use travel guides taking you in this instance, on a relaxed but informative tour of Lincolnshire and Nottinghamshire. Lincolnshire, although it is the second largest county in England remains relatively unknown. It is a rural county and has some of the richest farmland in the country producing potatoes, sugar beet and flowers. The county has strong historical connections with Holland and Scandinavia and is blessed with many picturesque villages and towns such as the majestic county capital Lincoln, historic Stamford (proclaimed as *"the finest stone town in England"*) and Grantham, the birthplace of Margaret Thatcher. Lincolnshire also possesses an extensive coastline, which was the haunt of smugglers in the 17th and 18th centuries and is now the home of a number of traditional seaside resorts.

The county of Nottinghamshire is an interesting combination of rural landscapes and industrial history. The River Trent winds its way through much of Nottinghamshire and forms an attractive backdrop to the historic city of Nottingham. The famous Forest of Sherwood still forms a green spine through the centre of the county. To the east are many pleasant villages set in rolling countryside whilst to the west are the mining towns,and villages which are very much a part of this county's industrial heritage. Both counties are a haven for "hidden places" and the book provides the reader with plenty of interesting historical facts and stories.

This edition of *The Hidden Places of Lincolnshire and Nottinghamshire* is published *in full colour*. All *Hidden Places* titles are now published in colour which ensures that readers can properly appreciate the attractive scenery and impressive places of interest in this county and, of course, in the rest of the British Isles. We do hope that you like the new format.

Our books contain a wealth of interesting information on the history, the countryside, the towns and villages and the more established places of interest in these counties. But they also promote the more secluded and little known visitor attractions and places to stay, eat and drink many of which are easy to miss unless you know exactly where you are going.

We include hotels, inns, restaurants, public houses, teashops, various types of accommodation, historic houses, museums, gardens, garden centres, craft centres and many other attractions throughout the area, all of which are comprehensively indexed. Most places are accompanied by an attractive photograph and are easily located by using the map at the beginning of each chapter. We do not award merit marks or rankings but concentrate on describing the more interesting, unusual or unique features of each place with the aim of making the reader's stay in the local area an enjoyable and stimulating experience.

Whether you are visiting the area for business or pleasure or in fact are living in the counties we do hope that you enjoy reading and using this book. We are always interested in what readers think of places covered (or not covered) in our guides so please do not hesitate to use the reader reaction forms provided to give us your considered comments. We also welcome any general comments which will help us improve the guides themselves. Finally if you are planning to visit any other corner of the British Isles we would like to refer you to the list of other *Hidden Places* titles to be found at the rear of the book and to the Travel Publishing website at www.travelpublishing.co.uk.

Travel Publishing

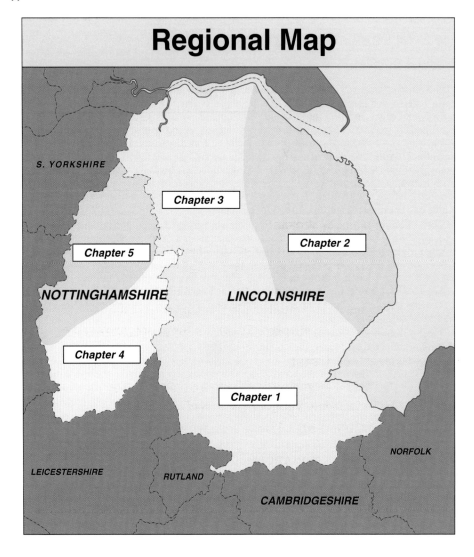

Regional Map

S. YORKSHIRE

Chapter 3

Chapter 2

Chapter 5

NOTTINGHAMSHIRE

LINCOLNSHIRE

Chapter 4

Chapter 1

NORFOLK

LEICESTERSHIRE

RUTLAND

CAMBRIDGESHIRE

Contents

1 South Lincolnshire and the Fens

The Elizabethan writer Michael Drayton must have deterred many of his contemporaries from visiting southeast Lincolnshire by his vivid word picture of the "foggy fens". It was, he wrote, *"a land of foul, woosy marsh...with a vast queachy soil and hosts of wallowing waves"*. It can't have been quite that bad - the Romans farmed extensively here, for example. Since Drayton's day, various drainage schemes, from the 16th century onwards, have reclaimed many thousands of waterlogged acres. The resulting waterways, often unappealingly called "drains", are today noted for the quality of their coarse fishing, particularly for bream, roach, rudd, pike and zander. Chub, gudgeon and carp are also plentiful. And the level terrain makes this area ideal for non-strenuous cycling. A useful leaflet available from TICs features 15 suggested routes ranging between 13 and 38 miles, most of them on minor roads with little traffic.

The area is remarkable for its wealth of outstanding churches. Crowland Abbey is now a moodily impressive ruin, but Boston's St Botolph's, the famous Boston Stump, still provides an unmistakable landmark for mariners and wayfarers alike.

And the fenland road from Spalding to the county boundary is famous for the string of modest villages all boasting magnificent churches. An attractive spring event is the Church Flower Festival when up to 20 parishes in South Holland bedeck their churches with glorious displays of spring flowers designed around a variety of themes.

Spalding itself of course is known around the world

Tulip Fields, Spalding

for its annual Tulip and Spring Flower Festival when a procession of floats, adorned with millions of tulip heads, progresses through the town.

Until well into the 1900s, the flat landscape of the Fens was regularly interrupted by a wind or water-mill. Today, only two are still working in this part of the county - both near Boston and both well worth seeing.

The area is also well-provided with museums, amongst them Spalding's Ayscoughfee Hall Museum, housed in a lovely medieval mansion; Boston's Guildhall, with its Pilgrim Fathers connections; Gordon Boswell's Romany Museum near Spalding; and the unusual Museum of Entertainment at Whaplode St Catherine.

The landscape of the south-western corner of the county divides into two distinct areas. Grantham and Stamford lie in the gently rolling hills that form the continuation of the Leicestershire Wolds; while to the east, Bourne and the Deepings stand on the edge of the Fens. Historically, this has always been one of the more prosperous parts of the county, a wealth reflected in the outstanding churches at Stamford, Grantham and Corby Glen.

Babbling Brook, South Lincolnshire

The Great North Road, now the A1, brought Grantham and Stamford a constant stream of travellers and trade, a traffic whose legacy includes some fine old coaching inns. One visitor during the early 1800s regarded this as *"the only gentrified region"* of Lincolnshire. Belton House, Belvoir Castle, Grimsthorpe Castle and the breathtaking Elizabethan splendour of Burghley House are four of the grandest stately homes in England, while the Victorian extravaganza of Harlaxton Manor is almost unique in its unrestrained mock-medieval exuberance. Isaac Newton's birthplace, Woolsthorpe Manor, is on a much more modest scale but fascinating as the home of the great scientist who was recently voted "Man of the Last Millennium".

SOUTH LINCOLNSHIRE AND THE FENS

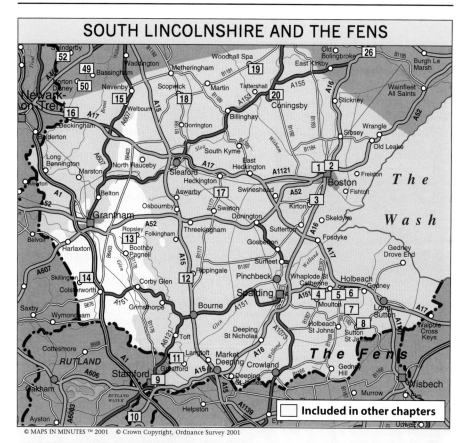

© MAPS IN MINUTES ™ 2001   © Crown Copyright, Ordnance Survey 2001

PLACES TO STAY, EAT, DRINK AND SHOP

BILLINGHAM'S

47 Wide Bar Gate, Boston, Lincolnshire PE21 6SH
Tel: 01205 311811

Conveniently located right in the heart of the town, close to the large car park where the Wednesday and Saturday markets are held, **Billingham's** is a combined bakery and tea rooms where the delicious aroma of fresh baking wafts through the bright and cheerful rooms.

The 26-seater restaurant serves an appetising selection of meals, snacks and teatime treats with the delicious home made cakes a major attraction. Also popular are the hot puddings which include such traditional favourites as Spotted Dick, Jam Sponge & Custard and Apple Pie & Custard. The menu also offers a breakfast selection - croissants, cereals, eggs or beans on toast, toasted tea cake and mega baps. At lunchtime, tuck into a salad platter, ploughman's, more mega baps, jacket potatoes or one of the soups which is served with a bread roll fresh from the bakery at the rear of the premises. During the winter, the regular menu is supplemented by such Winter Warmers as Lasagne, Curry 'n' Rice and Pizza canoes.

At teatime, all year round, in addition to those marvellous cakes, there's also a choice of savouries. Rob Billingham, who owns and runs this quality tea room together with his wife Sally, is the master baker and his tasty breads can also be sampled at their sandwich shop at 56, Pen Street which is just around the corner.

NEW ENGLAND HOTEL

49 Wide Bar Gate, Boston, Lincolnshire PE21 6SH
Tel: 01205 365255 Fax: 01205 310597
e-mail: newengland@fsmail.net

The New England Hotel is situated only a short walk from the famous Boston Stump. It is a traditional town house hotel, full of character and warmth. It stands across from the Market Place which is busy with markets each Wednesday and Saturday. This is also the venue for the several special markets held in May and December, and other fairs which take place throughout the year.

The hotel's traditional style restaurant, with its classical Roman columns and models of historic ships such as the *Mayflower*, is well known locally for its excellent cuisine which offers a wide choice of English and international dishes. The table d'hôte menu changes daily, there's a Carvery on Sundays and also an extensive bar menu. In addition to a wide range of beers and other popular beverages, the restaurant also boasts a long and interesting wine list.

The hotel has 29 tastefully furnished en suite rooms, all with modern facilities including internet access. The hotel also offers a wide range of services to guests on business. There are Conference Rooms available with differing capacities, and the hotel is experienced in catering for seated functions with up to 120 guests and buffets for up to 160.

BOSTON

An important inland port on the River Witham, Boston's fortunes reached their peak during the Middle Ages when the town was second only to London in the amount of taxes it paid. Today, it's a prosperous market town of around 37,000 inhabitants and the administrative centre for the region. The market, more than 450 years old now and the largest open air market in Lincolnshire, takes place every Wednesday and Saturday.

The town's most famous landmark is St Botolph's Church, much better known as the **Boston Stump**. "Stump" is a real misnomer since the tower soars 272ft into the sky and is visible for thirty miles or more from land and sea. Building of the tower began around 1425 and was not completed for a hundred years. The body of the church is older still - it dates back to 1309 and is built mainly in the graceful Decorated style of architecture. St Botolph's is the largest parish church in England (20,070 square feet in all) and its spacious interior is wonderfully light and airy. The church is noted for its abundance of often bizarre medieval carvings in wood and stone - a bear playing an organ, a man lassooing a lion, a fox in a bishop's cope taking a jug of water from a baboon. One of St Botolph's greatest treasures is a superb collection of medieval manuscripts which are housed in the Library above the south porch. Outside, on the church green, a prominent statue commemorates Herbert Ingram (1811-60) who served as the town's MP and also founded the Illustrated London News in 1842.

The Stump looks especially fine when viewed from the river. Boats can be hired from the Marina upstream and river cruises are also available.

Boston Guildhall Museum

One of Boston's most striking secular buildings is the 15th century **Guildhall** which for 300 years served as the Town Hall and now houses the town museum. The most popular attraction here is connected with the Pilgrim Fathers. In 1607 this famous band of brothers tried to escape to the religious tolerance of the Netherlands but were betrayed by the captain of their ship, arrested and thrown into the Guildhall cells. The bleak cells in which they were detained can still be seen, along with the old town stocks. Other exhibits range from archaeological finds to a portrait of the botanist Sir Joseph Banks, a local man who sailed with Captain Cook and later introduced sheep to Australia. A recent addition to the museum's attractions is a virtual reality simulation which permits visitors to

Boston Market and Town Centre

"walk" through Boston as it was in the 16th century. You can chat with a variety of local characters ranging from the Elizabethan composer John Taverner to Lord Hussey, Lord of the Manor and friend of Henry VIII.

Right next to the museum is **Fydell House**, a stately Georgian mansion which contains the American Room opened by the US Ambassador Joseph Kennedy in 1938. The house is now an adult education centre but visits are possible by appointment.

Another impressive building is the **Maud Foster Windmill**, the tallest working windmill in Britain and unusual in having 5 sails, or "sweeps". Visitors can climb to the top of the mill, see the machinery and millstones in action, and enjoy some fine views from the outside balcony. There's a tea room and a Mill Shop that sells the mill's own stone-ground organic flour as well as local books and souvenirs.

If you enjoy seeking out architectural curiosities, then there's a splendid one in a quiet back street of the town. The frontage of the **Freemason's Hall** represents a miniature Egyptian temple, complete with columns crowned by papyrus fronds. Half a century earlier, following Napoleon's Egyptian campaign there had been a spate of such monumental buildings, but Boston's temple, built in the 1860s, presents a very late flowering of the style.

For a town of its size Boston is well-provided with arts venues. The "Cultural Quarter" lies just south of the Market Place, beside the river. Here you'll find the spectacular **Shodfriars Hall** with its half-timbered 15th century gables overhanging the street, and the Old Custom House (1725) which now houses the Blackfriars Arts Centre. Nearby, a converted seed warehouse provides a spacious auditorium for the Sam Newsom Music Centre where concerts are held throughout the year.

The town itself hosts a wide variety of events, beginning with the **May Fair** in the first week of that month. The Summer Festival and the Boston Carnival with its Caribbean flavour both take place in June. July sees the "Party in the Park" with live musicians catering for every kind of musical taste, and also **Boston Bike Night** when motorcyclists from all over the country congregate here to show off both vintage cycles and the latest models. The year's festivities conclude with a Christmas market in early December.

AROUND BOSTON

SIBSEY
5 miles N of Boston on A16

Standing a mile west of Sibsey, the famous **Sibsey Trader Mill** was the last windmill to be built in Lincolnshire, back in 1877. Constructed by Saundersons of Louth, the mill is an impressive sight - six storeys high and with six sails. The mill closed in 1953 but has been restored to working order by English Heritage and is open to the public on certain milling Sundays. (Tel: 01205 820065).

STICKNEY
7 miles N of Boston on A16

There's a very strong French connection here. The poet Paul Verlaine taught French, Latin and drawing at the village school. Verlaine fled here from Brussels where he had been sentenced to two years hard labour for wounding his fellow poet Rimbaud. He left in 1876, apparently depressed by the English climate but otherwise in good spirits.

A mile further up the A16 is Stickford, home of the **Allied Forces Museum**, a large private collection of World War II and post-war British and American military vehicles. The display includes personnel carriers, tracked vehicles, field guns and motorcycles.

FREISTON
3 miles E of Boston off A52

Freiston takes its name from the Frieslanders who settled here in Saxon times. At that time their colony was on the coast but the sea is now 2 miles distant. In the mid-1700s, Freiston Shore was quite a popular bathing resort for the leisured classes and a palatial hotel was built near the beach. The hotel is still there but several fields now separate it

from the sea. Interestingly, Freiston Shore's patrons deserted it for Skegness - because it was quieter there.

In Freiston itself the most remarkable building is the grand Perpendicular church. It has a striking clerestory with 8 huge windows and, inside, a beautifully carved font cover.

FISHTOFT
3 miles SE of Boston off A52

This tiny village has just one claim to fame. It was from an obscure creek near the village that the Pilgrim Fathers made their first attempt to escape England's oppressive religious laws. A simple monument is inscribed with the words:

Near this place in September 1607 those later known as the Pilgrim Fathers set sail on their first attempt to find religious freedom across the seas.

KIRTON
3 miles S of Boston on B1397

The large village of Kirton was once a market town but its market faded away in the early 1800s. However, the old market place still provides an open area just across from the church. The church itself is very large and originally was larger still. The story goes that when restoration was under way around 1804, the architect decided to remove a portion of the old building with gunpowder. He misjudged the quantity of explosive and managed to demolish a goodly part of the chancel.

About 30 years earlier, Kirton was at the heart of the anti-drainage riots. In the winter of 1763, all 22,000 acres of Holland Fen were flooded, causing immense economic disruption. The Government passed an Act authorising the draining and enclosure of the fen. Local people, fearing that their livelihoods were at risk, rioted. Sluices were destroyed, fences ripped up and at one point a mob of

STAG & PHEASANT

1 High Street, Kirton, Boston,
Lincolnshire PE20 1DR
Tel: 01205 724198

Located in the heart of this large village,
close to the impressive church of St Peter
and St Paul, the **Stag & Pheasant** was
originally built as a public house around
1850 with large dormitories on the first
and second floors to accommodate farm
workers.

Today, this welcoming hostelry, owned
and run by Yvonne Gerard, has been
completely renovated, the former
dormitories now provide 5 comfortable
bed & breakfast guest rooms, (3 of them en suite), while the ground floor is now a spacious open plan
bar. Part of this area is a non-smoking restaurant serving a good choice of main meals and snacks. The
specialities of the house are its delicious home made burgers which are available in a choice of regular
and Manly sizes! An All Day Breakfast is also served and to accompany your meal there's a wide range
of real ales, draught beers and all the popular beverages. Customers can enjoy their refreshments
either in the bar with its open wood fire or, in good weather, on the pleasant patio.

If you are visiting the Stag & Pheasant on a Friday evening, you'll usually find live entertainment
on the programme, and if you are taking advantage of the inn's accommodation there's plenty to do
and see in the neighbourhood. The Lincolnshire Cycle Path passes close by and the historic town of
Boston with its famous church, the Boston Stump, is just a couple of miles or so up the road.

around a thousand were only prevented
from putting Boston to the torch by the
presence of the Scots Greys. The drainage
project went ahead and its enormous
benefits became plain for all to see. When
another drainage scheme, for **Wildmore
Fen**, was proposed a few years later the
work took place without trouble.

SWINESHEAD
7 miles SW of Boston on A52

Swineshead is one of only a couple of
Lincolnshire villages to get a mention in
Shakespeare, although the Bard did
misname it "Swinstead". The reference
occurs in Act V, Scene VII of *King John*.
The king has just lost all his treasure and
baggage while crossing The Wash and is
resting in the orchard of "Swinstead
Abbey". John did in fact stay at the
Cistercian Abbey for a few hours on
October 12th, 1216, before riding on to
Newark where he died a week later.

During the Reformation, the Abbey was
almost completely destroyed and much of
the fabric was used to build the present
private house which still bears the name
"Swinstead Abbey".

DONINGTON
10 miles SW of Boston on A52

A small market town, Donington boasts
some elegant Georgian buildings,
amongst them the former Grammar
School, and a huge church which was
bountifully re-endowed in the 14th
century when Donington was flourishing
as the centre of trade in flax and hemp.
Like Deeping St James, mentioned earlier,
the church has its own rather elegant
hude, or movable hut. If inclement
weather co-incided with a burial, the hut
would be moved to the graveside.
Standing inside the shelter (complete with
its own coat hook) the parson could
smugly observe the mourners being

drenched. Inside the church there are a number of memorials to the Flinders family. Their most famous son, Matthew, was born at Donington in 1774 and later became celebrated for his exploration of the Australian coastline. Returning from Australia to England via the Indian Ocean in a decrepit ship, Flinders put in at Mauritius for repairs. At that time, Mauritius was governed by the French who had watched British expansion in Australasia with alarm. They arrested Flinders as a spy and it was seven long years before they allowed him to continue his journey back to England and his home town of Donington.

SPALDING

This small market town is known around the world for its annual Flower Parade which attracts half a million visitors each year. Established in 1959, the Festival is held in early May when marching bands lead a succession of colourful floats, each adorned with thousands of tulip heads and spring flowers, through the town. The floats are then displayed at **Springfield Gardens** whose 30 landscaped acres include marvellous show gardens, a carp lake and a sub-tropical palm house.

The two weeks around the **Flower Parade** co-incide with the **South Holland Arts Festival** featuring open air concerts, workshops, exhibitions and a host of other activities and performances. The festival is based on the South Holland Centre, a stylish venue which is active throughout the year and also has a café-bar on the first floor overlooking the Market Place.

Spalding itself is an interesting place to stroll around, with Georgian terraces lining the River Welland and with many of the buildings revealing Dutch architectural influences. Before the days of

mass car ownership, most visitors to the Tulip Festival arrived by excursion trains and a great mesh of sidings stretch to the north of the town. To cross them, the longest iron footbridge in Lincolnshire was built. Two, actually, because another equally impressive construction stands south of the station, spanning the main line and a now defunct branch line.

The present parish church of St Mary & St Nicholas was built on a cathedral scale as part of the Benedictine Priory that existed in Spalding from 1051 to its dissolution in the 1530s. By that time the church was in a ruinous condition and there are reports of elaborate plays being performed in the **Sheep Market** to raise funds for its repair. Later, the St Thomas Chapel served as the town's Grammar School. The Victorians carried out some "improvements" in the 1860s and more

Springfield Gardens, Spalding

recent additions include some modern stained glass windows and decorations on the chancel ceiling.

The jewel in Spalding's crown, however, is undoubtedly **Ayscoughfee Hall Museum and Gardens**, a well-preserved medieval mansion standing in attractive gardens by the river and with some venerable Yew tree walks. Pronounced "Asscuffy", the Hall was built around 1429 for Sir Richard Aldwyn. It later became the home of Maurice Johnson (1688-1755), a member of the Royal Society and a leading figure in the intellectual life of his day. In 1710, he founded the Gentlemen's Society of Spalding which still flourishes from its headquarters and small museum in Broad Street. Part of the Gentlemen's extensive collection of stuffed birds, dating back to 1800, is on display in Ayscoughfee Hall which also has a prominent exhibit honouring the explorer and oceanographer Capt. Matthew Flinders who has been mentioned earlier under his birthplace in Donington. Other galleries record Spalding's social and economic history.

Located in the lovely grounds of Ayscoughfee Hall is **Spalding's War Memorial** which stands at one end of an ornamental pool which in winters past would freeze over. Blocks of ice were hewn from it and stored in the icehouse which still survives, tucked away in a corner of the garden walls.

Connoisseurs of odd buildings should make their way down a lane off Cowbit Road to a red brick building that belongs to no recognisable school of architecture. Known as the **Tower House**, it was built in Victorian times but no one has any idea who built it, why or exactly when. It's a bizarre medley of medieval towers and crenellations, a random obelisk, Georgian-style windows and other bits and pieces. One writer described it as being " *like a giant Lego construction*". It is now a private house but the exterior can be enjoyed from the lane.

On the outskirts of the town can be seen more of Spalding's industrial heritage. The **Pode Hole Pumping Station** preserves one of the steam engines installed in 1825 to drain the local fens.

A couple of miles south of Spalding, the **Gordon Boswell Romany Museum** has a colourful collection of Romany Vardos (caravans), carts and harnesses along with an extensive display of Romany photographs and sketches covering the last 150 years. A slide show and conducted tour are available and there's also a fortune telling tent. Gordon Boswell and his wife Margaret also arrange Romany Days Out in a horse-drawn Vardo, a trip which includes a meal cooked over a traditional Romany stick fire. The museum is open from March to October but closed on Mondays (except Bank Holidays) and Tuesdays.

AROUND SPALDING

SURFLEET
4 miles N of Spalding off A16

The River Glen provides an attractive feature in this popular village with its yachts on the water and holiday homes on the banks. Surfleet church has a tower that leans at an alarming angle, more than 6ft out of true, the result of subsidence in the boggy ground. The north door is pockmarked with musket shot, a permanent reminder of an unwelcome visit from Cromwell's soldiers during the Civil War.

PINCHBECK
2 miles N of Spalding on the B1356

For an interesting insight into how the **South Holland Fen** has been transformed by man, a visit to the **Pinchbeck Engine**

and Land Drainage Museum is strongly recommended. The star exhibit here is the Pinchbeck Engine, a sturdy monster which was built way back in 1833. Each year for almost 120 years, up until 1952, the 20hp engine lifted an average of 3 million tons of water from the soggy fens at a rate of 7,500 gallons per minute.

In 1988 the Drainage Board and South Holland Council restored this superb piece of machinery and it now operates regularly, the centrepiece of the museum which is open daily from April to October.

Also in Pinchbeck is the **Spalding Bulb Museum** which follows the growth of the bulb-growing industry down the years with the aid of tableaux and artefacts, as well as audio-visual and seasonal working demonstrations.

A third attraction is **Spalding Tropical Forest**, actually a water garden centre but promising *"a tropical paradise full of plants, waterfalls, fountains and streams"*.

Spalding Tropical Forest

MOULTON
5 miles E of Spalding off A151

A large village with attractive tree-lined roads and parkland, Moulton once had its very own castle of which just a few lumpy mounds remain. It does however still possess a fine church with a splendid nave *"like an avenue of stone"*. Indeed, the road from Spalding to Kings Lynn, the

THE SWAN

13 High Street, Moulton,
nr Spalding, Lincolnshire PE12 6QB
Tel: 01406 370349

Standing opposite Moulton's famous windmill, **The Swan** is an attractive whitewashed building located in the heart of this large village just off the A151, about 4 miles east of Spalding. The oldest part of the inn, now known as the Elizabethan Bar, dates back to the 1800s and the olde worlde atmosphere created by its low ceilings, window seats and open fire is enhanced by the fact that the bar, tables and chairs were all constructed from a single oak tree.

There's a pool table here and the bar serves an excellent selection of real ales that includes Old Speckled Hen, Greene King Abbot and Marston's Pedigree. The other part of the inn houses a stylish 45-seater restaurant with a striking colour-coordinated decor in terracotta with a fleur de lys motif. Open every lunchtime (11am to 2.30pm) and evening (6pm to 9pm), the restaurant is well-known for its lobster dishes, fish specialities and an exceptional vegetarian menu. Children also have their own menu and there's an extensive wine list to complement the grown-ups' meals. Should you prefer something that's not listed, the Green family will be happy to provide it so long as you give them sufficient notice. Caroline and Kevin Green, aided by their daughter Claire and son Kirk, have made this traditional country inn a popular destination for *"a good meal out"* and also for weddings and other special functions when the large enclosed garden at the rear, weather permitting, provides additional space.

THE CROWN HOTEL

5 West End, Holbeach, Spalding,
Lincolnshire PE12 7LW
Tel/Fax: 01406 423941

Opposite All Saints Church with its curious tower flanking
the north porch, **The Crown Hotel** is also of considerable age
- the main building is around 300 years old and the cellars are
believed to be almost as old again. Many of the original beams
are still in place and the original fireplace now provides a cosy
seating area.

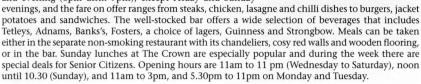

The Crown is run by a welcoming lady who has built up
the inn's reputation for good food and drink and comfortable
accommodation. There are 8 guest bedrooms, (2 doubles, 2
twins, 3 singles and 1 family), all of them en suite apart from
two of the single rooms, and all comfortably furnished. Guests
stay on a bed-only basis during the week, with an evening
meal offered instead of breakfast, but bed & breakfast is
available at weekends.

Quality food is served every lunchtime (noon until 2pm)
and evening (6pm until 9pm), except Friday and Sunday
evenings, and the fare on offer ranges from steaks, chicken, lasagne and chilli dishes to burgers, jacket
potatoes and sandwiches. The well-stocked bar offers a wide selection of beverages that includes
Tetleys, Adnams, Banks's, Fosters, a choice of lagers, Guinness and Strongbow. Meals can be taken
either in the separate non-smoking restaurant with its chandeliers, cosy red walls and wooden flooring,
or in the bar. Sunday lunches at The Crown are especially popular and during the week there are
special deals for Senior Citizens. Opening hours are 11am to 11 pm (Wednesday to Saturday), noon
until 10.30 (Sunday), and 11am to 3pm, and 5.30pm to 11pm on Monday and Tuesday.

THE RED LION

6 Spalding Road, Holbeach, Spalding,
Lincolnshire PE72 7HG
Tel/Fax: 01406 425534

Built in traditional red brick, **The Red
Lion** has been a pub for more than
170 years and is today a listed building.
The original indentures for the pub are
on display inside, along with copies
of old newspapers chronicling some
of the town's history. Low beamed
ceilings, open fires and dark wood
furniture all contribute to the old
world atmosphere.

The Red Lion is a family business
run by brothers George and Mark, and
Georges wife Dee, all providing a warm and friendly welcome. Dee is the chef and her menu is based
on fresh meat and vegetables supplied by local traders, with all dishes freshly prepared to order.
Specials include a 2 course set meal and a popular Sunday lunchtime Carvery. Dee's sweets are renowned
and include old favourites such as Treacle Sponge and Spotted Dick as well as Peach Melba or Black
Forest Sundaes. Food is served every lunchtime (noon until 2pm) and evening (6pm to 9pm, later at
weekends) and can be enjoyed either in the upstairs bar/restaurant or in the non-smoking restaurant
downstairs. A free house, The Red Lion offers a wide selection of beverages, including a well-chosen
selection of wines.

An unusual feature of the pub is the decor in the toilets where gents can study walls covered with
Beano comics, and ladies will find a display of theatrical memorabilia.

A151, is famous for its string of villages each of which boasts a church which is outstanding in some way.

WHAPLODE ST CATHERINE
5 miles E of Spalding on B1165

A great find here is the **Museum of Entertainment**, a fascinating collection of mechanical musical instruments, and gramophone and phonograph records. One of the stars of the show is a theatre organ brought here from the Gaumont Cinema in Coventry.

Museum of Entertainment

HOLBEACH
7 miles E of Spalding on A151/B1168

Located deep in the heart of the Fens, Holbeach stands at the centre of one of the largest parishes in the country. It extends some 15 miles from end to end and covers 21,000 acres. Holbeach is a pleasing little town with a market on both Thursday and Saturday and also boasts an impressive church with a lofty spire visible for miles across the flat fields. The curious entrance porch, with its two round towers, is believed to have been "borrowed" from the now vanished Moulton Castle, a few miles to the west.

When William Cobbett passed through Holbeach on his *Rural Rides* in the 1840s he was delighted with the *"neat little town,*

a most beautiful church, fruit trees in abundance and the land dark in colour and as fine in substance as flour". Surprisingly little has changed since William visited.

GEDNEY
10 miles E of Spalding off A17

Of all the fine churches in this corner of the county, **St Mary's** at Gedney is perhaps the most spectacular. It is supernaturally light inside, an effect produced by its magnificent clerestory in which the medieval masons reduced the stonework to near-invisibility. The 24 three-light windows drench the interior with light, brilliantly illuminating the carvings and bosses of the roof, and the interesting collection of monuments. The best known of these is a brass in the south aisle which depicts a lady who died around 1400 with a belled puppy crouching in the folds of her gown.

LONG SUTTON
13 miles E of Spalding on B1359

Long Sutton is a very appropriate name for this straggling village. St Mary's Church has an unusual 2-storeyed porch, the upper floor of which was once used as a school, and a rare, lead-covered spire 160ft high. A popular visitor attraction here is the **Butterfly & Falconry Park**. In addition to the hundreds of butterflies in tropical houses and daily displays of falconry, the park has an animal centre, honey farm, ant room, wallaby enclosure, insectarium and reptile land. A great place for a family day out, the park also provides a mini-assault area for the kiddies, a picnic area and tea room. The town is also home to a large Antique and Crafts Centre.

The surrounding area borders The Wash and is a favourite place with walkers and naturalists, especially bird-watchers. One of the most popular routes is the **Peter Scott Walk** - during the 1930s the

Butterfly and Falconry Park

celebrated naturalist lived in one of the two lighthouses on the River Nene nearby. Another route, King John's Lost Jewels Trail, covers 23 miles of quiet country roads and is suitable for cyclists and motorists. It starts at Long Sutton market place and passes Sutton Bridge where the unfortunate king is believed to have lost all his treasure in the marsh. Sutton Bridge itself is notable for the swing bridge over the River Nene. Built in 1897 for the Midland and Great Northern Railway, it is one of very few examples still surviving of a working swing bridge.

SUTTON ST JAMES
12 miles SE of Spalding on B1165

An odd survival here is a quite substantial medieval cross, its shaft supported by 3 buttresses. Known as St Ives Cross, it was at one time used by local women as a stall from which they sold dairy produce to passers-by. Also rather unusual is the

HERON COTTAGE

Frostley Gate, Holbeach Fen, Spalding,
Lincolnshire PE12 8SR
Tel: 01406 540435

Enjoying a quiet and peaceful location in the heart of the Fens, **Heron Cottage** is a small caravan park offering 28 touring pitches. Set on level ground beside the Little Holland Drain (river), the site provides excellent fishing from purpose-built stands. The 5-star facilities include a modern amenity block with toilets and free hot showers, electric hook-ups to all pitches, a disabled toilet and an information centre. Also available are fully equipped, non-smoking 2-berth holiday caravans at all-inclusive rates.

FOREMAN'S BRIDGE

Sutton St James, Spalding, South Lincolnshire PE12 0HU
Tel/Fax: 01945 440346 www: foremans-bridge.co.uk

Foreman's Bridge is located alongside the South Holland Main Drain which makes these two self-catering cottages ideal for keen anglers. Both cottages are beautifully appointed with high quality furniture, soft furnishings and fixtures so it's regretted that smoking and dogs are not permitted. Grebe Cottage has a lounge/kitchen, one double bedroom with a walk-in shower which is suitable for disabled visitors. Coot Cottage has a dining kitchen, lounge, one double and one twin bedroom plus a bathroom with a shower cubicle. Available all year, both cottages are equipped with television, radio, refrigerator, gas cooker and microwave oven, and both have a patio and parking area. E.T.C. 4 stars.

Crowland Abbey

The abbey buildings have suffered an unusually troubled history. Nothing but some oak foundations remain of the first abbey - the rest was destroyed by Danish invaders. The monastery was rebuilt in Saxon style in about 950 when the community began to live according to the rule of St Benedict. That abbey was also destroyed, on this occasion by a great fire in 1091. An earthquake in 1117 interrupted the rebuilding. Some 50 years later, the third abbey was completed, in the Norman style. Parts of this splendid building can still be seen, notably in the dog-tooth west arch of the central tower. Another fire caused massive damage in 1143 and the restoration that followed provides most of the substantial ruins that remain. They present an impressive sight as they loom forbiddingly over this small fenland village. Happily, the abbey's

village church where the tower stands separate from the chancel. The nave which once linked them was destroyed in Cromwell's time and never rebuilt.

CROWLAND
10 miles S of Spalding on the A1073

It was in 699AD that a young Mercian nobleman named Guthlac became disillusioned with the world and took to a small boat. He rowed off into the fens until he came to a remote muddy island, (which is what the name Crowland means). Here he built himself a hut and a small chapel. Guthlac's reputation as a wise and holy man attracted a host of visitors in search of spiritual guidance He died in 714 and shortly afterwards his kinsman, King Ethelbald of Mercia, founded the monastery that became known as **Crowland Abbey**.

Trinity Bridge, Crowland

former north aisle survived and now serves as the parish church.

Crowland is also noted for its extraordinary "Bridge without a River", also known locally as the "Three Ways to Nowhere Bridge". When it was built in the 1300s, **Trinity Bridge** provided a dry crossing over the confluence of three small streams. Hence its unique triangular shape. But the streams dried up and the bridge now serves no purpose apart from being extremely decorative. At one end, there's a large seated figure, possibly of Christ and almost certainly pilfered from the West Front of the abbey where a surprising number of these 15th century statues are still in place.

STAMFORD

Proclaimed as *"the finest stone town in England"*, Stamford was declared the country's first Conservation Area in 1967. Later, "England's most attractive town" (John Betjeman's words), became familiar to millions of TV viewers when its wonderfully unspoilt Georgian streets and squares provided an authentic backdrop for the BBC's dramatisation of George Eliot's *Middlemarch*. Stamford is a thriving little town with a wide variety of small shops, (including a goodly number of antique shops), and a bustling street market on Fridays.

A dubious local legend asserts that Stamford was founded in the 8th century BC by the Trojan king of Britain, Bladud, and continued as a seat of learning until the 14th century AD when it was supplanted by the upstart universities of Oxford and Cambridge. Whatever its past, what gives the present town its enchanting character is the handsome Georgian architecture, evidenced everywhere in private houses and elegant public buildings such as the Town Hall,

the Assembly Rooms, the theatre and the well-known George Hotel whose gallows sign spans the main street.

The town is also celebrated for its rich cluster of outstanding churches: **St Mary's** with its spectacular spire and marvellous stained glass; **St Martin's**, built in 1430 and a gem of the late Perpendicular style; and **St George's** which has a centuries-old association with the Knights of the Garter. It was re-endowed in 1449 by William de Bruges, the first Garter King of Arms, who gathered together the heraldic emblems of the 200 founder members of the Order. These were later incorporated into the great chancel window to create the most impressive collection of heraldic glass in the country.

Also well worth a visit is the 13th century All Saints Church, notable for its multiple arched wall arcading and semi-detached tower and spire. All Saints was extensively rebuilt in the 1400s by John and William Browne, prosperous wool merchants who are commemorated in the church by life size brasses.

Stamford's most ancient ecclesiastical building however is **St Leonard's Priory**, founded by the Benedictines in the 11th century and a fine example of Norman architecture with an ornate west front and north side arcade.

Secular buildings of note include Browne's Hospital in Broad Street which was founded in 1494 by the same Browne brothers mentioned above. It now houses the **Museum of Almshouse Life** - the ground floor presenting aspects of almshouse life; the upper hosting various exhibitions.

The town is well-provided with museums. The **Stamford Museum** (free) includes an exhibit celebrating one of the town's most famous visitors. Daniel Lambert earned a precarious living by exhibiting himself as the world's heaviest man. As an additional source of income he would challenge people to race along a course of his choosing. Daniel would then set off along the corridors of the inn, filling them wall to wall and preventing any challenger from passing. When he died at Stamford in 1809 his body was found to weigh almost 59 stones. He had been staying at the Waggon & Horses Inn and the wall of his bedroom had to be demolished in order to remove the body.

Other exhibits at the museum trace the history and archaeology of Stamford, including an industrial section featuring agricultural implements and machines, and the short-lived locally produced Pick motor car. Glazed Stamford ware was highly regarded in the Middle Ages and a collection forms part of the medieval display. It was manufactured in the town from about 850AD to the 13th century. Later, for a short period during the Victorian era, terracotta was produced: this too is on show.

Railway buffs will want to pay a visit to the **Stamford East Railway Station**. The station was built in 1855-6 for the branch line of the Great North Railway. Because the land was owned by the Marquess of Exeter, of nearby Burghley House, the architect William Hurst was obliged to build in the classical style using the local honey-coloured stone. The result is surely one of the most elegant small stations in the country.

A rather more specialised museum is the **Stamford Steam Brewery Museum** which has a collection of original 19th century brewing equipment. The museum is housed in the malt house and brewery which was established by William Burn in 1825 and continued brewing right up until 1974. It is now open to the public by prior arrangement.

Two more of Stamford's famous residents should be mentioned. Buried in the town cemetery is Sir Malcolm Sargent,

PENNIES FROM HEAVEN

17 Maiden Lane, Stamford,
Lincolnshire PE9 2AZ
Tel: 01780 481634

Heather Windsor had wanted to own a teashop since she was a child. Having worked for the previous owner for two years, she bought **Pennies from Heaven** in the autumn of 1998.

Part of a brick-built terrace of houses dating from the 17th century, it's a charming, cosy spot with 30s and 40s decor (hence the name), a picture of Bing Crosby, George VI coronation pottery, 1940s adverts on the walls, a 1930s dresser with a working valve radio, and pretty linen tablecloths with china cups and saucers to match. Heather makes all the delicious cakes (fruit, chocolate, carrot, Bakewell tarts), while on the savoury side there's a wide choice of sandwiches, plain or toasted, and light snacks. A home-made soup is available every day except Sunday, and children have a little menu of their own.

A chilling footnote: No.12 Maiden Lane, just along the road, was the home of John Haig, the 1940s acid bath murderer believed to have been responsible for the deaths of five women. Also close by is the town's Museum with its fascinating exhibit dedicated to Daniel Lambert who, when he died at Stamford in 1809, weighed 52st 11lbs (336kgs), and was believed to be the largest man who had ever lived until then.

Stamford Town Houses

windows. Clear glass was still ruinously expensive in the 1560s so Elizabethan grandees like Cecil flaunted their wealth by having windows that stretched almost from floor to ceiling. Burghley House also displays the Elizabethan obsession with symmetry - every tower, dome, pilaster and pinnacle has a corresponding partner.

Contemporaries called Burghley a "prodigy house", a title shared at that time with only one other stately home in England - Longleat in Wiltshire. Both houses were indeed prodigious in size and in cost. At Burghley, Cecil commissioned the most celebrated interior decorator of the age, Antonio Verrio, to create rooms of unparalleled splendour. In his "Heaven Room", Verrio excelled even himself, populating the lofty walls and ceiling with a dynamic gallery of mythological figures.

the "pin-up" conductor of the Henry Wood Promenade Concerts in the 1960s and '70s. The cross on his grave is inscribed with the Promenaders' Prayer. And in St Martin's Church is the splendid tomb of William Cecil, 1st Lord Burghley, who was Elizabeth I's Chief Secretary of State from her accession until his death in 1598. Cecil's magnificent residence, Burghley House, lies a mile south of the town.

"The largest and grandest house of the Elizabethan Age", **Burghley House** presents a dazzling spectacle with its domed towers, walls of cream coloured stone, and acres of

Burghley House

Burghley House

The eighteen State Rooms at Burghley house a vast treasury of great works of art. The walls are crowded with 17th century Italian paintings, Japanese ceramics and rare examples of European porcelain grace every table, alcove and mantelpiece, and the wood carvings of Grinling Gibbons and his followers add dignity to almost every room. Also on display are four magnificent State Beds along with

important tapestries and textiles.

In the 18th century, Cecil's descendants commissioned the ubiquitous "Capability" Brown to landscape the 160 acres of parkland surrounding the house. These enchanting grounds are open to visitors and are also home to a large herd of fallow deer which was first established in Cecil's time. Brown also designed the elegant Orangery which is now a licensed restaurant overlooking rose beds and gardens.

A more recent addition to Burghley's attractions is the **Sculpture Garden**. Twelve acres of scrub woodland have been reclaimed and planted with specimen trees and shrubs and now provide a sylvan setting for a number of dramatic artworks by contemporary sculptors.

Throughout the summer season, Burghley hosts a series of events of which the best known, the Burghley Horse Trials, takes place at the end of August.

AROUND STAMFORD

GREATFORD
6 miles NE of Stamford off A15 or A16

A charming little village where the River Glen flows gently past grey stone cottages, Greatford has some additional attractions for visitors. Around the village are dotted an extraordinary collection of carved

THE ROYAL OAK HOTEL

Duddington, nr Stamford, Lincolnshire PE9 3QE
Tel: 01780 444267 Fax: 01780 444369

Situated in open countryside with extensive views of the Welland Valley, **The Royal Oak Hotel** is a welcoming family-run hotel offering excellent food and comfortable accommodation. The restaurant serves morning coffee, bar meals, lunches and evening meals and the hotel has recently been upgraded to provide 6 superb bedrooms. Each bedroom has a private bathroom/shower and is equipped with colour television, tea maker, alarm clock and telephone. The historic town of Stamford is only 5 miles away, Rutland Water with its fishing, sailing and windsurfing about 10 miles, and the magnificent Elizabethan mansion of Burghley House also about 5 miles distant.

Hare & Hounds

Main Street, Greatford, Stamford, Lincolnshire PE9 4QA
Tel: 01778 560332

Just across from Butterbridge and the River Glen, the **Hare & Hounds** is a charming old hostelry dating back to the 1600s. The interior has some interesting olde worlde features, including an unusual Quaker bible chair and some stained glass windows but the major attraction at this free house is the imaginative food created and prepared by the owner Nick Hards. The seasonal menu changes frequently, with game dishes as a speciality, and the regular house beers (including Charles Wells, Bombardier, Eagle & Adnams) are supplemented by guest ales.

stones - obelisks, mushrooms, coronets, stone sofas, elephants and other bizarre objects. They date from the 1930s when the owner of Greatford Hall (private) had them carved for exhibition as garden ornaments at the Chelsea Flower Show in order to attract custom for his business. Also of interest is a fine Nollekens' bust in the church. It commemorates a local doctor, Francis Willis, who in 1788 cured King George III of his first bout of madness. Francis' sons, Robert and John, were also doctors and they successfully treated the king's next attack in 1801. At that time the Willis family ran a lunatic asylum in the village and another in the neighbouring parish of Braceborough.

THE DEEPINGS
8 miles E of Stamford off A16

There are four Deepings in all and they lie alongside the River Welland which here forms the county boundary with Cambridgeshire. The largest is **Market Deeping** which was once an important stop on the London to Lincoln coaching route. The triangular town centre has some imposing Georgian buildings, a large antique and craft centre, and a church dating back to 1240.

Today, **Deeping St James** merges imperceptibly with its larger neighbour. The old village sits on the banks of the Welland which at this point is controlled by two locks. The **Priory Church of St**

James is an impressively large structure and was originally built as a satellite cell of Thorney Abbey. Amongst its possessions is a *hude* - a small shelter rather like a sentry box which was designed to keep the Vicar dry when conducting burial services in the rain. Another interesting curiosity is the small square building in the centre of the village. It was originally the Market Cross but was converted into a lock-up in 1819 to contain village drunks and other troublemakers. Three semi-circular stone seats with chains can still be seen through bars in the doors. Incongruously, the rather elegant little building is topped by a graceless modern street lamp.

West Deeping has a picturesque main street running down to a bridge over the Welland. The two main buildings of note here are the 13th century church and, nearby, a Grade II listed, moated manor house that was once owned by the mother of Henry VII.

North of the village, on the other side of the A16, lie **Tallington Lakes**, a 200-acre site of water-filled pits where the action includes fishing, sailing and windsurfing.

BOURNE
10 miles N of Stamford on A6121

A small attractive town, Bourne has a fine church, an impressive Town Hall of 1821 with an unusual staircase entry, delightful

Memorial Gardens, and a variety of family shops, craft and antiques emporia, as well as modern shopping precincts. A colourful market takes place every Thursday and Saturday.

It was the springs of clear water that enticed the Romans to settle here. Today, the springs flow into St Peter's Pool from which a small stream known as the Bourne Eau runs into the town and Memorial Gardens. Here, willow trees border the crystal clear water, home to fish, wildfowl and small roosting houses. En route, the Bourne Eau passes Baldocks Mill which functioned between 1800 and the 1920s, and now houses the **Bourne Heritage Centre.**

Bourne's most famous son is undoubtedly William Cecil, Elizabeth I's chief minister and builder of the sumptuous Burghley House near Stamford. Cecil was born here in 1520 in a house that now forms part of the Burghley Arms inn. An earlier hero, Hereward the Wake, is also reputed to have begun life at Bourne. There's no doubt about a later celebrated figure, Raymond Mays, who was responsible for the pre-war ERA racing cars and the post-war BRMs. A rather less creditable figure was William Dodd, son of the Vicar of Bourne, who was born here in 1729. He became a man about town, popular preacher and chaplain to the King. But, falling into debt, he signed Lord Chesterfield's name to a bond for £4000 and was hanged for forgery.

When the town had its own branch railway line, the Bourne and Essendine Railway, it also boasted one of the most elegant stationmaster's houses in the country. The railway company acquired for this

purpose Red Hall, a fine Elizabethan mansion built around 1601 by a local merchant. Red Hall is now a community centre and functions building.

A mile west of the town, beside the A151, stands **Bourne Wood**, 400 acres of long-established woodland with an abundant and varied plant and animal life. Once part of the great Forest of Brunswald, it's a great place for walking or cycling, and has some interesting modern sculpture in wood and stone. The waters around Bourne and the Deepings are credited with curative properties and the Blind Well, on the edge of the wood, is reputed to be particularly efficacious in healing eye complaints.

About 4 miles south of Bourne, near the village of Witham on the Hill, stands the **Bowthorpe Oak** which is believed to be the largest in terms of its girth than any other tree in Britain. When last measured, the oak was just over 39ft around. The tree is hollow and it's claimed that on one occasion 39 people stood inside it.

GRIMSTHORPE
5 miles NW of Bourne on A151

Grimsthorpe Castle is definitely two-faced. Seen from the north, it's a stately 18th century demi-palace. Viewed from the south, it's a homely Tudor dwelling.

Grimsthorpe Castle

Grimsthorpe Castle Gardens

presence was tarnished by the adultery that allegedly took place here between Henry's fourth wife, Katherine Howard, and an attractive young courtier, Thomas Culpepper. In Tudor times, royal misbehaviour of this nature constituted an act of high treason. The errant Queen and her ardent courtier paid a fatal price for their nights of passion at Grimsthorpe Castle. Both were condemned to the executioner's axe.

The Tudor part of the house was built at incredible speed in order to provide a convenient lodging place in Lincolnshire for Henry VIII on his way north to meet James V of Scotland in York. The royal visit to Grimsthorpe Castle duly took place in 1541 but the honour of the royal

The imposing Georgian part of Grimsthorpe Castle was built in the early 1700s. The 16th Baron Grimsthorpe had just been elevated by George I to the topmost rank of the peerage as Duke of Ancaster. It was only natural that the new

THE BULL

3 High Street, Rippingale, Lincolnshire PE10 0SR
Tel: 01778 440054

The Bull in Rippingale is a classic English pub with an eye-catching whitewashed brick exterior and a warm and pleasant atmosphere within. Comfortably and tastefully furnished and decorated, it provides the perfect place to enjoy a relaxing drink or delicious meal.

Real ales available at this hospitable pub include Theakstons, John Smith's Extra Smooth and a choice of local ales. There is also a very good wine list ranging from French to New World vintages. The menu boasts a variety of home-cooked and freshly prepared dishes - everything from soups, sandwiches and salads to superb main courses such as grilled whole lemon sole, sirloin steaks, rack of lamb, Caribbean chicken and savoury vegetable pie, all of them sure to tempt the palate. The Sunday lunch is a particular gastronomic treat.

Booking advisable for Friday and Saturday evenings. Open: seven days a week; meals served at lunch and dinner.

Duke should wish to improve his rather modest ancestral home. He commissioned Sir John Vanbrugh, the celebrated architect of Blenheim Palace and Castle Howard, to completely redesign the building. As it happened, only the north front and the courtyard were completed to Vanbrugh's designs which is why the castle presents two such different faces.

There's no such confusion about the grounds of Grimsthorpe Castle. These could only be 18th century and were landscaped by whom else than "Capability" Brown. His fee was £105, about £100,000 in our money. In return for this substantial "consideration" Brown miraculously transformed the flat fields of south Lincolnshire into an Arcadian landscape of gently rolling hills, complete with an artificial lake and a sham bridge.

Seventeen generations of the Willoughby family have been Lords of the Manor of Grimsthorpe since they first arrived here in 1516. During that time they have borne a bewildering variety of other titles. All have held the Barony but at different times have also been Earls of Lindsey, Dukes of Ancaster and, later, Earls of Ancaster. The Willoughby genealogy is further complicated by the fact that the Barony is one of the very few peerages in Britain that can descend through the female line. A marriage in 1533 between the 49-year-old Duke of Suffolk and the 14-year-old Margaret Willoughby added yet another title, Duchess of Suffolk, to the Barony's pedigree.

GRANTHAM

In a radio poll during the 1980s, Grantham was voted *"the most boring town in England"*. It seems a rather unfair judgement on this lively market town set beside the River Witham. Turn a blind eye to the charmless environs that surround the town from whichever direction you approach. Make your way to its centre which boasts a pleasing core of old buildings. These cluster around the town's famous church, **St Wulfram's**, whose soaring spire, 282ft (86 metres) high, has been described as *"the finest steeple in England"*. When completed in 1300 it was the loftiest in England and is still the sixth highest. St Wulfram's interior is not quite so inspirational, dominated as it is by uncharacteristically drab Victorian stained glass, but the rare 16th century chained library of 150 volumes is occasionally open to the public and well worth seeing.

Just across from the church, **Grantham House** in Castlegate is a charming National Trust property, parts of which date back to around 1380. Additions were made in the 16th and 18th centuries. The house stands in 25 acres of garden and grounds sloping down to the River Witham and although the house itself is not open to the public there is a right of way through the meadows on the opposite bank of the river.

Also in Castlegate, look out for the only living pub sign in the country. In a lime tree outside the **Beehive Inn** is a genuine bee hive whose bees produce some 30lbs of honey each year. This unique advertisement for the pub has been in place since at least 1830.

After St Wulfram's Church, Grantham's most venerable building is that of the **Angel and Royal Hotel** in High Street. The attractive 15th century façade still bears the weather-beaten sculptured heads of Edward III and Queen Philippa over its central archway. King John held his court here and it was in one of the inn's rooms that Richard III signed the death warrant of the 2nd Duke of Buckingham in 1483.

Sir Isaac Newton

A hundred yards or so from the inn stands an unusual Grantham landmark. The **Conduit** is a miniature tower built by the Corporation in 1597 as the receiving point for the fresh water supply that flowed from springs in the nearby village of Barrowby. At the southern end of the High Street stands a monument to Sir Isaac Newton who was born nearby and educated at the town's King's School. It's an impressive memorial, cast in bronze from a Russian cannon captured during the Crimean War. Behind the statue is the ornate Victorian Guildhall (1869) which now houses the **Guildhall Arts Centre.** Originally, the building incorporated the town's prison cells but these now serve as a box office for the Arts Centre.

Just around the corner, the **Grantham Museum** (free) provides a fascinating in-depth look at local history - social, agricultural, industrial, and has special

exhibits devoted to Sir Isaac Newton, and to Lady Thatcher, the town's most famous daughter. When elevated to the peerage she adopted the title Baroness Thatcher of Kesteven - the local authority area in which Grantham is located. She still retains close links with the town and once declared *"From this town I learned so much and am proud to be one of its citizens"*.

There is another connection with the former Prime Minister in **Finkin Street Methodist Church,** just off the High Street. Inside this imposing building with its pillared entrance and spacious balcony is a lectern dedicated to Alderman Alfred Roberts, a Methodist preacher, grocer, and father of Margaret Thatcher who worshipped here as a child.

The Thatcher family lived over Alderman Roberts' grocery shop in Broad Street. For a while this became The Premier Restaurant but is currently unoccupied.

Margaret Thatcher was Britain's first woman Prime Minister, but Grantham can also boast another distinguished lady who was the first in her profession. Just after World War I, Edith Smith was sworn in as the country's first woman police officer. Edith was reputed to be a no-nonsense lady who made the lives of the town's malefactors a misery.

Before leaving the town, do try to track down the local delicacy, **Grantham Gingerbread**. It was created in 1740 by a local baker who mistakenly added the wrong ingredient to his gingerbread mix. The unusual result was a white crumbly biscuit, completely unlike the regular dark brown gingerbread. Traditionally, the sweetmeat was baked in walnut-size balls and until the 1990s was always available at Catlin's Bakery and Restaurant whose baker possessed the secret recipe. Sadly, Catlin's is now closed and Grantham Gingerbread is no longer easy to find.

AROUND GRANTHAM

BELTON
3 miles N of Grantham on A607/A153

"An English country-house at its proudest and most serene", **Belton House** stands in 1000 acres of parkland surrounded by a boundary wall 5 miles long. Built in 1685 of honey-coloured Ancaster stone and in the then fashionable Anglo-Dutch style, Belton was the home of the Brownlow family for just under 300 years before being given to the National Trust in 1983. The Trust also acquired the important collections of pictures, porcelain, books and furniture accumulated by 12 generations of Brownlows. With its Dutch and Italian gardens, orangery, deer park, woodland adventure playground and indoor activity room, Belton provides a satisfying day out for the whole family.

The adjacent Church of St Peter and St Paul is crammed with monuments to the Brownlows and their ancestors, the Custs, and includes a fine memorial to Sophia, Lady Brownlow, by Canova.

Anyone interested in follies should make a short detour from Belton to the village of Londonthorpe. The original purpose of the *"heavily rusticated stone arch with a horse on the top"* has long since been forgotten but it now serves as a bus shelter.

MARSTON
7 miles N of Grantham off A1

Marston is a village of redbrick houses, a 14th century church, almshouses and a fine manor house, **Marston Hall**. The Hall is the home of the Thorold family, one of the oldest in Lincolnshire. Pillaged and virtually destroyed by Cromwell's soldiers in 1643, it has now been restored as a family home with a wealth of family pictures and possessions. Visitors are welcome by appointment only, (tel: 01400 230225). If you do visit, look out for the summerhouse in the garden. It was originally built in the 18th century as a gazebo and restored in 1962 with its crenellations and pinnacles all in pristine condition. Inside, there are some delightful murals by Barbara Jones depicting phoenix, flamingos, penguins and her trademark owls, including an Owl and a Pussycat over the door.

OSBOURNBY
8 miles E of Grantham on A15

Set in rolling hill country, *"Ozemby"* is an attractive village with a pleasing mix of architectural styles from the 16th to the 19th centuries. The large church, unusually for Lincolnshire, has a tower rather than a spire and is also notable for its fine collection of medieval bench ends. Hanging on the wall of the nave are paintings of Moses and Aaron of which Pevsner enquires: *"Are they the worst paintings in the county? Anyway, one cannot help liking them"*.

FOLKINGHAM
8 miles E of Grantham on A15

Once a market town and an important coaching stop, Folkingham was also the venue until 1828 of the Kesteven Quarter Sessions which were held in the former Greyhound Inn facing the Market Square. Convicted prisoners were confined in the nearby **House of Correction** of which only the forbidding gatehouse-cum-governor's house survives. This surprisingly roomy edifice is now available to rent as a holiday "cottage" through the Landmark Trust. Also recalling the penal provisions of the past are Folkingham's village stocks which are preserved in St Andrew's Church. (The Greyhound Inn is now an Antiques and Craft Centre, open daily and with more than 50 stalls).

ASWARBY
9 miles E of Grantham off A15

Briefly a spa town, Aswarby was also the birthplace of the explorer George Bass who accompanied Mathew Flinders on his journeys to Australia, helping him to map the coast. Together with Flinders, Bass was the first to circumnavigate Tasmania and the passage between the island and the mainland, the Bass Strait, is named after him.

Aswarby Parish Church

THE ROPSLEY FOX

23-25 Grantham Road, Ropsley, Lincolnshire NG33 4BX
Tel/Fax: 01476 585339 e-mail: chrisspj@compuserve.com

Built in creamy-grey local stone and with a history going back to 1657, **The Ropsley Fox** presents a very inviting appearance with its steep tiled roof, shuttered windows and brilliantly colourful display of window boxes and hanging baskets.

The attractive traditional exterior, however, provides no indication of the wonderful and fantastical decor to be found inside. The main bar for example has a striking vaulted roof whose beams and supporting walls are hung with an eclectic display of memorabilia - bicycles, sewing machines, brass pots and pans, and even a giraffe perched on top of the bar with its Latin inscriptions in Gothic script. This begins to seem quite normal when you walk into the restaurant, a kind of baronial Hall where a vintage "bubble car" is parked under the eaves. In the inglenook fireplace, an old-fashioned "range" is flamed by a half-life size model of a gorgeously attired Oriental figure. Pool players can enjoy their game in a room decorated in the fashion of a Gentlemen's Club with a blue baize table, blue lamps and a blue carpet.

Quite apart from its unique decor, The Ropsley Fox is also well worth visiting for its excellent food and real ales. A typical menu might include trout, fish, duck and game dishes, a choice supplemented by daily specials which, if they prove popular, are added to the regular menu. Understandably, the restaurant is very popular so booking ahead is strongly advised. In addition to the main restaurant, there's a second dining area in a charming conservatory which leads to vast gardens where customers can enjoy their refreshments on sunny days.

This outstanding hostelry is owned and run by Paul Jarram, who was formerly with the Rolls Royce company in China, and his Chinese wife, Chrissie. A friendly and welcoming couple, they have made The Ropsley Fox a "not to be missed" destination for any visitor to this corner of the county.

ROPSLEY
6 miles E of Grantham off A52

Described in Elizabethan times *as "a considerable village remarkably situated as it were in a bason with hills all around"*, Ropsley was famous then as the birthplace of Richard Fox (1448-1528), a trusted advisor of Henry VII. Fox was appointed to a succession of bishoprics, two of which, Exeter and Wells, he never visited. But he did spend the last 12 years of his life in Winchester as its bishop. Fox founded Corpus Christi College at Oxford, and also established the King's School in Grantham where Sir Isaac Newton was later educated. The house in which Fox was born still stands on Ropsley High Street.

BOOTHBY PAGNELL
5 miles SE of Grantham on B1176

Boothby Pagnell Manor House is regarded as one of the most important Norman buildings of its kind still surviving in England. A Grade I listed building, the manor house is all that remains of a much larger mansion. The rectangular building with its two arched cellars and first floor Hall was owned by the de Boby, or de Boothby, family, hence its name. It is now the property of Lady Netherthorpe and open all year by appointment (tel: 01476 585374).

CORBY GLEN
10 miles SE of Grantham on A151

Until 1955 this hillside village was known simply as Corby: the "Glen" was added to avoid the rather unlikely confusion with the much larger town of Corby in Northamptonshire. A sizeable, stone built village, Corby Glen still holds an annual sheep fair in October, a popular event which first took place in 1239. **The Church of St John the Evangelist** is distinguished by a large number of beautifully preserved medieval wall paintings, including an 11ft high representation of St Christopher. Corby Glen's former Grammar School, founded in 1671, is now the Willoughby Art Gallery.

WOOLSTHORPE BY COLSTERWORTH
7 miles S of Grantham off A1 at Colsterworth

Recently voted "Man of the Last Millennium", Isaac Newton was born in 1642 in the modest Jacobean farmhouse, **Woolsthorpe Manor,** which has scarcely changed since he lived here. It was at Woolsthorpe that the "Father of Modern Science" later made some of his greatest inventions and discoveries. The Manor is now owned by the National Trust which has furnished the rooms to reflect life of the period and has converted a 17th century barn into a **Science Discovery Centre** which helps explain the achievements of one of the country's most famous men. Almost as famous is the legendary apple tree which helped clear Newton's thinking about the laws of gravity: the apple tree in the garden here is said to have been grafted from the original tree beneath which Newton was sitting when the apple fell on to his head.

A rather strange memento of the young Newton is preserved in the church at nearby Colsterworth. It's a sundial crafted by Newton when he was 9 years old. It seems odd to place a sundial *inside* a church and even odder to install it upside down.

SKILLINGTON
7 miles S of Grantham off A1

Tucked away in rolling countryside near the Leicestershire border, Skillington is a compact little village grouped around a green dominated by an imposing stone-built Methodist chapel of 1847. Nearby, **St James's Church** retains some evidence of its Saxon origins but is more interesting for its connections with two celebrated Englishmen. The first was Sir Isaac Newton who began his education in a small school held in the transept. The second was Skillington's Vicar in mid-Victorian times, the Revd. Charles Hudson. An accomplished mountaineer, Hudson formed one of the party led by Edward Whymper which, in 1865, was the first to reach the summit of the Matterhorn. Incredibly, one of the seven man team was a climbing novice and on the descent he slipped and fell. The rope linking him to the others snapped, hurtling five of the climbers onto a glacier 4000ft below. The Revd. Hudson was one of those killed and two windows in St James's Church record his glorious but fatal exploit.

HARLAXTON
4 miles SW of Grantham off A607

One of the most extraordinary architectural fantasies in the country, **Harlaxton Manor** was the brainchild of Mr Gregory de Ligne Gregory, a local landowner who spent many years acquainting himself with other stately homes across Europe before embarking on its construction in the 1830s. Built in glowing-white Ancaster stone, and on a colossal scale, the Manor combines Elizabethan, Jacobean and baroque styles to create an endearingly flamboyant result. The interior of Harlaxton, says Pevsner, *"must be seen to be believed. It is without any doubt the wildest and most fanciful mansion of the 1830s"*. Access to the Manor is limited however since it is now the British Campus of the University of Evansville, USA. The house is open for just two days in the summer; at other times, parties of 20 or more can visit by

THE BLUE HORSE

The Square, Skillington,
Lincolnshire NG33 5HB
Tel: 01476 860423

Overlooking the village green and directly opposite the church where Sir Isaac Newton attended school as a boy, **The Blue Horse** is a delightful old inn built in the attractive creamy- grey local stone and bedecked with hanging baskets of flowers. Originally three cottages, the interior features antiques, memorabilia and vintage pieces such as a well-preserved washer called a "Darling" which dates back to the late 1800s. Open fires, converted oil lamps and cosy alcoves where you may find yourself sitting alongside an antique sewing machine all add to the charm.

Mine hosts, Mick and Tarina, have made The Blue Horse a hub of village life and also one of the best eating places in the area. The chef has worked all around the world and her frequently changing menus offer an appetising choice of dishes based on local produce. Do try the house speciality, "Skilli Pie", a unique combination of steak, Guinness, onions, mushrooms and horseradish topped with puff pastry. The inn arranges various theme nights - Valentine's, a 40s Night, an Italian evening for example, when the whole place is appropriately decorated. There's also an attractive function room, ideal for small parties and conferences. In good weather, the lawn outside provides a perfect vantage point for watching activities on the village green or to admire Mick's vintage A35 van in its Blue Horse livery! (Please note that The Blue Horse is closed all day on Mondays).

appointment. However, the gardens, which have been restored to provide a horticultural "walk around Europe", are open between April and October, Tuesday to Sunday, and on Bank Holiday Mondays.

BELVOIR
8 miles SW of Grantham off A607

In Victorian times, the Dukes of Rutland could stand on the battlements of **Belvoir Castle** comfortable in the knowledge that, in whichever direction they looked along the pastoral Vale of Belvoir, everything in sight formed part of their estate, some 30,000 acres in all, (plus large holdings in other parts of the country). William the Conqueror granted this spectacular site to his standard-bearer at the Battle of Hastings, Robert de Todeni and, more than 900 years later, his descendants, now the Dukes of Rutland, still live here. Perched on the hilltop, the present castle looks convincingly medieval with its great tower, turrets and castellations, but it was in fact built in the early 1800s and is the fourth to occupy the site. The opulent interior contains some excellent paintings, including works by Gainsborough, Reynolds and Poussin, and the familiar portrait of Henry VIII by Holbein. In the 130ft long Regent's Gallery are some remarkable Gobelin tapestries, while other magnificent rooms display elegant Regency furniture, a dazzling ceiling copied from the Church of Santa Maria Maggiore in Rome, a dramatic array of 18th century weaponry and a monumental silver collection which includes a wine cooler weighing more than 112lbs. The castle also houses the Museum of the Queen's Royal Lancers. The grounds provide a marvellous setting for special events, amongst which the medieval jousting tournaments are undoubtedly the most colourful.

(Incidentally, Belvoir Castle lies just across the county boundary, in Leicestershire, but has always been

Jousting, Belvoir Castle

regarded as a Lincolnshire attraction. Another stately home, Burghley House, historically belongs to Lincolnshire but was transported over the border into Cambridgeshire during the Local Government reorganisation of 1974).

SLEAFORD

The history of this busy market town stretches back to the Iron Age. In Roman times there was a massive mint here, (730 coins were discovered in one dig), and when a railway was being constructed in

Victorian times a vast Anglo-Roman cemetery was uncovered. Later, the Normans built a sizeable castle of which only a small portion of a wall remains, but much of their other major contribution to the town, the **Church of St Denys**, still survives. Its tower, 144ft high and dating from around 1200, stands separate from the main body of the church, and is among the oldest stone-built towers in England. The interior is notable for the superb 14th century tracery in the north window, two magnificent monuments to the local Carre family, some stained glass by William Morris, and a striking rood loft restored by Ninian Comper in 1918.

Collectors of old inn signs will be interested in the **Bull and Dog** pub in Southgate. Set in the wall above its ground floor is a stone bearing the date 1689 and depicting a bull being baited by dogs. The scene is thought to be unique in the country and the stone itself the oldest surviving pub sign in England.

Sleaford also boasts one of the most unusual locations for a Tourist Information Centre. It is housed in **Money's Mill**, a 70ft high, 8-storeyed building erected in 1796 when the Slea Navigation canal allowed large quantities of corn to be brought by barge and offloaded right outside the door. On the eastern edge of the town, **Cogglesford Mill** (free) has been restored to working order and is open to the public. Probably built around 1750, the Mill contains an exhibition detailing its history.

Other features of interest in Sleaford include the 15th century Vicarage near the church, the landmark **Handley Monument**, a memorial erected to the town's MP in 1846 and reminiscent of an Eleanor Cross, and the Old Playhouse, purpose-built as a theatre in 1824 and now home to the local theatre company.

AROUND SLEAFORD

NAVENBY
10 miles NW of Sleaford on A607

One of the county's most unexpected attractions is **Mrs Smith's Cottage**, just off the High Street of this village where Hilda Mary Craven was born on October 28th, 1892. After spending her childhood in Navenby, Hilda moved out of the county but returned in the 1920s to live in a tiny cottage in East Road. At the age of 64 she married, becoming Mrs Smith, but her husband Joseph died less than 4 years later. Hilda stayed on in the cottage, resisting any change she thought unnecessary, until she was 103. During her 80 years of living here, she created a spellbinding time warp. The original ladder access to the first floor is still in place; Hilda's rocking chair and shawl still remain in her favourite place by the

View from Escarpment, Wellingore

range; the original outside privy and washhouse can still be viewed. Opening times are restricted: for more details telephone 01529 414294.

WELBOURN
9 miles NW of Sleaford off A607

This pleasant village has two parallel streets forming a cul-de-sac off the A607 Lincoln to Grantham road. A few earthworks betray the site of a 12th century castle, there's a handsome 17th century Manor House, and a fine 14th century church with a crocketed spire. A memorial tablet inside the church honours a famous soldier who was born, in 1860, in a small house at the other end of the village. At the age of 17, William Robertson joined the Army as a private. His aptitude and diligence marked him out as a rising man. William's career steadily progressed and he became the first man ever to serve in every rank of

the British Army, an astonishing record that culminated in his appointment as Commander-in-Chief of the British Army of the Rhine in 1919. By now Robertson was a Field Marshal, and a baronet, and the government also awarded him a very substantial honorarium of £10,000. He died in 1933.

NORTH RAUCEBY
5 miles W of Sleaford off the A17

Generations of RAF personnel have trained at the Royal Air Force College, Cranwell. When it opened on February 5th, 1920, it was the first Military Air Academy in the world and it later chalked up another first when a jet plane designed by Frank Whittle, a Cranwell graduate, took off from the runway here in 1941. In the nearby village of North Rauceby the **Cranwell Aviation Heritage Centre** (free) tells the Cranwell story and that of the other numerous RAF bases in the

JOINERS INN

High Street, Welbourn,
Lincolnshire LN5 0NH
Tel/Fax: 01400 272430

Located in the heart of this attractive village, a few miles south of Lincoln, the **Joiners Inn** is a traditional red brick building believed to be nearly 200 years old. The interior reflects its long history - old black beams, open fires at each end of the bar and lots of interesting memorabilia that includes vintage carpentry tools, a collection of jugs, another of old cameras and there's even a crossbow.

This friendly hostelry is owned and run by Cliff and Beryl Freeman who took over here in September 2000 but are familiar faces locally since they have been in the licensed trade around here for more than ten years. A free house, the Joiners stocks a wide range of quality beverages, amongst them real ales which are changed regularly and an excellent cellar. The small but excellent menu always includes one red meat dish, one white meat, one fish, one vegetarian and one special. Popular favourites are the Thai Fish Curry, the Beef Stew with Dumplings, and the Stilton & Leek Pie. There's also a good selection of light lunches such as soup, filled baguettes and ploughman's. Meals can be enjoyed either in the small, 18-seater dining area with its wood-burning stove or in the bar area. (Please note that food is not served on Sunday evenings, all day Monday, and Tuesday lunchtime).

BLACK SWAN BISTRO

Hillside, Beckingham,
Lincolnshire LN5 0RQ
Tel: 01636 626474

Located just off the A17, about 5 miles east of Newark, the **Black Swan Bistro** is owned and run by Trudy Hallam and Nick Winter whose declared aim is "to serve the finest food in the area accompanied by specially chosen wines from around the world"

The family moved here in March 1999 and to judge by the popularity of their charming bistro, a former inn set beside the River Witham, they have clearly achieved their aim. Nick is the chef and his dishes, based on French and modern English quality cuisine, all have a distinctive flair. Both the à la carte and table d'hôte menus change according to season. Winter main courses include Loin of Venison served with Poivrade Sauce & Blackcurrants, and melt-in-the-mouth Rolled Fillets of Plaice with a smoked salmon & chive sauce. Amongst the popular desserts are Bread & Butter Pudding with Crème Anglaise, and Chestnut Bavarois with chocolate sauce. To complement your meal, there's an excellent wine list, which is predominantly French but also offers other European and New World wines.

Guests can enjoy a pre-dinner drink in a comfortable lounge area with a large open fire before taking a table in the non-smoking restaurant with its old beams. Sparkling silver and glassware, crisp linen tablecloths, and courteous and efficient staff, all add to the appeal of this outstanding eating place.

THE NAGS HEAD

2 The Green, Helpringham, Sleaford,
Lincolnshire NG34 0RJ
Tel: 01529 421274

Just along the road from Helpringham's splendid medieval church and facing the village green is **The Nags Head**, an inviting-looking traditional inn with a reputation for serving excellent food and well-maintained real ales. Hanging baskets and window boxes of flowers add colour to the whitewashed exterior during the summer months and there are picnic tables outside from which to watch life pass by on the chestnut-lined village green. Inside, old beams dotted

with horse brasses and traditional furniture create a welcoming atmosphere. Mine hosts, Paul Breese and Fran Horrocks, took over here in March 2000 and their success is due in no small part to the friendly staff - Pat, Sarah, Jan, Davina, Sue, Kirsty and Michelle, all of whom come from the village.

Quality food is served every lunchtime and evening, except on Sunday evenings and Monday lunchtime, unless it's a Bank Holiday. Tuesday evenings are designated as Lamb Steak Sizzler night, the Wednesday special is a 3-course Curry, and on Friday, Rump Steak Sizzler takes pride of place. There are usually 3 real ales on tap, along with a good choice of wines available by the glass or bottle. All the time-honoured pub games - darts, pools, dominoes and cards, are on hand and on Friday nights the inn hosts a Topical Quiz. In good weather, customers can enjoy the pleasant beer garden which has its own barbecue area.

region, with the help of photographs, exhibits and film. The museum is open Wednesday, Thursday and Sunday afternoons during the season.

BECKINGHAM
15 miles W of Sleaford on A17

This pleasant village on the River Witham has a fine church with a sturdy 15th century tower and a notable Norman doorway, and some handsome Georgian houses, including a stately former Rectory.

HECKINGTON
5 miles E of Sleaford off A17

There's plenty of variety and interest here, in particular the tall Church of St Andrew, the Victorian almshouses and the magnificent eight-sailed **Heckington Windmill** by the railway station. When built in 1830 the mill's sails numbered a modest five, but after storms damaged the mill in 1890, eight sails were removed from another mill nearby and installed here. The only surviving eight-sailed mill in Britain rises to five floors and was in use up until 1942. It is now owned by Lincolnshire County Council and can be visited on weekend afternoons, Thursday and Friday afternoons in the season, and at other times by appointment. A few steps away, the **Pearoom** is a contemporary craft centre housed in an old mill building four storeys high.

Heckington's other major attraction is its early-14th century **Church of St Andrew** which is famous for the wealth of stone carvings on its tower. Inside, there's an outstanding Easter Sepulchre on which medieval master masons depicted the events of Christ's Crucifixion and Resurrection. The same masons were also responsible for the nearby sedilia (stone seats), beautifully carved with scenes from village life and figures of saints.

SOUTH KYME
7 miles NE of Sleaford on B1395

A quiet village, well off the beaten track, South Kyme has two buildings of note: the Priory, built at the end of the 19th century and incorporating parts of a 12th century Augustinian community; and South Kyme Tower, a four-storey 77ft high tower built in the 1300s, which stands in solitary splendour in a field near the church.

BILLINGHAY
8 miles NE of Sleaford on A153

This substantial village on the edge of the Fens was once well-known for its springs which were reputed to have healing properties. Today, the main attraction is **Billinghay Cottage and Craft Workshop**, housed in an attractive limewashed and thatched 17th century cottage, and with a blacksmith's workshop next door.

DORRINGTON
5 miles N of Sleaford on B1188

Run entirely by volunteers, **North Ings Farm Museum** is a fascinating place where vintage tractors, stationary engines, a narrow-gauge railway and a small foundry are among the attractions. The museum is open Sundays during the summer and steam train rides are operational on the first Sunday of each month.

SCOPWICK
9 miles N of Sleaford on B1188/B1191

Stone cottages line the main street of this small village and a stream splashes alongside the road. In 1838, the Revd George Oliver noted in his booklet, *Scopwickiana,* that the stream invariably overflowed in wet weather making progress along the street possible only by means of stepping stones. This

THE ROYAL OAK

2 Brookside, Scopwick,
Lincolnshire LN4 3PA
Tel: 01526 320285

Standing opposite the beck that ripples through this attractive village, **The Royal Oak** is a charming old building of grey stone and pantiled roof. It has been dispensing hospitality to locals and visitors for some 250 years, ever since it was built as a coaching inn, and now enjoys the status of a Grade II listed building

Mine hosts, Angela and Stuart Robinson, took over here in February 2000. Both of them are Lincolnshire born and bred: Stuart worked as an agricultural contractor, Angela is an experienced caterer, a fact which is clearly demonstrated by the excellent food on offer. The extensive menu ranges from a mighty 16oz T-bone steak, through fish, meat and poultry dishes, to appetising salads, pasta and vegetarian options. The lunchtime menu also includes a wide choice of sandwiches, ploughmans, burgers and omelettes. Meals can be enjoyed either in the separate, non-smoking dining room with its open fire, or in the spacious lounge bar which also has its own open fire. To accompany your meal, the beverages on offer include real ales such as Tetley's bitter and a guest ale which changes regularly.

This friendly and welcoming inn also offers darts and pool, and is the unofficial "headquarters" of the village cricket team and the local Lotus Car Club whose members hold "Meets" here from time to time.

OGLEE GUEST HOUSE

16 Stanhope Avenue, Woodhall Spa,
Lincolnshire LN10 6SP
Tel: 01526 353512

The Oglee Guest House is owned and run by Tonia Oldham and naturally one of the first things her bed and breakfast guests ask is "What does 'Oglee' mean?" In fact it means "Our God loves everyone, everywhere".

The house is a fine example of an Edwardian property, with spacious rooms, a striking polished wood staircase and an interesting stained glass window on the landing. Guests are welcome to relax in the attractive, mature garden or in the large, comfortable residents' lounge, perhaps while enjoying a drink from the licensed bar.

The traditional English breakfast includes the choice of free range eggs and tasty Lincolnshire sausages but Tonia is also happy to cater for vegetarian and other diets. Packed lunches and evening meals are available by arrangement. There are 4 guest bedrooms - 2 family rooms (one with a balcony), 1 double, and 1 twin. Two of the rooms have en suite facilities, (the large family room and the double), the other two rooms share a spacious bathroom and shower. Children and pets are welcome - Tonia has her own pet, Millie, a delightful non-racing greyhound.

Oglee is conveniently close to many leisure facilities. Amongst them are the Woodhall Spa championship golf course, tennis, bowls, swimming, fishing on the nearby River Witham, and there are many attractive walks in the neighbourhood. In addition, no holiday in this area would be complete without a visit to the unique Kinema in the woods.

inconvenience continued until fairly recent times. The Revd. Oliver also recorded that the village's only ale house was kept in good order by a formidable landlady who permitted her customers no more than a couple of pints before sending them home to their wives.

Just south of Scopwick is **RAF Digby** which was the first Lincolnshire airfield to be attacked by the Luftwaffe in World War II. In the RAF Digby Operations Room Museum the wartime setting has been recreated, complete with plotting table, maps and personnel, and the airfield's story is told with the help of many exhibits, photographs and documents. Guided tours take place on summer Sundays: further details on 01526 327503

METHERINGHAM
9 miles N of Sleaford on B1188

Just outside this large, straggling village is the Metheringham Airfield Visitor Centre. This was one of many Lincolnshire airfields established by the RAF during World War II. A leaflet available from local TICs gives details of the North Kesteven Airfield Trail which includes Metheringham. Here, the Centre's exhibits, photographs and documents tell the story of the airfield and of 106 Squadron, Bomber Command, whose base it was.

WOODHALL SPA

Woodhall Spa is something of an anomaly – a chunk of the Home Counties transplanted to the heart of Lincolnshire. Surrounded by pine and birch woods, spacious Victorian and Edwardian villas are set back from tree-lined avenues and it's said that not a single house in the town is older than the 1830s. Woodhall became a spa town by accident when a

shaft sunk in search of coal found not coal but mineral-rich water. In 1838 a pump room and baths were built, to be joined later by hydro hotels. Here, real or imagined invalids soaked themselves in "hypertonic saline waters" heated to 40°C (103° F). The arrival of the railway in 1855 accelerated Woodhall's popularity, but by the early 1900s the spa had fallen out of favour and the associated buildings disappeared one by one. But this beautifully maintained village has retained its decorous spa atmosphere, pleasantly relaxed and peaceful, and also boasting a Championship golf course.

One interesting survivor of the good old days is a former tennis pavilion, now the **Kinema in the Woods**. When it was converted to a cinema during World War II, it inevitably became known as the "Flicks in the Sticks". It's one of very few back projection cinemas in the country and the entertainment on offer includes performances on an original Compton Organ. The **Cottage Museum** on Iddesleigh Road, also the Tourist Information Centre, tells the story of the establishment of the town as a spa resort.

Woodhall Spa had close connections with 617 Squadron, the "Dambusters", during World War II. The Petwood House Hotel was used as the officers' mess. Memorabilia of those days are displayed in the hotel's Squadron Bar, and in Royal Square a memorial to those intrepid airmen takes the form of a 20ft long model of a breached dam.

There are several sites of interest outside the town. To the north stand the ruins of a 15th century hunting lodge called the **Tower on the Moor**, built for Ralph, Lord Cromwell of Tattershall Castle. And, standing all alone on Thimbleby Moor in the hamlet of Reeds Beck, is a 36ft high memorial to the Duke of Wellington, erected in 1844 and topped by a bust of the Iron Duke. The column celebrates the successful cultivation of Waterloo Woods, an oak forest planted just after the battle in 1815.

At Kirkstead, off the B1191, stands a towering piece of brickwork, the only visible remains of a 12th century Cistercian Abbey. Close by is the fine 13th century Church of St Leonard, *"a gem of Early Gothic...with an interior like a cathedral aisle"* according to Simon Jenkins. Originally built as a *"chapel outside the gates"* for visitors to the abbey,

St Leonard's was closed in 1877, but restored in 1914 by the Society for the Protection of Ancient Buildings. Miraculously, its beautifully carved chancel screen has survived intact. Dating back to the 13th century, it is believed to be the second oldest such screen in England.

THE LEA GATE INN

Leagate Road, Coningsby,
Lincolnshire LN4 4RS
Tel: 01526 542370 Fax: 01526 345468
Website: www.theleagateinn.co.uk

The records show that **The Lea Gate Inn** is the oldest continuously licensed premises in the county. Built in 1542 as a Fen guide house, it stands at the start of the road across Wildmore Fen to New York.

The inn used to keep a blazing beacon attached to the gable wall on dark and dangerous winter nights to guide travellers across the treacherous bogs and marshes of the Lincolnshire fens. The bracket can still be seen. The yew tree in the garden is as old as the pub itself while inside, beams, real fires and lots of memorabilia create a lovely old-world atmosphere. The inglenook fireplace, priest hotel and evidence of the true stories about nearby Gibbets Nook and its highwaymen, the bar is absolutely soaked in atmosphere and history.

In the separate restaurant, once stables and barns, a wide-ranging menu is available: house specialities include lasagne, chicken chasseur and the all-time favourite, Steak & Kidney Pie. Chef Marcus is always prepared to prepare your meal to your particular taste and preference. A selection of open sandwiches is available for quicker snacks and to accompany your meal there's a wide choice of great ales, fine wines and spirits. When the weather permits, refreshments can be enjoyed out in the garden where a feature pond is home to some beautiful koi carp. Children are very welcome, have their own menu and, outside in the secure play, there are swings and slides where they can burn off their surplus energy.

The pub has been in the family of current owners Sharon and Mark Dennison for 16 years. They have recently added 8 luxury suites, each beautifully appointed and each with its own individual style - from the Millennium Suite with its jacuzzi bath and 4-poster bed to the specially equipped suite for disabled persons which has wheelchair access.

A visit to the inn can easily be combined with an excursion to nearby Tattershall Castle, a striking red brick tower built in the 1440s by Lord Chancellor Ralph Cromwell.

AROUND WOODHALL SPA

CONINGSBY
4 miles S of Woodhall Spa on A153

The centre of this large village, which started life as a Danish settlement, is dominated by the church tower of St Michael, notable for its enormous single-handed clock; at over 16ft in diameter, this 17th century clock claims to be the largest working example of its kind. South of the village is RAF Coningsby, a major Tornado base and also home to the Battle of Britain Memorial Flight. Created in memory of the gallant airmen who flew in that crucial battle, the Flight operates a Lancaster, (one of only two in the world still flying), five Spitfires, two Hurricanes and a Dakota. These historic World War II aircraft are not just museum pieces - they are all still flying and can be seen at a variety of air shows during the summer months. Visiting them on their "home territory" however provides an added dimension and knowledgeable guides provide informative tours. The Centre is open throughout the year, Monday to Friday, and at weekends for special events. More details on 01526 344041.

TATTERSHALL
4 miles S of Woodhall Spa on A153

Tattershall lies on the opposite bank of the River Bain from Coningsby and is known all over the world for the astonishing keep of **Tattershall Castle**. Its 6 storeys rise 110ft, a huge rectangular slab built in local red brick. In the 1400s it must have appeared even more formidable than it does now. Construction began around 1445 on the orders of the Lord Chancellor, Ralph Cromwell, and it was clearly designed more as a statement of his power and wealth rather than for defence.

Military fashion had moved on from such huge Keeps and in any case the peaceful heart of 15th century Lincolnshire had no need for fortifications on this scale. Originally, the Keep was surrounded by a large complex of other buildings but these have almost entirely disappeared and the tower stands menacingly alone. Despite its magnificence, Tattershall had fallen into near ruin by the early 1900s. There was a very real possibility that it would be dismantled brick by brick, transported to the United States and re-erected there. Happily, the tower was rescued by Lord Curzon who bequeathed it to the National Trust on his death in 1925. In the shadow of the castle is Tattershall Country Park, set in 365 acres of woods, parks and lakes and offering all sorts of sporting facilities.

As well as this superb castle, Tattershall boasts one of the county's finest churches. **Holy Trinity** was also commissioned by Ralph Lord Cromwell. That was in 1440: the church was finally completed in 1480, long after Ralph's death. Constructed of Ancaster stone, this "glasshouse church" is dazzlingly light and airy inside, but because of its scale and the absence of all but a few adornments, more imposing than likeable. Amongst the items of note is a striking brass of Ralph himself, but sadly his image is headless.

2 The Lincolnshire Coast and Wolds

Stretching from Wainfleet and Skegness in the south to Cleethorpes and the mouth of the Humber to the north, the Lindsey Coastal Plain runs for about 40 miles, north to south, and extends between five and ten miles wide, east to west. The rich pastures of the plain produce excellent grass - for generations farmers would bring their cattle here to be fattened up before going to market. The area's other main attraction, the splendid sandy beaches running virtually the whole length of the coast, didn't come into their own until the railways arrived in the mid-1800s. The coastal villages of Skegness, Mablethorpe and Cleethorpes have grown steadily to become popular resorts for East Midlanders, each one offering a wide range of family entertainment.

There are few grand houses in the area. A notable exception however is the charming William & Mary-style Gunby Hall, near Spilsby, hereditary home of the Massingberd family. In Wainfleet is the impressive Magdalen College School of 1484 while Alford's Manor House, built around 1660, claims the title of being the largest thatched manor house in England. Alford also

Nettleton, North Wolds

boasts a majestic 6-storeyed working windmill and there are other, non-working, mills at Alvingham and Burgh le Marsh.

The area also includes the largest town in the county, Grimsby (pop. 92,000), once one of the busiest fishing ports in the world and now an important centre of the food processing industry. A striking reminder of Grimsby's days of glory is the magnificent Dock Tower rising high above the town.

The Plain offers a good range of animal sanctuaries and nature reserves, and there are some interesting connections with the Poet Laureate Tennyson and with Captain John Smith, founder of the State of Virginia, whose name is inextricably linked with that of the Indian princess Pocahontas.

One Victorian traveller who had spent some days in the Fens described her first sight of the Wolds as being like *"the first sight of land after a long sea journey"*. Although they never rise above a height of 550ft, these chalk uplands are generally regarded as the most picturesque part of the county. A continuation of the East Yorkshire Wolds, the hills extend some 40 miles in a tear drop shape, about 5 miles wide in the north, and broadening to about 15 miles in the south.

In the past, especially after the Danish and Saxon invaders arrived, the area was comparatively well-populated. The many place names ending in *–by* bear witness to those hardy colonists. Today, the Wolds are sparsely inhabited. The largest town, Louth, has a population of less than 15,000 while the pleasant little market towns of Horncastle and Spilsby register 4,200 and 1800 respec-

Vikingway Path, The Wolds

tively. Dozens of unspoilt villages are tucked away in the folds of the hills, sleepy little places whose quiet charm makes a visit to this part of the county particularly refreshing and relaxing.

There are no grand houses in the Wolds but scores of fine churches, most notably the Church of St James at Louth whose 295ft high spire is the tallest of any English parish church. We begin our tour in the north of the region at Caistor and travel southwards to Spilsby.

THE LINCOLNSHIRE COAST AND WOLDS

© MAPS IN MINUTES ™ 2001   © Crown Copyright, Ordnance Survey 2001

PLACES TO STAY, EAT, DRINK AND SHOP

SKEGNESS

In the early 1800s, when the Tennyson family used to visit Skegness with the future Poet Laureate, Alfred, in tow, it was still a tiny fishing village but already famous for its miles of firm sandy beaches and its "oh-so-bracing" sea air. As late as 1871, the resident population of Skegness was only 239 but two years later the railway arrived and three years after that the local landowner, the Earl of Scarborough, built a new town to the north of the railway station.

A huge pier, 1843ft long, was erected. This survived for almost one hundred years before a gale on the night of January 11th, 1978 left it sadly truncated. Other amenities provided by the Earl of Scarborough for visitors included the Lumley Hotel, St Matthew's Church and a grand promenade. The Jubilee Clock Tower on the seafront was added in 1899, and in 1908 the town fathers amazed even themselves by a stroke of advertising genius - their adoption of the Jolly Fisherman as the town's mascot.

The Jolly Fisherman has an interesting story behind him. In 1908 the Great Northern Railway purchased an oil painting of the plump and prancing fisherman for £12. After adding the famous slogan "Skegness is so Bracing", they used the painting as a poster to advertise trips from London to Skegness (fare, 3/- - 15p). Almost a century later the same Jolly Fisherman is still busy promoting Skegness as a holiday resort. There are two statues of him in town, one at the railway station, another in Compass Gardens, and during the summer months he can also be seen strolling around the town.

Naturally, the town is well-provided with funfairs - Bottons, Fantasy Island, and Butlin's, the latter two of which are actually in the contiguous town of Ingoldmells. It was in 1936 that Billy Butlin opened his very first holiday camp with the slogan "A Week's Holiday for a Week's Wage" - about £2.50 in those days. The price included accommodation, meals and entertainment and the holidays were understandably popular with workers - a new law had just guaranteed them a statutory week's leave with pay. Just three years later, World War II erupted and the holiday market imploded. But Billy Butlin still prospered. The government bought his camps to use as army barracks, appointed him Director-General of Hostels, and at the end of the war sold the camps back to him at a knock-down price. The camp is still operating, now named the Butlin's Family Entertainment Resort, and day visit tickets are available.

Alongside the obvious attractions of the beach and all the traditional seaside entertainment, Skegness and Ingoldmells have other places of special interest. **Church Farm Museum**, a former farmhouse, is home to a collection of old farm implements and machinery, re-created village workshops, a paddock of Lincoln Longwool sheep and a fine example of a Lincolnshire "mud and stud" thatched cottage brought here from the nearby village of Withern. Craft demonstrations can be viewed on most Sunday afternoons and a programme of special events - sheep shearing, steam threshing and so on, continues throughout the season. Teas and snacks are available and the toilets, complete with facilities for those with special needs, claim to be "the best in the area!"

Natureland Seal Sanctuary on North Parade provides interest and fun for all the family with its seals and baby seal rescue centre; aquarium; tropical house with crocodiles, snakes and tarantulas; a pets corner and Floral Palace and including a large greenhouse teeming with plant, insect and bird life, including butterflies and flamingoes. A popular attraction is the seal feeding which takes place four times a day during the summer months: twice daily in winter. There's also a Sea Life exhibit - a 25ft tank containing 5000 gallons of seawater and a ceaselessly rotating cast of performers that includes British sharks, rays, lobsters, crabs and other species of marine life.

On the northern outskirts of Ingoldmells, **Hardy's Animal Farm** is a working farm set in 7 acres of Lincolnshire countryside. Attractions include a large children's adventure playground, horse and cart rides, and children are welcome to feed, fuss over and make friends with all the farm animals. There's also a tea room and shop.

Serious birdwatchers should head south along the coast to **Gibraltar Point National Nature Reserve**, a field station among the salt marshes and dunes with hides, waymarked routes and guided tours.

AROUND SKEGNESS

WAINFLEET
5 miles SW of Skegness on A52

Formerly a thriving port, Wainfleet now finds itself several miles from the sea. Narrow roads lead off the market place with its medieval stone cross, making this a place you really have to explore on foot. Wainfleet is perhaps best known as the home of the family-run **Bateman's Brewery**, established in 1874. The original old copper, milling machines and mash tun are still in use and the visitor tour takes you through the whole brewing process from raw materials to tasting. The

former windmill is now a café/bar and there's also a beer garden set beside the River Steeping. Other attractions include a unique beer poster display; one of the most extensive collections of bottled beers in the world, (more than 4500 of them); a games room and shop.

The most striking building in the town is the former **Magdalen College School**, built in dark red brick in 1484 for William of Wayneflete, Bishop of Winchester and Lord Chancellor to Henry VI. William first founded Magdalen College, Oxford and later established the college school in the town of his birth. It continued as a school until 1933 but now houses the public library, a small museum, a tea room and a walled tea garden.

This attractive little town has a Friday market, held in the unspoilt Market Place with its Buttercross and Clock Tower, and amongst the variety of family-run shops here is one which offers an unusual culinary treat: - traditional fish and chips cooked on a coal range.

A curious feature lies about a mile south of the town, on the western side of the A52. Rows and rows of small, rounded mounds are all that remain of an important industry that flourished here from the Iron Age to the 1600s - the extraction of salt from sea water. Throughout these long centuries, salt was an expensive, but absolutely vital, commodity, both as a preservative and a condiment. During the Roman occupation of Britain, part of an Imperial soldier's remuneration was a pouch of salt - his *salarium*, or salary. When the mounds at Wainfleet were excavated in the 1950s they were found to contain *salterns* - low hearths surrounded by brick in which fires were lit to evaporate pans of sea water and leave behind the precious salt.

BURGH LE MARSH
4 miles W of Skegness on A158

Pronounced *"Borough"*, this small town was once the terminus of a Roman road from Lincoln. Although Burgh is now several miles inland, it was from here, centuries ago, that travellers boarded a ferry to cross The Wash and join the Peddars Way in Norfolk.

Burgh has two buildings of special interest to look out for. **Dobson's Mill**, 5 storeys high, has an unusual arrangement of five left-handed sails, was built in 1833 and worked until 1964. A year later the County Council bought the mill and it is now open to visitors on the second and last Sunday of each month. The majestic **Church of St Peter and St Paul**, almost entirely 15ᵗʰ century, is notable for its colourful clock face inscribed with the injunction *"Watch and Pray for Ye Know not When the Time is;* a fine peal of eight bells; some splendid Jacobean woodwork; and an impressive wooden eagle lectern carved in 1874 by the local barber and antiquarian, Jabez Good, author of *A Glossary of Lincolnshire*. The church is also prolific with carvings of that rather sinister pagan symbol, the Green Man. There are no fewer than ten representations of him on the wooden roof of the nave.

About 3 miles northwest of Burgh, **Gunby Hall** (National Trust) is reputed to be the setting Tennyson had in mind when he wrote of

"an English home – gray twilight pour'd
On dewy pastures, dewy trees
Softer than sleep – all things in order stored,
A haunt of ancient peace".

Built in 1700 and extended in the 1870s, Gunby Hall is a delightful William & Mary house of plum-coloured brick surrounded by sweeping lawns and flower gardens. The Hall has long been associated with the Massingberd family whose portraits, including several by Reynolds, are on display along with some very fine English furniture. The walled garden is particularly charming and beyond it the Church of St Peter contains some life-size brasses of early Massingberds.

WILLOUGHBY
11 miles NW of Skegness on B1196

Willoughby is best known as the birthplace of Captain John Smith, founder of what is now the State of Virginia in the USA. A farmer's son, Smith was born in the village in 1580 and educated in nearby Louth. He left England as a young man and, after a spell as a mercenary in Europe, set sail with other optimistic colonists for Chesapeake Bay in 1607. A forceful character, Smith was elected Governor of the new settlement but his diplomatic skills proved unequal to the task of pacifying the local Red Indians. They took him captive and were intent on killing him until one of the chieftain's daughters, Pocahontas, interceded and saved his life. Pocahontas later married one of Smith's fellow colonists, John Rolfe, and returned with him to England. Beautiful and intelligent, the dark-skinned Pocahontas was welcomed as an exotic celebrity. King James I graciously allowed her to be presented at his Court but within a few months the lovely Indian princess died "of a fever". Four hundred years later, the romantic tale continues to furnish the material for songs, stories, plays and musicals.

Willoughby village celebrates its most famous son with a fine memorial window in the church, (a gift from American citizens), and in the Willoughby Arms pub where a portrait painted on an outside wall and, inside, accounts of his adventures may be seen.

ALLSOPP'S LICENSED RESTAURANT

Vine Road, Chapel St Leonard's, Lincs. PE24 5TD
Tel: 01754 872316

Enjoying a countrywide reputation for outstanding food, **Allsopp's Licensed Restaurant** is located in the heart of this popular little town. Such is its renown that customers from all around the world return time and time again. Brian and Tina Allsopp have owned and run the restaurant for the past ten years, offering an extensive bill of fare that ranges from sandwiches to a full roast. The roasts, incidentally, are available every day.

Brian is the chef and one of his specialities is succulent fish dishes. All the meals are served in generous portions and at very reasonable prices. The restaurant is

attractively furnished and decorated with lots of flowers all around, including vases on each table. Some non-smoking tables are available. Children are very welcome here: they have their own menu and outside there's a secure and well-equipped play area. The restaurant is open every day from 10am to 6pm, but closed from November to March. Please note that credit cards are not accepted.

If you are just looking for an ice cream, Tina's Ice Cream Parlour is right next door and offers a good choice of quality ices.

THE FOOD DEN

10 St Lawrence Street, Horncastle, Lincolnshire LN9 5BJ
Tel: 01507 527805   e-mail: foodden@aol.com

Located in a cobbled street off the Market Place, **The Food Den** is a charming traditional tea room housed in a Grade II listed timber-framed building with the Regency bow windows which are such a feature of this historic little town. Andrew and Mary Kennedy opened their tea room at Christmas 1999, a bright and cheerful non-smoking place with traditional pine furniture and soft music playing in the background.

The Food Den quickly established a fine reputation for quality catering in addition to offering an outstanding choice of teas and coffees. Mary is an accomplished cook whose "Cakes and other Naughties", all baked on the premises, are irresistibly delicious and can also be specially ordered for special occasions such as birthdays, anniversaries and other celebrations. Her menu also includes a wide choice of appetising main meals and light snacks - omelettes, salads, jacket potatoes, ploughman's, hot or cold savouries, filled baps and baguettes, as well as daily home made specials. Sandwiches to take away are also available. Andrew is the coffee expert whose aromatic brews are all freshly ground and prepared to order. Just try a glass of the Mochaccino - fresh ground coffee and chocolate in hot milk, or the Iced Latte Coffee with a choice of flavourings that includes Amoretto, Irish Cream, Butter Rum or Brandy. A similar range of quality teas is also available and other beverages include herbal and fruit teas, Den Cream Sodas and Den Ice Cream Sodas.

At nearby Mawthorpe there is a nature reserve and the privately run **Mawthorpe Museum** which is concerned primarily with aspects of rural life and features an extensive collection of tractors and farm equipment. Also on display are relics from the East Lincolnshire Railway that used to run past the rear of the premises. The old railway line to the coast, long since devoid of track, is now a thriving wildlife area and provides great walking.

CHAPEL ST LEONARDS
6 miles N of Skegness off A52

Much smaller than its neighbours, Ingoldmells and Skegness, Chapel St Leonards nevertheless provides a full range of family entertainments and, of course, a superb beach where lifeguards are on duty during the season and donkey rides are available. At its centre is a charming village green with rose gardens, swings and slides. An especially good time

to visit Chapel St Leonards is August when the village holds its own week-long carnival.

HORNCASTLE

"Few towns of Horncastle's size can have so many Regency bow-windows", noted Nikolaus Pevsner. These attractive features, and the houses that went with them, were a direct result of the town's increased prosperity and the building boom that followed the opening of the Horncastle Navigation Canal in 1802. The town also has an unusual number of hotels for its population, currently about 4,500. The hostelries were built to accommodate visitors to the annual Horse Fair which started some time in the 1200s and continued until 1948. Its modern successor is the Horncastle Town & Country Fayre, a popular event that takes place each June.

OLD NICK'S TAVERN

8 North Street, Horncastle,
Lincolnshire LN9 5DX
Tel: 01507 526862

A coaching inn 200 years ago, **Old Nick's Tavern** still has the arched entrance through which the coaches used to pass, (as well as a resident ghost from those times!) and it remains a place where hospitality is dispensed in good measure.

David Dean operates a cheerful, well-stocked bar, whilst Monday to Saturday, Pams Kitchen provides splendid home-cooked lunchtime food with vegetarian options and usually includes a roast of the day. They were runners up in the Lincolnshire Life Best Pub Meal 2000/2001! Every evening except Monday and Friday there's a selection of tasty, freshly made pizzas which are also available to take away. One semi-partitioned area of the pub away from the bar is designated non-smoking at lunchtime, making it an ideal place for children to eat with their parents.

Some of the pub's decor has a mystical theme and includes some interesting designer mosaic tables. Background music plays gently at lunchtime while the mood in the evening depends on the day of the week. There's a games room with pool table, dartboard and pinball machine but Old Nick's provides much more in the way of entertainment. Wednesday and Sunday nights bring live music that could be anything from jazz, folk or indie; to piano nights and even string quartets - all the events providing a platform for local musicians. The pub raises money for various charities by organising events such as karaoke and quiz nights, auctions and an annual treasure hunt.

According to some historians, the town's name derives from the fact that there was a Roman *castle* here, sited at the meeting of two small rivers, the Bain and the Waring, which curve towards each other in the shape of a pair of cattle *horns*.

In Roman times the settlement was called Banovallum and parts of the Roman walls surrounding the 7 acre site still survive near St Mary's Church, with another part incorporated into the library on Wharf Road. In truth, neither of these fragments is particularly exciting.

St Mary's Church *does* have some interesting features. Outside the north porch is the ground level tombstone of a 19th century local doctor. This is an unconsecrated quarter of the churchyard but the doctor insisted on being buried here. It was his personal gesture of solidarity with suicides to whom, at that time and until very recently, the Church of England refused interment in hallowed ground. Inside the church there's a brass

CROSS KEYS INN & PLATES RESTAURANT

Salmonby, nr Horncastle, Lincolnshire LN9 6PX
Tel/Fax: 01507 533206

The building now occupied by the **Cross Keys Inn & Plates Restaurant** started life inauspiciously. It was erected in 1850 as the first station on the Horncastle to Skegness railway but the track was never

completed because of problems with a gradient. Nowadays, it's a much more useful destination, drawing visitors from all over the country with its terrific atmosphere, excellent real ale and fine food.

The owners are Rhodesian-born Ian Jenkinson and his partner Barbara Norton, both of whom have long experience in the catering trade. Ian is in charge of the kitchen which produces an extensive and varied range of dishes to be enjoyed in the 36-cover restaurant whose walls are adorned with a splendid collection of plates. The menu, which is full of jokey references, includes plenty of old favourites and some less familiar choices such as Chicken Breast stuffed with

Stilton and Chives wrapped in Bacon, or Chinese-style lemon vegetables. Dishes from the charcoal grill are popular - especially the T-bone steaks of either Lincolnshire or Scottish beef. There's also a snackier bar menu. The walls of the bar are hung with the owner's paintings of previous establishments in Cheshire and Northumberland, and with caricatures of snooker players

A grand old juke box plays vintage 45s and feeds on old 10p and 50p coins which can be obtained from the bar. The pub is a lively meeting place for local pool, darts and dominoes teams who pride themselves on their social rather than their playing skills. Recent additions include bar skittles and a very useful Link cashpoint machine.

In the pub's grounds are a beer garden with solid cedar tables and chairs, and a site for 5 touring caravans with electrical hook-up and washing facilities. As we go to press, plans are under way to add a motel-style extension which will provide quality accommodation in modern rooms, all with en suite facilities.

portrait of Lionel Dymoke, dated 1519. The Dymokes were the hereditary King's Champions who, at the coronation feast of medieval monarchs, challenged anyone who disputed the validity of the king's succession to mortal combat. Above an arch in the south aisle hang 13 scythe blades. These agricultural tools were the only arms available to the local people who took part in the Pilgrimage of Grace of 1536. This was a mostly northern protest against Henry VIII's policy of closing down every monastery in the country. Their rebellion failed. The king graciously pardoned those who had taken part and the rebels returned peacefully to their homes. Once the crisis had been defused, Henry ordered the summary execution of the most prominent leaders and supporters of the uprising.

Horncastle cannot claim any particularly famous son, although the celebrated botanist Sir Joseph Banks, co-founder of Kew Gardens, had a town house here, a dark red brick house that still stands on the south-east corner of the Market Place. But Horncastle has to admit to being the home town of a much less admirable character. During the 1870s and 1880s, William Marwood worked here as a successful shoemaker and cobbler. Somehow, William also found the time to pursue an interesting part-time job as public executioner. To begin with, his very competent hangings were mostly carried out in local gaols but William's reputation for avoiding such unprofessional and distressing side effects of hanging as ripping the condemned man's head from his body soon spread far and wide. William was the first hangman to carefully study the important relationship between the body weight of a condemned criminal and a "drop" that would leave the body very dead but still entire. William Marwood's career peaked in 1882

when he was summoned to Dublin to *"dispatch into eternity"* the republican activists who had murdered England's two most senior resident officials in the city's Phoenix Park. William's tiny cobbler's shop still stands in Church Lane, near the Church of St Mary.

AROUND HORNCASTLE

SALMONBY
5 miles NE of Horncastle off A153 or A158

Within the undulating hills of the south Wolds lies a clutch of picturesque villages - Fulletby, Oxcombe, Tetford and Salmonby amongst them. Some of the surrounding hills open up grand views, most notably from Belchford Hill. Salmonby is a tiny place without even a church of its own. It used to have one but St Margaret's was demolished in 1978. The village does have an excellent inn though, *(see panel opposite)*, the Cross Keys, which began life as a railway station.

TETFORD
7 miles NE of Horncastle off A153 or A158

This sizeable Wolds village is laid out in the form of an irregular figure of eight with an old Roman road slicing through the crossover point. In the 1770s the White Hart Inn was the venue for the monthly meetings of the Tetford Club when the local gentry gathered to enjoy skittles, bowls, *"the thoughtful pipe and wit-inspiring bowl"*. On one occasion they were joined by the sociable Dr Samuel Johnson who even tried his dexterity at skittles. The bar still contains an old settle on which the learned Doctor is reputed to have sat and held forth.

To the north of the village rises **Tetford Hill**, 468ft high and scheduled as being of outstanding botanical importance. And a

The George & Dragon

Main Road, Hagworthingham,
Lincolnshire PE23 4NX
Tel: 01507 588255

The locals at the **George & Dragon** jokingly refer to mine hosts, Mandy and Richard Baxter, as "Basil" and "Sybil" - the fearsome couple in charge of Fawlty Towers. In fact, Mandy and Richard could hardly be more different from those "hoteliers from Hell" as the popularity of this friendly old inn with its open fires and snug bar bears witness.

A major attraction at the George & Dragon is the quality and range of the food on offer. Vegetarians will find half a dozen choices, steak lovers have the option of anything from an 6oz cut up to a daunting 32oz chunk, during the season specialist game dishes such as Venison Baden-Baden are on offer, Haddock and Chips is the dish of the day on Fridays, and other choices include lasagne, moussaka, steak & kidney pudding or Spaghetti Bolognese. A unique speciality of the house is a local delicacy, Chine of Ham stuffed with herbs and served with roast potatoes. There's also a special menu for children. Food is available every evening, except Monday all year, and Thursday to Sunday lunchtimes from November to March. A free house, the inn stocks a good selection of beverages including John Smith's cask ales, Scrumpy, Fosters, Castle Eden, and a choice of 3 red and 3 white wines.

Outside, there's a huge, secluded garden with extensive views over the Lincolnshire countryside. During the summer, a marquee is often set up here for special events.

The White Hart Hotel

Market Square, Spilsby, Lincs. PE23 5JP
Tel: 01790 752244 Fax: 01790 754445

Occupying a prominent position in Spilsby's unspoilt Market Square, **The White Hart Hotel** is a delightful old coaching inn dating back to the 1500s but with an attractive 18th century façade. An interesting feature on this outside wall is an antique letter box dated 1842 and believed to be one of the oldest still surviving. Inside, you may well receive a welcome in the form of a shrill whistle from "Major", the resident African grey parrot who is now in his late twenties and boasts an extensive vocabulary! Cosy log fires add to the warmth of the welcome, and a snooker room and big screen TV provide entertainment. Mine hosts at The White Hart are Glen Hillaby and Emma Roode who took over here in 2000 from Glen's mother who had run the business for 14 years.

Good old-fashioned home cooking is the order of the day here with a wide choice of main meals served in the separate non-smoking restaurant, and an appetising selection of hot and cold snacks available in the bar. Customers come from miles around for the melt-in-the-mouth Grimsby Haddock, cooked in a special beer batter. Real ales are served, with Kimberley Brewery Best Bitter permanently on tap, supplemented by guest ales such as Frolicking Farmer and Guzzling Goose. If you are planning to stay in this peaceful corner of the county, The White Hart has comfortable en suite accommodation available and, if you have a special event upcoming, there's also a large function room.

couple of miles further north is the hamlet of **Ruckland**, whose church, rebuilt in 1885, is claimed to be the smallest in Lincolnshire. It is dedicated to St Olave, the first Christian king of Norway, who reigned around 1000AD.

SOMERSBY
7 miles NE of Horncastle off A158

For pilgrims on the Tennyson trail, a visit to Somersby is essential. The poet's father, Dr George Clayton Tennyson, was Rector of the village and the adjoining parish of Bag Enderby. Alfred was born here in 1809 and for most of the first thirty years of his life Somersby Rectory was his home. Many of his poems reflect his delight in the surrounding scenery of the Wolds, Fens and coast. When the family left Somersby in 1837, following the death of Dr Tennyson, Alfred wrote:

> We leave the well-beloved place
> Where first we gazed upon the sky;
> The roofs, that heard our earliest cry,
> Will shelter one of stranger race.

The Rectory, now Somersby House (private), still stands, complete with the many additions Dr Tennyson made to accommodate his family of 10 children. He is buried in the graveyard of the small church where he had been minister for more than 20 years and which now contains a fine bust of his famous son. Also in the graveyard, where a simple tombstone marks the Doctor's burial place, stands a remarkably well-preserved medieval cross.

The nearby village of **Bag Enderby** is associated with another celebrated figure, John Wesley. He preached here on the village green beneath a noble elm tree. The hollow trunk still stands. The church also has a special treasure: a beautifully carved 15th century font "worth crossing Lincolnshire to see". The carvings include a tender Pietà, a hart licking the leaves of a tree growing from its back, and a seated figure playing what appears to be a lute.

SPILSBY
10 miles E of Horncastle on A16

A pleasant little market town with a population of about 2000, Spilsby sits near the southern edge of the Wolds. Market day is Monday, (with an open air auction as part of the fun), and there's an annual May Day Carnival with dancing round the may pole in the market square. The **Church of St James** has many interesting features, most notably the incredible array of tombs and memorials of the Willoughby family from the 1300s to the early 1600s. Perhaps the most striking of them, a 1580s memorial to the Duchess of Suffolk and

Woodmans Cottage, Somersby

Richard Bertie, fills the whole of the original chancel arch. Another monument honours Spilsby's most famous son, the navigator and explorer Captain Sir John Franklin, who lost his life while in charge of the expedition that discovered the North West Passage. A handsome bronze of the great man stands in the square facing the market hall of 1764. Also of note is the stately Sessions House and prison (1824) with its imposing Doric portico. The building is now the Spilsby Theatre. Almost opposite is the entrance to Eresby Avenue, an elegant tree-lined road that was originally the approach to Eresby Hall, a mansion of the Willoughbys which was destroyed by fire in 1769.

OLD BOLINGBROKE
8 miles SE of Horncastle off A155 or B1195

Old Bolingbroke is the site of **Bolingbroke Castle** (free), now in the care of English Heritage. Originally built in the reign of William I it later became the property of John of Gaunt whose son, afterwards Henry IV, was born at the castle in 1367. During the Civil War, Bolingbroke Castle was besieged by Parliamentary forces in 1643, fell into disuse soon after and very little now remains.

EAST KIRKBY
8 miles SE of Horncastle on A155

The airfield beside the A155 is the setting for the **Lincolnshire Aviation Heritage Centre**, based in the old control tower. Displays include an Avro Lancaster bomber, a Shackleton, cockpits from Canberras, military vehicles and a wartime blast shelter.

LOUTH

One of the county's most appealing towns, Louth is set beside the River Lud on the eastern edge of the Wolds in an Area of Outstanding Natural Beauty. Louth can make the unusual boast that it stands in both the eastern and western hemispheres since the Greenwich Meridian line passes through the centre of the town.

There was a settlement here long before the Romans arrived. By the time of the Domesday Book, in 1086, Louth was recorded as a prosperous market town. It still is. There's a cattle market on Fridays; a general market on Wednesdays (with an open air auction), Fridays and Saturdays; and a Farmers' Market, selling every kind of produce from eggs to ostrich meat, on the last Wednesday of each month.

The town is a pleasure to wander around, its narrow winding streets and alleys crammed with attractive architecture and bearing intriguing names such as Pawnshop Passage. Westgate in particular is distinguished by its Georgian houses and a 16th century inn. A plaque in nearby Westgate Place marks the house where Tennyson lodged with his grandmother while attending the King Edward VI School. Founded in the 1200s, the school is still operating and amongst its other famous old boys are Sir John Franklin and Captain John Smith of Pocahontas fame. Broadbank, which now houses the **Louth Museum**, is an attractive little building with some interesting artifacts including some amazing locally-woven carpets that were displayed at the 1867 Paris Exhibition. And Tennyson fans will surely want to visit the shop in the market square that published *Poems by Two Brothers* and is still selling books.

But the town's pre-eminent architectural glory is the vast **Church of St James** which boasts the tallest spire of any parish church in England. Nearly 300 feet high and built in gleaming Ancaster stone, this masterly example of the mason's art was constructed between 1501 and 1515. The interior is noted for its glorious starburst tower vault, beautifully restored Georgian pine roof, a wonderful collection of Decorated sedilia, and a fascinating array of old chests. On summer afternoons, visitors can climb to the base of the spire for a panoramic view that stretches from the Wolds to the North Sea.

An interesting addition to the town's attractions is currently being developed. The **Louth Art Trail** will link commissioned works of art, each of which will have some significant connection with the town's history. Already in place are sculptures around the Louth Navigation Canal and the River Lud. Both waterways have made important contributions to the town's prosperity although the Lud has also brought disaster. In 1920 a flash flood destroyed hundreds of homes and killed 23 people. A plaque on the side of the town watermill shows how high the river rose during that disastrous inundation. Another Art Trail commission is based on the theme of the Greenwich Meridian, and the summer of 2001 should see a further sculpture located in **Hubbards Hills**, a picturesque public park lying in a 125ft-deep glacial valley to the west of the town.

AROUND LOUTH

COVENHAM ST BARTHOLOMEW
6 miles N of Louth off A16

The dominant presence here is Covenham Reservoir, a huge expanse of

WAINGROVE COUNTRY COTTAGES

Fulstow, Louth, Lincolnshire LN11 0XQ
Tel/Fax: 01507 363704
e-mail: macandstephanie@waingrove.demon.co.uk
website: www.lincolnshirecottages.com

Guests arriving at **Waingrove Country Cottages** find awaiting them a bottle of chilled wine, a tea tray with home made Lincolnshire "Plum Bread" and a slice of locally produced Poacher Cheese (traditionally eaten together), local magazines and a TV guide on the coffee table and, as a final welcoming touch, fresh flowers. Mac and Stephanie Smith, the owners of these three charming cottages, have shown the same kind of customer care in furnishing and equipping the properties. Country style furnishings in pretty colours, pine doors and beams complement pale walls, attractive table lamps and thoughtfully chosen furniture. All three cottages are superbly equipped - kitchens with fridge-freezer, auto washer-dryer, microwave, coffee-maker, toaster; bathrooms with electric showers over the bath, soaps, bath gels and towels; and sitting rooms with video player and colour television. (In the courtyard is the "Tourist Information

Room" which stocks a selection of video films, as well as brochures, maps, books and guides to the area). Garden furniture is provided for sunny days and there are barbecues for the outdoor chef. "The Old Farmhouse", with its original beams and doors, and open fire, can accommodate up to 6 guests; "Bramble Cottage" and "Hawthorn Cottage", created from a traditional Lincolnshire barn and both single storey, are suitable for up to 4 guests. They overlook a paved and gravelled courtyard planted with tubs and flowers. Please note that all the cottages are non-smoking inside, and are not suitable for children under 10 or for pets.

water combining a nature reserve with a recreational area offering all kinds of water sports.

ALVINGHAM
5 miles NE of Louth on minor roads

This small village set beside the River Lud has two features of special interest. **Alvingham Mill**, dating back to 1755, is unusual in having a "breast wheel" in which the incoming water strikes the paddles halfway up the wheel. Even stranger is the fact that there are two churches in the single churchyard. St Adelwold's is Alvingham's church; St Mary's belongs to the parish of North Cockerington which lies on the other side of the river but whose boundary runs through the churchyard. St Adelwold's is the only church in England dedicated to this Saxon saint who became Bishop of Lindisfarne. Another curious fact: for almost a hundred years, St Adelwold's was abandoned: its doors locked and its fabric neglected. Then in 1933 it was beautifully restored in memory of a local MP, Robert Armstrong Yerburgh.

MABLETHORPE
13 miles E of Louth on A52 &A1104

Mablethorpe is the northernmost and most "senior" of the three Lincolnshire holiday resorts that almost form a chain along this stretch of fragile coast which has frequently been threatened by the waves, and whose contours have changed visibly over the years. Much of the original village of Mablethorpe has disappeared into the sea, including the medieval Church of St Peter. In the great North Sea flood of January 31st, 1953, seven Mablethorpe residents were drowned.

The young Alfred Tennyson was a frequent visitor to Mablethorpe between 1828 and 1843. It was then just a tiny village set beside a wonderful stretch of sands and dunes.

How often when a child I lay reclined:
I took delight in this fair land and free,

The youthful poet stayed with a Mrs Wiliman at Marine Villa. Her house is now called Tennyson's Cottage and although private is visible from the road.

Long popular with day trippers and holidaymakers, Mablethorpe offers all that could be asked of a traditional seaside town, and a little more. One of the most popular attractions is the **Animal Gardens, Nature Centre & Seal Trust** at North End. This complex houses creatures of all kinds, with special wildcat and barn owl features, and includes a seal and seabird hospital, as well as a nature centre with many fascinating displays. The lynx caves are particularly interesting, displaying 3-dimensional scenes of Mablethorpe as it was 9,000 and 20,000 years ago, along with prehistoric tools and fossils. The cave walls are covered with full size replicas of prehistoric art and the sound system relays the cries of wolves and mammoths. The centre is open every day from Easter to October.

A unique collection is on view at **Ye Olde Curiosity Museum** where Graham and Sue Allen have amassed an astonishing collection of more than 18,000 curios. One of the oddest is an 1890 "fat remover" which looks like a rolling pin with suction pads and was used in massage parlours. The star exhibits however are Sue's 400 or more Pen Delfin figurines, Burnley-made ceramics of rabbits that Sue has been collecting for almost 30 years. Almost everything in the museum is on sale - apart from Graham's beloved Morris Minor!

Rather similar but on a smaller scale is **Newstead Lodge** where Lila Sells has stocked her family living room with all her family treasures and heirlooms. Decorative glassware and old gramophones vie for space with family china, linen, books and other treasures. Included in the collection is what is believed to be the world's oldest surviving gramophone record - a recording of Chopin's Funeral March played by an orchestra in a village hall.

SUTTON ON SEA
15 miles E of Louth on A52

Although virtually a suburb of Mablethorpe nowadays, Sutton on Sea still retains an individual character. The enormous beach with its firm golden sands was the only one along the whole of the East Coast to be awarded the prestigious Blue Flag in 2000 and it provides a wonderful playground for young and older folk alike.

The sea here hasn't always been so benign. Half a century has passed since Sutton suffered the most disastrous episode in its history. On January 31st,

1953 a sudden North Sea flood swept across the beaches and deluged the town, claiming the lives of eleven people. Most of the town's residents were evacuated to Louth while troops and workmen laboured to dump 25,000 tons of slag into the breaches of the sea defences. A curious legacy of this tragedy is the Maple Leaf paddling pool which was presented to Sutton by the Canadian people.

A less forbidding aspect of the sea is revealed at very low tides when the remains of a 4500-year-old submerged forest briefly appear above water here and at Huttoft Bank a few miles to the south.

LEGBOURNE
4 miles SE of Louth on A157

In the heyday of the railways, the East Lincolnshire Coast Railway had a station at Legbourne. Today the station building has been restored as the **Legbourne**

WAGGON & HORSES

Main Road, South Reston, Louth, Lincolnshire LN11 8JQ
Tel: 01507 450364 Fax: 01507 450730

Scattered along the A157, the small village of South Reston is well worth seeking out in order to visit its popular hostelry, the **Waggon & Horses**. This striking building began life as a coaching inn and its former stables still stand although now converted into a cottage.

Sandra Owen has owned and run the pub since 1997 and she provides a warm welcome to one and all, a welcome seconded by Kate, Sandra's

friendly black Labrador. Over the years, Sandra has built up the inn's excellent reputation for good food and quality ales. Food is served every lunchtime (noon until 2pm) and evening (7pm to 9pm) from Tuesday to Sunday, with a menu offering a wide choice of wholesome, freshly prepared home cooked food. There's an extensive selection of beverages on offer, including cask ales and an impressive wine list. The spacious, brightly decorated dining room can seat up to 70 diners but even so Sunday lunch in particular is so popular that booking ahead is strongly advised.

The Waggon & Horses is a children-friendly pub - they have their own area inside and outside there are swings and a trampoline on the lawn. Entertainment for the grown-ups includes pool, darts and game machines. The inn doesn't have any letting rooms but at the rear of the garden there's a caravan site which has electric hook-ups for 5 vehicles.

Railway Museum and now houses a model railway and almost 2000 items of railway memorabilia, with a working signal box close by.

LITTLE CAWTHORPE
4 miles SE of Louth off A157

This delightful little village has a ford, a picture-postcard duck pond and a lovely mellow brick manor house built in the 1670s. Twin Ice Age boulders are set in the wall by the entrance.

Claythorpe Wildfowl Gardens

ABY
10 miles SE of Louth on minor roads

Claythorpe Watermill & Wildfowl Gardens are a major draw for visitors of all ages to this small village on the edge of the Wolds. A beautiful 18th century

watermill provides the central feature, surrounded by attractive woodlands inhabited by hundreds of waterfowl and other animals. Built in 1721, the mill is no longer working but it provides a handsome setting for a restaurant, gift

---

PARK FARM HOLIDAYS

Withern, Alford, Lincolnshire LN13 0DF
Tel/Fax: 01507 450331
e-mail: alan@park-farm-holidays.fsnet.co.uk

Situated about 6 miles from the coast, between Alford and Louth, **Park Farm Holidays** offers a choice of self-catering holiday accommodation in wonderfully peaceful surroundings. Four of the properties are attractive log cabins set in woodland but, as the owners Alan and Elsie Burkitt, point out, "they are not built of tree trunks notched at the ends so they fit together, with gaps stuffed with moss and mud to keep the Arctic winds out"! Double glazed and centrally heated, they can accommodate either up to 4 or 6 people. All are very well-equipped, (colour TV, electric cooker, microwave, fridge, etc), and all have garden tables and chairs on the verandahs. A separate building has a washing machine, tumble drier, ironing facilities and a pay phone.

Also on the farm are 2 semi-detached cottages which have been converted from former farm workers houses and provided with all modern amenities, including double glazing and central heating. Each has 3 bedrooms, one with a double bed and two with a single in each, all with blankets, not duvets. There's a bathroom upstairs, and downstairs a comfortable lounge/dining area with a settee, easy chairs and television, a well-equipped kitchen and a shared utility area. Garden tables and chairs are also provided. The cottages are not suitable for the disabled; the Cabins, although they do not have a Disability rating, are suitable for someone in a wheelchair with assistance.

Claythorpe Water Mill

with markets that were first established in 1238 still taking place on Tuesdays and Fridays. These are supplemented by a regular Craft Market every Friday throughout the summer.

Small though it is, Alford boasts some outstanding buildings. **Alford Manor House**, built around 1660, claims the distinction of being the largest thatched manor house in England. It's an attractive building with brick gabling and a beautifully maintained thatched roof. It serves now as a folk museum where visitors are invited to step back into the past and take a look at local life through time-warp shops, an old-fashioned veterinary surgery and a Victorian schoolroom. Reaching even further back into the past, the History Room contains a collection of interesting Roman finds and also displays from the salt works that once prospered in this part of the county. Another exhibit explores the still-flourishing connections between Alford and the USA.

An even more tangible link with the past is provided by **Alford Tower Mill** on the eastern side of the town. It was built by a local millwright, Sam Oxley, in 1813. Standing a majestic six floors high, it has

shop and Country Fayre shop. Open daily between March and October, the gardens also have a Bygone Exhibit Area.

ALFORD
12 miles SW of Louth on A1114

Often described as Lincolnshire's Craft Centre, Alford is a flourishing little town

THE OLD LIBRARY RESTAURANT & TEA SHOP

4 High Street, Alford, Lincolnshire LN13 9DS
Tel: 01507 462180

Located in the heart of this lively market town, **The Old Library Restaurant & Tea Shop** offers visitors a choice of tasty home baked cakes and scones as well as a good choice of snacks, lite bites and hot lunchtime meals. Coral Westall who, together with her husband Jim, owns and runs the restaurant, is a former cookery editor and her menu is based on traditional, time-honoured recipes using good, fresh ingredients. The interior is bright and cheerful with honey-coloured pine walls, an abundance of books to browse through and nostalgic music of the 40s playing quietly in the background.

Alford Manor House Museum

back in full commercial operation, complete with a vintage oven producing bakery items with the full flavour that only the old-fashioned methods seem able to produce. Other attractions here include a wholefood shop, tea room and garden.

Alford's handsome medieval **Church of St Wilfrid** dates from the 14th century and amongst its treasures are a curiously carved Jacobean pulpit, the marble tomb of the former Manor House residents, (the

five sails and four sets of grinding stones. This sturdy old mill came perilously close to total destruction in 1955. Thanks to the efforts of local enthusiasts it is now

THE HALF MOON HOTEL & RESTAURANT

25/28 West Street, Alford, Lincolnshire LN13 9DG
Tel: 01507 463477 Fax: 01507 462916

A listed building with a history going back some 400 years, **The Half Moon Hotel & Restaurant** has been run by the same family for some 37 years. Dave and Jill Dixon, assisted by their son Geoff, have made their hostelry a lively social centre where Alford's Rotary Club, Horticultural Society, Bridge Club and Folk Club all hold their meetings, with local Morris Dancers also making the inn a regular port of call.

Another long-serving member of the team is chef Nick Foxwell whose culinary skills have gained a dedicated following. His menu offers customers a very wide choice beginning with an extensive range of exciting and cosmopolitan starters, followed by specialities in poultry, fish and meat dishes as main courses, as well as vegetarian options and a children's choice, all served either in the separate non-smoking restaurant, or in the smoking bar area. Also available is a good selection of Light Bites, (omelettes, sandwiches, baguettes, ploughmans, jacket potatoes and rice dishes), and do look out for the speciality of the house - Nick's delicious home made pies and world famous haddock. To accompany your meal a wide range of beverages, including cask ales and an interesting selection of wines from around the world, is available.

There are darts, pool and a juke box in the public bar and, for those special events, the hotel has a very spacious function room which can accommodate up to 100 guests.

Alford Windmill

DONINGTON-ON-BAIN
10 miles SW of Louth via A153/A157

Country roads lead westward into wonderful walking country at Donington-on-Bain, a peaceful Wolds village on the **Viking Way**. This well-trodden route, which was established in 1976 by Lincolnshire County Council, runs 147 miles from the Humber Bridge to Oakham in Rutland and is waymarked by Viking helmet symbols. While in Donington, have a look at the grand old water mill and the 13th century church. There is a story that it was usual at weddings for old ladies to throw hassocks at the bride as she walked up the aisle. This boisterous custom was ended in 1780 by the rector after he was hit by a misdirected hassock!

To the east of Donington and south of Goulceby is the celebrated **Red Hill Nature Reserve**. The hill itself is an

Christopher family), and an amazing collection of tapestry kneelers. With so many parish churches nowadays locked for most of the time, it's good to know that St Wilfrid's is open daily from 9am to 4pm. In August, St Wilfrid's hosts a Flower Festival, part of the **Alford Festival** which began in 1974 and over the years has attracted a growing variety of craftspeople, joined nowadays by dancers, singers, poets and actors.

The Viking Way

THE WILLOW RESTAURANT & TEA ROOMS
128/129 West Street, Alford, Lincolnshire LN13 9DR
Tel: 01507 462179

Housed in a listed building near the town centre, **The Willow Restaurant & Tea Rooms** has a very cosy, olde worlde atmosphere, with walls covered with a profusion of collectable jugs, mugs and plates. Partners Chris Arnold and Bob Smith offer a very extensive menu that includes hearty main courses, lite bites, omelettes, salads, baps and jacket potatoes, as well as daily specials. Vegetarian and children's meals are also available. The restaurant is licensed and there are separate smoking and non-smoking areas.

Scamblesby Nature Reserve

across the Wolds. The hill also provides the setting for a Good Friday procession when the vicar of Asterby and three parishioners carrying crosses climb the steep lane. The three crosses are erected above a chalk pit and a short service takes place with music provided by the Horncastle Brass band.

GRIMSBY

outcrop bearing a vein of spectacular red chalk that is rich in fossil finds. The small reserve is home to several species of butterflies and moths, the meadow pipit, common lizard and grass snake. From the clifftop there are some wonderful views

According to tradition it was a Dane called Grim who founded the town. He had been ordered to drown the young Prince Havelock after the boy's father had been killed in battle. Grim could not

THE GREEN MAN

Old Main Road, Scamblesby, Louth, Lincolnshire LN11 9XG
Tel/Fax: 01507 343282 e-mail: thegreenman@onetel.net.uk

Set in lovely countryside and enjoying open views of the Wolds, **The Green Man** stands on what used to be the main coach road between Horncastle and Louth but is now a peaceful village lane. Believed to be more than 200 years old, the inn has a small, intimate interior with open log fires, lots of horse brasses and amongst the banquettes and stool seating the unusual feature of a vintage rocking chair.

Anne and Tim Eyre, who own and run this friendly and hospitable hostelry, have both spent a considerable amount of time in Australia - Tim for 16 years, Anne for 30, and they bring a relaxed "Down Under" atmosphere to the inn. A motorcycle enthusiast, Tim is the proud owner of a Ducati. (Handily, the Cadwell Park Circuit is just a couple of miles up the road). Anne is the chef and offers a

menu of wholesome traditional pub food which also includes vegetarian options such as a Brie, Potato, Courgette & Almond Crumble. All dishes are freshly prepared and cooked to order. There's a wide selection of cask ales, amongst them Shepherd Neame Master Brew, Spitfire, Black Sheep Best and guest ales.

The Green Man also offers accommodation - 2 comfortable rooms (1 twin, 1 double) which share a bathroom. Guests also have the use of a relaxing lounge. Walkers, especially, will feel at home here since the Viking Way is just a few steps away.

bring himself to murder the child so he set sail for England. After a tempestuous crossing of the North Sea, Grim and the boy arrived at the Humber estuary where he used the timbers of their boat to build a house on the shore. They lived by selling fish and salt, thus establishing the foundations of an industry for which Grimsby would become known the world over.

But until 1848, Grimsby didn't even rank among Lincolnshire's ten largest towns. That was the year the railway arrived, making it possible for fish to be swiftly transported to major centres of population inland. Only four years later, the town's most famous landmark, the elegant, Italianate **Dock Tower**, was built, soaring more than 300ft above the busy docks. The Tower now enjoys Grade I listed building status, ranking it alongside such national treasures as Buckingham Palace and Chatsworth House. The tower's original function was purely utilitarian, the storage of 33,000 gallons of water to operate the hydraulic system that worked the lock gates. But shortly after it was built in 1852 it was discovered that water in a pressurized tube worked just as well so the tower became redundant. On open days, visitors can undertake the gruelling climb up the inside of the tower to enjoy the breathtaking views from the top.

The Tower stands beside Alexandra Dock which enjoyed its heyday during the 1950s when Grimsby was the world's largest fishing port. The story of those boom days is told in vivid detail in the **National Fishing Heritage Centre** in Alexandra Dock, where visitors are challenged to navigate the icy waters of the Arctic, experience freezing winds, black ice, and lashing rain as the trawler decks, literally, heave and moan beneath your feet. A popular all-in arrangement is **The Fishy Tour**. This begins with an early morning visit to the fish auction, (white coats and wellies provided), followed by a traditional haddock and poached egg breakfast. Then on to the fish filleting and smoking houses, after which there's a guided tour of the Heritage Centre and an exploration of the *Ross Tiger*, a classic fishing trawler from the 1950s. A fish and chip lunch rounds off the trip.

The Time Trap (free), housed deep in old prison cells of the Town Hall, recreates the seamier side of life on dry land, and has proved a very popular annexe to the Heritage Centre. Visitors pass through dark, twisting corridors, explore mysterious nooks and crannies, discovering en route some unexpected facets of the town. The **Town Hall** itself, built in 1863, is a dignified building whose frontage has a series of busts depicting Queen Victoria, Prince Albert, local man John Whitgift, later Archbishop

THE BUTTERY

14 Abbeygate, Grimsby, Lincolnshire DN31 1JY
Tel: 01472 242873 website: www.abbeygate.uk.com

Located within the Abbeygate Centre, Grimsby's premier shopping arcade, **The Buttery** offers a tempting choice of main meals and light snacks with specialities including home made soups, casseroles and salads. Children are welcome and a high chair is available. Alan and Linda Willey have been in the catering business for more than 12 years and are ably assisted by Linda's aunt, Jean. All three are accomplished cooks and, once a month, they host a food and wine themed evening. They also provide outside catering - anything from a children's party to a dinner party. Open Monday to Saturday 9.30am to 4.00pm.

of Canterbury, Edward III (who granted the land around here to the Freemen of Grimsby), the Earl of Yarborough, (local landowner and High Steward of the borough at that time), and the historian Gervase Holles who was Mayor of Grimsby in 1640.

Another imposing edifice from earlier days is **Victoria Mills** by Corporation Bridge, a large Flemish-style flour mill built between 1889 and 1906. The massive structure was converted into flats a few years ago.

Many Victorian buildings were destroyed during World War II but a surviving legacy from that era is the **People's Park** where the facilities include a heart-shaped lake, children's play area, bowling greens, croquet lawn, ornamental gardens and plenty of open space. There's also a Floral Hall (free) that is vibrant with colour all year round and houses both tropical and temperate species, and a large variety of house and garden plants, shrubs and conifers are on sale. Away from the centre, by the banks of the River Freshney, is **Freshney Park Way**, 300 acres of open space that attracts walkers, cyclists, anglers and birdwatchers as well as picnickers.

A popular excursion from Grimsby is to take one of the boat rides out into the Humber estuary, past the two First World War forts designed to protect the river from German submarines, and on to Spurn Point, the curling sandbar that sweeps out into the mouth of the estuary.

A final note for football fans. Be prepared for the question: Why does Grimsby Town Football Club play all its games away? Answer: Because the Mariners' ground is actually in Cleethorpes, a resort which has spread northwards to meet up with Grimsby itself.

AROUND GRIMSBY

IMMINGHAM
7 miles NW of Grimsby off A180

A small village until the early 1900s, Immingham's breakthrough came when a new port on the south bank of the Humber was proposed. Grimsby naturally thought that the honour should be hers but consultants favoured Immingham because the deep water channel of the river runs close to the shore here. The new Docks were opened by King George V in 1912 and rapidly grew in importance, especially when the Great Central Railway switched its passenger liner service from Grimsby. The Docks expanded yet further when the Humber was dredged in the late 1960s to accommodate the new generation of giant tankers and a huge refinery now stands to the west of the town. Not promising country for tourists but the heart of the old village has survived with St Andrew's Church at its centre.

The **Immingham Museum** traces the links between the Docks and the railways and there's also an exhibit about the group of Puritans who, in 1607, set sail from Immingham to the Netherlands. A memorial to this event, the **Pilgrim Father Monument**, was erected by the Anglo-American Society in 1925. It originally stood near the point of embarkation but is now located near the church. Most of the 20ft-high column is made from local granite but near the top is a block hewn from Plymouth Rock in New England where these religious refugees first landed.

EAST HALTON
13 miles NW of Grimsby off A160

This farming parish that commands a two-mile stretch of the Humber banks has

THE BLACK BULL

Townside, East Halton, nr Immingham, Lincolnshire DN40 3NL
Tel: 01469 540207

In times past the area around East Halton was notorious for its numerous witches and it's believed that one of the restless spirits they conjured up has taken up residence at **The Black Bull**. It's a good choice since this is a friendly and hospitable hostelry with a welcoming atmosphere that should cheer up the gloomiest soul. The inn has been run since March 2001 by the Heafields - Mick, who has lived in the village for the past 20 years, his wife Liz, and their family. Liz is the cook and her appetising menu is available every lunchtime and evening except Sunday evening. Enjoy your meal either in the separate restaurant or in the bar with its real fire. Even on Sunday evening you won't lack for sustenance - roast potatoes and gravy are supplied free. And on Saturday evenings there's also a free buffet to

accompany the live entertainment.

This lively inn also offers free pool on Tuesday evening, a darts and pool knockout competition on Thursday, and on Friday the juke box is also free. Children are very welcome and there are special toilets for the disabled. In good weather, customers can take advantage of the beer garden where barbecues are held in summer.

a church with a fine 15th century tower and parish records that go back to 1155. Delightful though it is, East Halton's church pales into insignificance beside the splendid ruins of **Thornton Abbey** (English Heritage, free), about 3 miles to the west. The massive gatehouse with its sculptured figures sheltering beneath ornate stone canopies is regarded as one of the finest 14th century structures of its kind. Beyond the 68ft high gatehouse are the ruins of the Augustinian abbey, founded around 1139, which include parts of the dormitory, refectory and a beautiful octagonal chapter house.

CLEETHORPES

1 mile S of Grimsby on A180

One of Cleethorpes' claims to fame is that it stands on zero longitude, i.e. on the Greenwich Meridian line. A signpost on the coastal path marks the Meridian line and points the way to London, the North

Pole and other prominent places, an essential snap for the family album.

Just south of Grimsby and almost merged with it, Cleethorpes developed from a little village into a holiday resort when the railway line was built in the 1860s. The Manchester, Sheffield & Lincolnshire Railway Company developed much of the town and also built the splendid promenade, a mile long and 65ft wide, below the cliff. Above the promenade they built the sham ruin known as **Ross Castle**, named after the railway's general secretary, Edward Ross. Swathed in ivy, the folly marked the highest point of the cliffs which the promenade now protects from erosion.

The railway company also funded the construction of a pier. This was opened on August Bank Holiday Monday 1873, when nearly 3,000 people paid the then princely sum of sixpence (2½p) for admission. The toll was reduced the next day to a much more reasonable penny (½p), and it is recorded that in the first five weeks 37,000 people visited. The pier, like many others, was breached during the Second World War as a defence measure to discourage enemy landings, and it was never restored to its full length. The pier now measures 355ft compared to its original 1200ft but the Edwardian pavilion of 1906 is still in place and is currently the largest nightclub in the area.

Cleethorpes offers a wide variety of traditional seaside amusements - donkey rides, a fun park (Pleasure Island), an 18-hole crazy golf course, an indoor children's play area called Fantasy World, an outdoor sandpit and paddling pool, a well-equipped Leisure Centre, and Jungle World, an indoor tropical garden inhabited by boas, pythons, parrots, toucans, monkeys, lizards and meerkats.

The town also boasts the last surviving seaside steam railway, the **Cleethorpes**

Coast Light Railway. This narrow-gauge steam railway runs along the foreshore and lakeside every day from Easter to September, and on weekends throughout the year. A recent addition to the town's attractions is the **Cleethorpes Humber Estuary Discovery Centre.** Here visitors can become time travellers, discover extinct creatures and submerged forests, and work off their aggression by participating in a Viking raid. The Lincolnshire clockmaker, John Harrison, who solved the problem of finding longitude is celebrated in one of the many exhibits and the complex also offers refreshments in the Boaters Tea Room.

Festivals have always played a major part in Cleethorpes' visitor attractions. From June onwards, one celebration follows another with the Carnival Week in late July/early August providing the highlight of the year. Other festivities include a classic car weekend; a jazz

GROSVENOR GUEST HOUSE

6 Isaac's Hill, Cleethorpes, Lincolnshire DN35 8JR
Tel: 01472 603516

The **Grosvenor Guest House** in Isaac's Hill has been welcoming bed & breakfast guests for more than 17 years. Colin and Jean Williamson took over this spacious Edwardian house in the spring of 2000 and have maintained the Grosvenor's reputation for providing comfortable accommodation and a warm welcome.

There are 6 guest bedrooms in all with two of the rooms, a family and a twin, located on the ground floor. Currently, none of the rooms has en suite facilities but that may have changed by the time you read this. A full English breakfast is included in the tariff and although Colin and Jean do not provide evening meals they can guide you to one of the many eating establishments within easy reach. The Grosvenor is open all year round and prices remain the same whatever the season. (Please note that credit cards are not accepted).

The guest house's location provides an excellent base for exploring the delightful countryside of the Lincolnshire Wolds and the famous sandy beaches that stretch for miles from Cleethorpes south to Skegness make this a popular base for family holidays.

weekend; a Monster Trucks exhibition; concerts; a steam weekend; Craft Fayres, sand sculpture contests and much more.

A curious survival from World War I is the **Haile Sand Fort**, close to the shore and clearly visible from the Cleethorpes Promenade. Haile was one of two such hexagonal forts built on either side of the Humber Estuary in 1915. A large net ran between them to stop German submarines entering the river. Both forts had 6-inch guns mounted on all sides but these were never fired in anger. The more distant fort, Bull Sand Fort, was much larger, capable of accommodating 200 officers and men. Both forts are now privately owned and their future use is as yet unknown.

NORTH SOMERCOTES
12 miles SE of Grimsby off A1031

Olney's Shrove Tuesday pancake races may be better known but those at North Somercotes are equally popular. Contestants run the length of this straggling village tossing their pancakes as they go. There are separate contests for adults and children.

To the east of the village is the **Donna Nook Nature Reserve** which stretches 6 miles south along the coast to Saltfleet. In summer it's a favoured nesting site for many species of birds, amongst them dunnock, little grebe and meadow pipits. Large colonies of brent geese, dunlin and other waders are attracted to the mudflats while common and grey seals pup on the sandflats. As well as marram grass and sea buckthorn, the dunes also provide a support for the much rarer pyramidal orchids.

WALTHAM
5 miles S of Grimsby on B1203

Primarily a commuter village, Waltham has retained its delightful green where

PROSPECT FARM & COTTAGES

Waltham Road, Brigsley, Grimsby,
Lincolnshire DN37 0RQ
Tel/Fax: 01472 826491

Set in the heart of the Lincolnshire countryside and surrounded by 40 acres of its own grounds, **Prospect Farm & Cottages** offers visitors the choice of either bed & breakfast or self-catering accommodation. Bed and breakfast guests stay in the spacious farmhouse, the home of Darrell and Janet Speight who had the house built. Occupying an elevated position, the farmhouse enjoys tranquil views of horses and sheep grazing in the pasture.

Three rooms are available - 1 double en suite, plus a double and a single, both of which have private bathrooms. Beautifully furnished, the rooms are provided with all kinds of pleasant extras such as fresh flowers, fruit, magazines, even shoe polish. Guests have the use of the snug with its open

fire and your day gets off to a good start with an Aga-cooked breakfast with eggs from the Speights' own hens. For those who prefer self-catering, the attractive old stable building has been imaginatively converted into 4 tastefully appointed cottages, each sleeping up to 6 people.

Opened at Easter 2001, the property has been designed with disabled users in mind and each unit has an extensively equipped kitchen with every conceivable need supplied. Children are welcome but no pets, and please note that both Prospect Farm and the cottages are all non-smoking.

CROSS KEYS

Brigg Road, Grasby, Barnetby,
Lincolnshire DN38 6AQ
Tel: 01652 628247

Set on the edge of the Wolds, the **Cross Keys** enjoys panoramic views not only of the gentle Lincolnshire hills but is also in a designated area of oustanding natural beauty. From the dining room, on a clear day, you can even see the towers of Lincoln Cathedral, an incredible 25 miles away.

Mine hosts, Tricia and Ian Parker, took over here in September 2000 and have made their welcoming old inn a favoured venue for all who enjoy good food. The speciality of the house is fresh Grimsby haddock, available on Thursdays and Fridays, but there's also an excellent choice of steaks and grills, a delicious home made steak and ale pie, and a good selection of dishes for vegetarians. The appetising menu is available every lunchtime and evening, except on Mondays (Bank holidays not included). Real ale fans will be pleased to find that traditional cask ales are available with the guest ale changed monthly.

Children are welcome, with a play area for them in the garden. Overlooking the garden, there's a spacious lounge bar with an open fire, and soft music playing in the background. Tricia and Ian organise a pub quiz once a week, and there's also live music every week. Popular with patrons from surrounding towns and villages, the Cross Keys also provides a convenient watering-hole for walkers along the Viking Way which passes close by.

THE SKIPWORTH ARMS

Station Road, Moortown,
nr Market Rasen,
Lincolnshire LN7 6HZ
Tel/Fax: 01472 851770

A warm welcome, good beer and good food are commodities you might expect from a pub, but **The Skipworth Arms** offers much more besides. This old railway pub which has traded almost continuously since the 1840s when it was named after Lady Skipworth on whose land it was built. Mine hosts Graham and Margaret Hicks arrived here a few years ago and they have completely refurbished the old tavern, building up the games side and offering bed & breakfast accommodation in 3 rooms - 2 doubles and 1 twin, all with private facilities. The lake at the back of the pub provides its most unusual attraction, namely coarse fishing for carp, tench and rudd. Day tickets for fishing can be obtained from the pub. Another amenity is the 4.5 acre caravan site which has standings for 5 caravans and is equipped with good on site facilities. On the food side, anglers, campers, caravanners and anyone else who pauses here will find a choice that runs from light snacks to 3-course meals. Margaret is particularly noted for her home made pies and her Sunday lunches are particularly popular. In addition to the regular menu a choice of Specials is available on Saturdays and Sundays. During the week, there are specially reduced prices for Early Eaters - anyone who eats here between 5.30pm and 7.30pm.

there's an anvil erected as a memorial to Henry Jackson, the village's last blacksmith. Just south of the village, the **Waltham Windmill and Rural Craft Centre** has as its focus the 1880 six-sailed windmill which was the last working mill in the area. It is now grinding corn again and its outbuildings have been converted into craft shops and studios. Visitors can learn the art of ceramic painting; sample old-fashioned confectionery in Ma Millers Sweet Emporium or settle back in a converted Pullman railway carriage and enjoy home made ice cream. Other attractions here include a museum recalling the bygone days of rural Lincolnshire and a small gauge railway.

CAISTOR
10 miles SW of Grimsby on A46

Caistor's market place stands on the plain, looking across corn fields to the distant towers of Lincoln Cathedral; but its narrow streets wind their way up the western slopes of the Wolds. Caistor's name makes it clear that this agreeable little market town did indeed start life as a small Roman camp. Just a few hard-to-find fragments of the once massive walls remain. However, it's known that the camp measured just 300 yards by 100 yards and that the present **Church of St Peter & St Paul** stands at the exact centre of the Roman enclosure. The church, whose oldest part is the Anglo-Saxon tower, contains a curiosity kept in a glass case. This is the famous Gad Whip, which until 1847 was *"cracked over the head of the vicar on Palm Sunday by a man from Broughton in payment for certain parcels of land"*. Another version of the tradition claims that the whip, which had a purse containing 2 shillings tied to it, was simply waved over the head of the clergyman while the latter read the second lesson. Either way, Victorian

THE BULL INN

Caistor Road, South Kelsey, Lincs. LN7 6PR
Tel/Fax: 01652 678417

South Kelsey may be well off the beaten track but the reputation of **The Bull Inn** has inspired many visitors to follow the winding Lincolnshire lanes to the village and its charming 18th century hostelry. Originally built as a coaching inn, (when it boasted a thatched roof), The Bull today is renowned for its excellent steaks and its outstanding wine list. Diners travel from miles around to sample the culinary delights and the pub is also convenient for walkers on the nearby Viking Way. Mine hosts at The Bull are Gwen and Keith Rogers, a friendly hospitable couple who are both Lincolnshire born and bred. In addition to the famous steaks, the menu offers some appetising fish and chicken dishes, as

well as some outrageously indulgent puddings. Wine lovers will be in their element here since there's a wide selection to choose from, and all the vintages are personally selected and highly recommended. Meals can be enjoyed either at the wrought iron and glass tables in the candlelit dining room with its beamed roof; in the beamed bar with its pew benches and open fire; or in the small snug bar with its log burning stove. In good weather, customers can take their drinks into the small garden.

LITTLE OWLS

North End Farm, Thornton Road,
North Owersby, Market Rasen,
Lincolnshire LN8 3PP
Tel/Fax: 01673 828116

Set around a charming paved courtyard colourful with flowers and with an ornamental fish pond, **Little Owls** is a group of farm buildings which has been ingeniously converted into attractive and comfortable bed and breakfast accommodation. Formerly a cattle shed and a waggon house, the buildings are part of North End farm and surrounded by more than 12 acres of garden and paddocks which guests are free to enjoy.

Arriving visitors receive a warm welcome from Henry and Marlene Burton, both of whom are Lincolnshire born and can guide you to all the local places of interest. Little Owls has 3 guest rooms, (2 twins and 1 single), one of them en suite, the others with private facilities. All the rooms are tastefully furnished and decorated, and provided with some friendly extra touches such as a bowl of fresh fruit. Guests have the use of a large comfortable lounge and a full English breakfast is included in the tariff - vegetarian and other diets can be catered for. Dogs are welcome by prior arrangement and kennelling can be provided. Little Owls is especially convenient for walkers along the Viking Way and for cyclists following the National Cycle Route from Hull to Harwich, both of which pass close by. Little Owls has secure parking for cars as well as bicycles.

opinion regarded the performance as not consistent with ecclesiastical decorum.

To the north of the church is the picturesque **Grammar School**, parts of which date back to 1631. The school's most famous alumnus is the poet Sir Henry Newbolt (1862-1928) whose patriotic poem, *Drake's Drum*, contains the immortal line *"Play up! Play up! and play the game"*. Near the Grammar School, a former Congregational church of 1842, impressive with its Doric columns, now serves as the school's library.

A fire ravaged Caistor in 1681; consequently, many of the buildings lining the market square are Georgian or early 19th century. A later addition is the cast iron pump erected here in 1897 to celebrate Queen Victoria's Diamond Jubilee.

A mile or so north of the town, **Pelham's Pillar** commemorates the planting of the surrounding woods by Charles Pelham, Earl of Yarborough. Between 1787 and 1828, the earl had planted 12,552,700 trees - at least that is what the inscription claims. The lofty tower cost a staggering £2,395 to build and when it was completed in 1849 no less a personage than Prince Albert came to view it. The tower is locked but if you want to climb up inside, a key can be obtained within reasonable hours from the Keeper's Cottage, Pillar Lodge.

The 147-mile long Viking Way passes through Caistor and about 5 miles south of the town climbs to **Normanby-on-the-Wold**, the highest village in Lincolnshire. The path continues through **Walesby** where All Saints Church is known as the Ramblers' Church because of its stained glass window depicting Christ with ramblers and cyclists, and on to the delightful village of Tealby.

MARKET RASEN
18 miles SW of Grimsby off A46

This pleasing little market town stands between the great plain that spreads north of Lincoln and the sheltering Wolds to the east. Now happily bypassed, the town still has a market on Tuesdays and throughout the year there are regular meetings at the **Market Rasen Racecourse**. Following the closure of Lincoln's racecourse in the 1960s, this is now the only horse racing track in Lincolnshire. Recently modernized, it's a popular venue with facilities that include a first class restaurant, children's playground, crèche, and a picnic area in the central area of the course.

Taking its name from the little River Rase, Market Rasen was once described by Charles Dickens as being *"the sleepiest town in England"*. Much of the central part is a conservation area and includes two ecclesiastical buildings of some note. The Centenary Wesleyan Chapel of 1863 has an impressive frontage with an Ionic portico and pediment; St Thomas's Church has a typical 15th century tower of local ironstone, an attractive modern stained glass window depicting the Nativity, and a font of Ancaster stone crafted in 1963 by Lawrence Bond who also made the cover. Just over 400 years ago, the church witnessed a dreadful deed. The vicar, William Storr, had taken the side of the poor against the lord of the manor, Francis Cartwright. Cartwright's son accosted the vicar outside the church porch and murdered him.

In the nearby village of West Rasen stands an interesting medieval survival, a narrow 3-arched packhorse bridge with a cobbled surface that crosses the tiny River Rase.

ASTON ARMS

Market Place, Market Rasen,
Lincolnshire LN8 3HL
Tel: 01673 842313

According to those who know about these things, Elton John's 1973 hit song *Saturday Night's for Fighting* was based on Market Rasen. Very odd, especially when you visit the quiet corner of the cobbled Market Place where the **Aston Arms** nestles close to the 15th century church. The interior of the inn is equally soothing with its beamed ceiling, leaded windows overlooking the square and its large open fire. Mine hosts, John and

Mary Bradley, are both Lincolnshire born and bred and their welcoming hostelry is very much a social centre for the town.

The local sports teams have made it their base and the pub also sponsors a local football team as well as having its own pool team. In the pub itself, the games area has two pool tables, a darts board and a large screen television. Real Ales are another of the attractions here, (with Theakstons XB permanently on tap along with a guest ale), and so too are the traditional home cooked pub meals which are served from midday until early evening every day. The menu offers a wide choice ranging from hearty main meals to appetising snacks and bar meals, all of them freshly prepared from top quality ingredients.

TEALBY
5 miles NE of Market Rasen on B1203

With its stone cottages set along winding lanes, the tiny River Rase flowing over a ford near a water mill, a 14th century thatched inn, small shops and tea rooms, and a fine church looking out across the Wolds, Tealby is about as unspoilt a village as 21st century England can provide. Sadly, Bayon's Manor, the flamboyant Gothic-style mansion built in 1834 by Charles Tennyson D'Eyncourt, a grandfather of Alfred Lord Tennyson, was blown up as a dangerous ruin in 1965. However, D'Eyncourt's taste in building styles lives on in the village school he designed and built in 1856: its beamed roof is copied from the one in Westminster Hall.

TEALBY TEA ROOMS
Front Street, Tealby, Market Rasen, Lincolnshire LN8 3XW
Tel/Fax: 01673 838261

With its narrow lanes and picturesque cottages, Tealby is well known as one of Lincolnshire's prettiest villages. **Tealby Tea Rooms** is a delightful traditional tea room offering delicious home made fayre. Richard Glover is a qualified baker and chef and has won many awards. This year The Tearoom is in 'The Guide to Good Food' 2000/2001. The Tearoom is open daily from April to October, (2.30pm-5.30pm, Monday to Friday; 10.30am to 5.30pm, Saturday, Sunday and Bank Holidays), and on Sundays only from 10.30pm to 5.30pm through the rest of the year. All groups booked to include, with no obligation, a free talk on Tealby history, famous for its paper mills and Tennyson connection.

THE OLDE BARN INN
Cow Lane, Tealby,
Lincolnshire LN8 3YB
Tel: 01673 838304
Fax: 01673 838750

Tealby has been described as the "most charming village in the Lincolnshire Wolds" so it's no surprise to find that it boasts a delightful traditional hostelry, **The Olde Barn Inn**. As the name suggests, it was originally built as a barn, some 400 years ago, and the locally quarried stone, now painted

white, provides a pleasant backdrop to the well kept gardens. In good weather, customers can relax here with their refreshments; in winter, a roaring log fire in the bar's inglenook fireplace creates a cosy, welcoming atmosphere. Soft music plays gently in the background, (no noisy game machines here), and Trev and Cathy King's excellent food makes The Olde Barn a place to linger.

The extensive menu has something for every palate, ranging from local specialities such as Tealby Toad in the Hole, (locally made sausage with Yorkshire pudding and onion gravy), through grills, poultry, meat and fish dishes, as well as bar snacks, vegetarian choices and a children's menu. All meals are freshly prepared to order and you can enjoy them either in the comfortable lounge or in the non-smoking restaurant with its vaulted beam ceiling. A choice of 4 hand pulled beers has earned The Olde Barn a prestigious Pub of the Season award from CAMRA, and the bar is stocked with a comprehensive range of other alcoholic and soft drinks.

CLICKEM INN

Swinhope, nr Market Rasen,
Lincolnshire LN8 6BS
Tel: 01472 398253

The tiny hamlet of Swinhope enjoys a quiet Wolds setting, hidden away in a deep valley just off the B1203, about 8 miles northeast of Market Rasen. It's well worth seeking out for the oddly-named **Clickem Inn** where you can be sure of a good pint of beer and something delicious to eat. Formerly known as The Talbot, the pub takes it present name from the click of the gate to the field opposite into which farmers drove their flocks before settling down for a friendly pint at the inn.

Today's customers are a good mix of ages from among the locals, plus ramblers, cyclists and tourists. Proprietors Terry and June Whitfield (he a former Grimsby fisherman, she once a deputy mess manager at nearby RAF Binbrook) put out the welcome mat for all comers. In the two comfortable, cosy bars and the non-smoking conservatory dining area excellent food is served, from light bar snacks to speciality steaks, seasonal lobster (24 hours notice needed) and roasts every day. On fairweather days, customers can enjoy their food and drink in the pleasant garden or on the patio. Darts and dominoes are popular, (the three man darts team has a combined age of over 200!), but tug o'war has all but died out, though there's a cabinet full of trophies from winning "tugs".

LUDFORD
6 miles E of Market Rasen on A631

Ludford used to consist of two manors, Ludford Magna and Ludford Parva, and had two churches. Today, the two villages are one, merging into each other along what is known as the Magna Mile. There's also just the one church, St Mary and St Peter's, designed in 1863, in the medieval style, by the renowned James Fowler of Louth.

3 Lincoln to the River Humber

Known to the Romans as "Lindum Colonia", Lincoln stood at the junction of two major Imperial thoroughfares, Fosse Way and Ermine Street. By the time of the Domesday Book, it had grown into a settlement of around 1000 households. William the Conqueror won few friends here by peremptorily ordering 166 of these houses to be destroyed to make way for an imposing castle. Around the same time, he authorised the building of a cathedral and made Lincoln the ecclesiastical centre of a vast bishopric that extended from the Humber to the Thames. The city reached its peak of prosperity during the Middle Ages but when Henry VIII visited in 1541 the town fathers were reduced to begging relief from taxation or *"they would be compelled in short time to forsake the city, to its utter desolation"*. Henry rejected their plea.

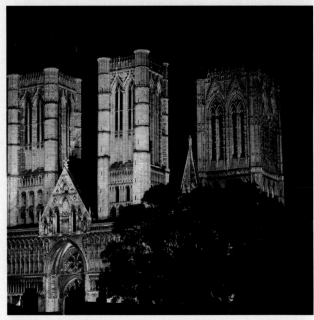

Lincoln Cathedral

When Daniel Defoe passed through Lincoln in the 1770s he found *"an ancient, ragged, decayed and still decaying city"*. Half a century later, another traveller dismissed the historic city as *"an overgrown village"*. Happily, improvements in roads and canals, and the arrival of the railway in the 1840s, returned the city to prosperity and Lincoln became a major centre for heavy engineering - steam engines, agricultural machinery, excavators, motor cars and other heavy duty items. The first Army tanks rolled off the assembly lines here. The downside of this industrial activity is an unlovely sprawl of buildings crowding the plain around the River Witham. But you only have to climb the hill to the old town to enter the serenity of the cathedral close, a tranquil enclave lying in the shadow of the noblest and most majestic of all English cathedrals.

The south bank of the River Humber is indeed Lincolnshire's most industrial area but that is only part of the story. As the North Lincolnshire District Council is proud to point out, almost 89% of the land here is in some form of agricultural use and more than half of this (54%) is rated as Land Quality Grades 1 and 2 - as against the average for England of around 16%. Rural north Lincolnshire is as peaceful and unspoilt as anywhere in the county, with scenery that ranges from the northern tip of the Wolds in the east, to the level plains of the Isle of Axholme in the west. A few miles up-river is the colossal Humber Bridge, the largest single span suspension bridge in Europe.

Steep Hill, Lincoln

Amongst more venerable buildings of note are Thornton Abbey with its monumental gatehouse, and Gainsborough Old Hall which dates back to the 1470s and is regarded as one of the best-preserved medieval manors in England.

During this tour of the area, we come across some interesting connections with the Pilgrim Fathers; with John Wesley, whose family lived at Epworth, near Scunthorpe; and with John Harrison who solved the ages-old riddle of how to compute longitude at sea.

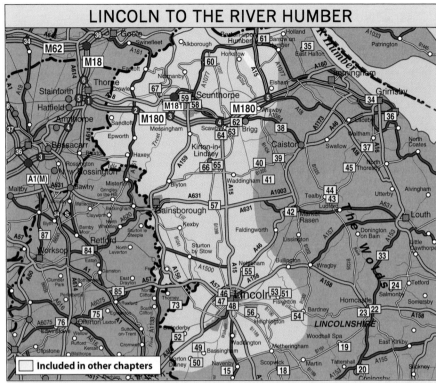

LINCOLN TO THE RIVER HUMBER

© MAPS IN MINUTES ™ 2001   © Crown Copyright, Ordnance Survey 2001

PLACES TO STAY, EAT, DRINK AND SHOP

LINCOLN

Apart from Durham, **Lincoln Cathedral** is the only one in England to occupy a magnificent hilltop location, its towers soaring high above the Lincolnshire lowlands and visible for miles around. William the Conqueror ordered the first cathedral to be built here but that was almost entirely destroyed by an earthquake on April 15th 1185. The rebuilding that followed, under the energetic direction of Bishop Hugh of Avalon, resulted in the creation of one the country's most inspiring churches. Among its many superb features are the magnificent open nave, stained-glass

Lincoln Cathedral

windows incorporating the 14th century Bishop's Eye and Dean's Eye, and the glorious Angel Choir, whose carvings include the Lincoln Imp, the unofficial symbol of the city.

The imposing ruins of the **Bishops Old Palace** (English Heritage) in the shadow of the Cathedral, reveal the sumptuous lifestyle of the wealthy medieval bishops whose authority stretched from the Humber to the Thames. Visitors can wander through splendid apartments, banqueting halls and offices, explore the dramatic undercroft, gaze at the views from inside the Roman city walls, and see one of Europe's most northerly vineyards.

A good way to explore the city is to follow the Lincoln Heritage Trail which takes in the city's "Magnificent Seven" tourist attractions. The cathedral, naturally, takes pride of place but close by is **Lincoln Castle** which dates from 1068. Visitors can climb to the ramparts, which

EDWARD KING HOUSE

The Old Palace, Minster Yard, Lincoln, Lincolnshire LN2 1PU
Tel: 01522 528778 Fax: 01522 527308 e-mail: ekh@oden.org.uk

Few bed and breakfast establishments occupy such a beautiful and historic setting as **Edward King House**, once the residence of the Bishops of Lincoln. It stands within the lee of the Cathedral and next to the medieval Old Palace, a quiet oasis with easy access to shops and the city's many places of interest. Each of the comfortable guest bedrooms has its own character and outlook, is equipped with central heating, hot and cold water, and tea/coffee-making facilities. Other amenities include a television lounge, an attractive and secluded garden and a car park.

THE ICE CREAM PARLOUR

3 Bailgate, Lincoln,
Lincolnshire LN1 3AE
Tel: 01522 511447

Just around the corner from the Cathedral and close to the Museum of Lincolnshire Life, **The Ice Cream Parlour** is owned and run by Claire Dennett whose family have been making quality ice cream in Lincolnshire for more than three quarters of a century.

The outside of the Parlour gives no indication of the wonderful vaulted room downstairs which was originally the cellar of a 14th century inn. The ribbed arches and an exposed stone wall make this a unique setting in which to enjoy the superb ice creams, yoghurts and sorbets on offer. They are all made with fresh milk or cream, completely natural with no artificial colours. The range includes no fewer than 26 different flavours of ice cream and Claire is always introducing new varieties - at the time of writing Honeycomb and Turkish Delight have joined the array of delights. Three or four different kinds of yoghurt and five sorts of sorbets make the choice even more difficult. The Parlour is open daily from 10.30am to 6pm, extended during the summer months until sunset. Out of season, it is closed on Wednesdays. Bookings are not essential but you can reserve a table downstairs if you wish. Children and dogs are welcome. The Parlour also supplies ice cream to other outlets across the country so do look out for them on your travels.

THE PRINCE OF WALES

77a Bailgate, Lincoln, Lincolnshire LN1 3AR
Tel: 01522 528894

Just a few moments walk from the majestic Cathedral, in the oldest part of this historic city, **The Prince of Wales** is a traditional hostelry with a history that goes back to the early 18th century when it started life as an alehouse. There's much more on offer nowadays. With its stone tiled floors and

exposed stone walls the inn has plenty of atmosphere and

it's also popular with local people because of the quality of the food on offer every lunchtime.

Meals are served between 11am and 3pm (Monday to Saturday), and from noon until 3pm on Sunday. Both the printed menu and the specials listed on the blackboard provide a good variety of main meals and snacks, with the pasta dishes and filled baguettes especially in demand. Children are welcome on the outside patio area. Kay Cockram took over here in 1998 and one of her priorities is maintaining the inn's reputation for serving real ales in top condition. There are always at least six of them on tap with Bass, Old Speckled Hen, John Smiths, Timothy Taylor's Landlord and Marston Pedigree as permanent fixtures. Sky TV is available in the bar and there's ample car parking nearby. Please note that credit cards are not accepted.

include Observatory Tower, to savour some fine views of the city. Interesting features abound, notably the keep, known as Lucy Tower, Cobb Hall, where the public gallows were located, and the Victorian prison whose chapel has separate pews like upright coffins. The building also houses an original version of Magna Carta.

Steep Hill, Lincoln

There are some fine Norman buildings on a lesser scale in **Steep Hill** and **The Strait**. **Jews House**, which dates from about 1170, is thought to be the oldest domestic building in England to survive intact. Its neighbour is Jews Court, a reminder of the time when there was a thriving Jewish community in Lincoln. Medieval splendour lives on in the black and white half-timbered houses on High Bridge, and in the old city Gateways, while the residences in the Cathedral Close and Castle Square are models of Georgian elegance.

The most impressive survival of the old town walls is **The Stonebow** which spans the High Street pedestrianised shopping mall. The 3-storey building houses the city's Guildhall, its Civic Insignia, royal Charters and other historic artefacts. The Mote Bell on the roof, dated 1371, is still rung to summon the City Fathers to council meetings.

Another place of interest is the **Greyfriars Exhibition Centre** (free), housed in a beautiful 13th century building. The Centre hosts themed exhibitions focused on the collections of

the City and County Museum which range from pre-historic times to 1750.

The Lawn (free), originally built in 1820 as a lunatic asylum and set in eight acres of beautiful grounds and gardens, is an elegant porticoed building whose attractions include an archaeology centre, a tropical conservatory with a display dedicated to the botanist Sir Joseph Banks, an aquarium, a specialist shopping mall and a fully licensed pub and restaurant.

Lincolnshire's largest social history museum is the **Museum of Lincolnshire Life** which occupies an extensive barracks built for the Royal North Lincoln Militia in 1857. It is now a listed building and houses a fascinating series of displays depicting the many aspects of Lincolnshire life. The Domestic Gallery turns the clock back to the beginning of the 20th century, showing what life was like in a middle-class home; settings include a nursery, bedroom, kitchen, parlour and wash house. The Transport Gallery shows the skills of the wheelwright and coachbuilder in such items as a carrier's cart and a horse-drawn charabier (hearse). It also contains a fully restored 1925 Bullnose Morris and a

Lincoln Elk motorcycle. In the Agricultural and Industrial Gallery notable exhibits include a First World War tank built by William Foster of Lincoln; a 20-ton steam ploughing engine; a steam traction engine and a number of tractors. Commercial Row features a builder's yard, a printing press, a village post office and several shops. All the above represent just part of the scope of this marvellous museum, where visitors can also pause for refreshment and perhaps a slice of the local speciality plumbread in the Hungry Yellowbelly café. (That peculiar name is applied to anyone born in Lincolnshire!)

Set in beautiful landscaped gardens, **The Usher Gallery** was built in 1927 with funds bequeathed by a Lincoln jeweller, James Ward Usher. It is a major centre for the arts, with collections of porcelain, glass, clocks and coins, and a display of memorabilia connected with the Lincolnshire-born Poet Laureate, Alfred Lord Tennyson. The gallery also houses an important collection of works by Peter de Wint and paintings by Turner, Lowry, Piper, Sickert and Ruskin Spear.

Ellis Mill is the last survivor of a line of windmills that once ran along the Lincoln Edge, a limestone ridge stretching some 70 miles from Winteringham by the Humber to Stamford on the county's southern border. This tower mill dates back to 1798 and is in full working order.

Lincoln stages several major annual events, including a flower festival in the Cathedral, the Lincolnshire Show at the Showground just north of the city, and the Jolly Water Carnival on Brayford Pool in the centre of the city. Raising money for charity is the purpose behind this aquatic event, which includes rowing and sailing races and a procession through the streets.

AROUND LINCOLN

Just southeast of the city are the popular open spaces of **Hartsholme Country Park** and **Swanholme Lakes Local Nature Reserve**, 200 acres of woodland, lakes and meadows to explore. A little way further south is **Whisby Nature Park**, set on either side of the Lincoln-Newark railway line and home to great crested grebes, teal and tufted duck. Also on the southern outskirts of the city is the **Lincolnshire Road Transport Museum** where 40 vintage cars, commercial vehicles and buses span more than 70 years of road transport history. Also on display is a wide variety of old road signs, ticket machines and early bus timetables.

About 5 miles west of Lincoln, **Doddington Hall** is a very grand Elizabethan mansion completed in 1600 by the architect Robert Smythson, and standing now exactly as then, with wonderful formal gardens, a gatehouse and a family church. The interior contains a fascinating collection of pictures, textiles, porcelain and furniture that reflect four centuries of unbroken family occupation.

BASSINGHAM
8 miles SW of Lincoln off A46

A pleasant little village with houses mostly of local warm red brick; an Elizabethan manor house (private) and, on one of the many little greens, an oak seat carved in the shape of a bull. This striking feature is part of an admirable enterprise masterminded by North Kesteven Arts to enhance both the natural and built-up areas of the District with all kinds of sculpture and art work. These imaginative pieces, many of them serving as public benches, range from the Dorrington Demons, based on a local legend, to the Scopwick Woman whose seat, in the lap of her skirt, has become a kind of letterbox with local people leaving tokens, messages or gifts for others to pick up. A booklet titled *In View,* which gives full details of these fascinating works, is available from TICs.

A couple of miles north of Bassingham, **Aubourn** is a charming Elizabethan and Jacobean manor house set in attractive gardens and notable for a finely carved oak staircase. Nearby, the tower of Aubourn's Victorian church stands alone,

all that was left after the church was demolished in 1973 and parishioners reverted to worshipping in the chancel of the old church amidst the clutter of memorials to the Meres and Nevile families.

NORTON DISNEY
10 miles SW of Lincoln off A46

Despite the name, there's no direct connection with Hollywood cartoons -

THE BUGLE HORN

19 Lincoln Road, Bassingham, Lincoln, Lincolnshire LN5 9HQ
Tel: 01522 788333

For those in search of a country inn with a genuinely traditional atmosphere, **The Bugle Horn** in the delightful village of Bassingham will fulfil all their expectations. Very much at the centre of village life, (the local cricket club has made it their headquarters), Russ and Gill Woodcock's welcoming hostelry is also well known for its excellent home made food. Chef Karen's extensive menu ranges from hearty steaks to vegetarian lasagnes, and her wonderful home made desserts include time-honoured favourites such as steamed puddings and crumbles. Definitely worth seeking out.

THE ST VINCENT ARMS

Main Street, Norton Disney, Lincoln LN6 9JU
Tel: 01522 788478

One of the most decisive engagements in the Napoleonic Wars was the Battle of Cape St Vincent in 1797 in which Admirals Nelson and Sir John Jervis defeated a fleet of French and Spanish ships twice their number. Jervis was later elevated to the peerage as Earl St Vincent and his glorious achievement was celebrated in the naming of **The St Vincent Arms,** just off the A46 southwest of Lincoln. This inviting old hostelry has a lovely beer garden where live bands play in summer, a children's play area and, inside, the welcoming atmosphere of a traditional English inn. The inn is well known for its excellent food, available every lunchtime and evening, with an extensive menu of main meals, snacks and

sandwiches supplemented by daily specials such as Poached Salmon, Sweet and Sour Pork, and Mushroom Stroganoff. There are two real ales on tap, along with a wide choice of other popular beverages. Children are welcome and there are non-smoking areas. Chris and Sheryll Thomson have made this a lively and popular inn, hosting a Sunday night Quiz from 9.15pm and a Bingo session once a month. The inn's most famous customer is commemorated by a display of photographs and newspaper cuttings recording the visit of Walt Disney to the village. He came here in 1949 in search of his ancestors who originated in the village.

THE CARPENTERS ARMS

High Street, Fiskerton, Lincoln, Lincolnshire LN3 4ET
Tel: 01522 751806

The little village of Fiskerton stands on the north bank of the River Witham, about 4 miles east of Lincoln, with the Viking Way long distance footpath and the National Cycle Route both passing nearby. Located in the heart of the village and originally built as two houses, **The Carpenters Arms** is believed to take its name from the wheelwright's shop which used to stand next door. That has long since gone, along with the adjacent blacksmith's and the site now provides a spacious car park for the inn.

The pub itself looks very inviting with its red-tiled roof and cream washed walls dotted with hanging baskets of flowers. The interior is just as welcoming - lots of old beams, comfortable upholstered seating and a display of paintings of local scenes, many of which are for sale. The popular games area offers pool, darts and Sky TV as well as traditional pub games such as dominoes and crib. Visiting darts players will need to watch out for the "Lincolnshire Board", an unusual variant which has no numbers on it and no trebles strip. The pub supports both a ladies' and a mens' darts team and also its own pool team. Other activities include a Quiz Night every Sunday evening and occasional live music.

The Carpenters is a family business, with the licensee Donna Welch aided by her parents, Jim and Julie, and manager Ben Crabb. Together, they have built up a reputation for serving good quality food at a reasonable cost and although their tasty home made pies (including a hearty "Desperate Dan")

are the speciality of the house, the extensive menu also offers steaks, fish dishes, large Yorkshire Puddings, curries, salads and filled baguettes. Vegetarians are well catered for with dishes such as Cream Cheese & Broccoli Bake or Vegetable Lasagne and from Tuesday to Friday, The Carpenters has a "Two Meals for £6.50" offer available between 5pm and 7pm. Food is available from 5pm to 9.30pm (Tuesday to Saturday, 9pm on Sunday), from noon until 2.30pm on Saturday, and from noon until 2pm on Sunday when a traditional Sunday roast lunch is served for which booking is strongly recommended. To accompany your meal, there's a short but attractively priced wine list, with house wine also available by the glass, and a range of cask ales that includes Masham Black Sheep Best Bitter, Tom Woods Highwood Brewery and Lincolnshire Legend.

The inn is open from 7pm to 11pm (Monday); 5pm to 11pm (Tuesday to Thursday); noon until 3pm & 5pm to 11pm (Saturday) and from noon until 10.30pm on Sunday. If you are living or staying within a 10-mile radius of The Carpenters, this customer friendly pub provides a free mini-bus service. Closed Mondays.

although Walt Disney did visit the village in the 1950s in search of his family roots. The name derives from a family who came over with William the Conqueror - their home town was Isigny, near Bayeux. If these Disneys were indeed Walt's ancestors, they left behind some impressive memorials in the church here. The oldest dates back to around 1300, depicting Joan d'Iseney in coif and wimple, but perhaps the most striking is a brass of around 1580. Three feet by two feet, it shows two generations of the Disney family who between them produced 21 children.

SWINDERBY
8 miles SW of Lincoln off A46

This small village boasts some good examples of 18th century houses and, a mile north of the village, a railway station which is one of the oldest surviving stations in the country. It was built in 1846 for the Great Midland Railway and is still in use.

Swinderby was the home of yet another RAF airfield in World War II and the RAF Swinderby Exhibition tells its story from its construction in 1941 until its closure in 1993. Unusually, the exhibition is located in a pub just across from the airfield, The Halfway House *(see also panel below)*.

FISKERTON
5 miles E of Lincoln off A158

This sizeable village lies close to the River Witham and it's possible to follow the riverside path all the way back to Lincoln. The village church has several Norman features and also a large brass, of around 1490, depicting a priest in a cope. Sometime in the 1600s, the brass went missing but was discovered almost 200 years later in an antiques shop by the

THE HALFWAY HOUSE

Newark Road, Swinderby, Lincoln, LN6 9HN
Tel: 01522 868206 Fax: 01522 868640

Conveniently located on the A46 between Lincoln and Newark, **The Halfway House** dates back to 1795. In those days, it served as a busy staging post on this major stage coach route with spacious stables and a blacksmith's forge on site. Standing in 5 acres of its own grounds, the Halfway House provides a pleasant beer garden and plenty of off-street parking.

More than 200 years after it opened, the inn is still dispensing hospitality and enjoys an excellent reputation for its quality food and ales. Meals are served all day from noon until 9pm (8.30pm on Sundays) and the extensive menu is displayed on blackboard with the fare on offer always changing. Home made steak and ale pie is a speciality of the house and to complement your meal there's wide

choice of beverages, including 2 real ales. The interior is full of character with a separate dining area, a non-smoking restaurant and a conservatory. The inn is disabled friendly with a ramped entry and disabled toilet. Children are welcome too with a childrens play area and even a baby-changing room.

An interesting feature is the small museum dedicated to RAF Swinderby which had many bases in this area during World War II. Photographs, paintings and memorabilia honour their contribution to the war effort and attract many visits from war veterans.

TYRWHITT ARMS & SHORT FERRY CARAVAN PARK

Ferry Road, Fiskerton, Lincoln LN3 4HU
Tel: 01526 398021 Fax: 01526 398102
website: shortferry.co.uk

Only 7 miles from the City of Lincoln and well situated for visits to the coastal towns of Skegness and Mablethorpe, the **Tyrwhitt Arms & Short Ferry Caravan Park** stand in almost 60 acres of attractive Lincolnshire countryside. Bordered by the Old River Witham and the Barlings Eau, both tributaries of the River Witham, the Park offers visitors a wide range of facilities, including a spacious hostelry serving a comprehensive menu with food for all tastes. There's a seasonal outdoor heated pool with sunbathing area, shuffleboard court, tennis court, children's play area, river and lake fishing, with a 9 hole pitch and putt, par 3 golf course and bowling green opening shortly. There are all the usual toilet and shower facilities, laundry room and a well-stocked shop selling groceries, frozen food, caravan accessories, fancy goods, newspapers, fishing tackle and bait, and much more. Most of the caravans are static, (some of them available for hire), but there's also a large touring site with electric hook-ups available and a dedicated shower/toilet block. Sited within the caravan park, The Tyrwhitt Arms has lounge bars, games room, dining room, snooker room and a children's room with adjacent patio and beer garden. With so much to do on site, it's tempting to just stay there but it would be a shame not to visit the historic city of Lincoln so close by, as well as the coast and the market towns of Newark, Boston and Louth.

THE BLACK HORSE B&B

16 Wragby Road, Bardney,
Lincolnshire LN3 5XL
Tel: 01526 398900 Fax: 01526 399281
e-mail: black-horse@lineone.net

Dating way back to the 16th century, **The Black Horse B&B** was for many years a public house but, after being completely refurbished, it re-opened in April 2000 as a fully licensed tea room and guesthouse.

During the summer months its frontage is ablaze with colourful tubs, urns and hanging baskets of flowers and it stands in half an acre of grounds which includes a grassed garden with a children's play area, room for a tent pitch or two, and a spacious car park. In the popular tea room, home made cakes and puddings are a speciality, along with traditional Cream Teas. An extensive snack menu is available all day which includes home made pasties, omelettes and a daily "special" lunch. Sandwiches, salads and baked potatoes are also available, either to eat in or take away, as indeed is everything on the menu. Evening dinner parties and private functions are welcome, while theme evenings and lunches are becoming ever more popular.

Accommodation for bed & breakfast guests comprises 4 comfortable rooms, (2 twins, 1 double, 1 family), all of them en suite and all equipped with remote control colour TV and hospitality trays. The tariff includes a 4-course English breakfast and packed lunches are available for walkers and cyclists or, in fact, for anybody who would like one!

Bishop of Lincoln. He restored the brass to its proper place.

BARDNEY
10 miles E of Lincoln on B1190/B1202

The dominating feature of this little town beside the River Witham is the British Sugar Corporation's towering beet processing factory. In medieval times, a more elegant structure distinguished the town, and was just as important to its prosperity. Bardney Abbey was famous then because it housed the holy remains of St Oswald, an 8th century King of Northumbria. Pilgrims flocked here in their thousands. The original Saxon abbey was demolished by Viking raiders in 870 and its Norman successor fared little better at the Dissolution of the Monasteries. Only the ground plan is now distinguishable. Some fragments from the abbey were incorporated into Bardney's Church of St Lawrence which is otherwise

mostly 15th century. Features of interest here include a tomb slab of Abbot Richard Horncastle, who died in 1508, and two unusual Charity Boards dated 1603 and 1639. These list benefactors of the parish, complete with colour portraits of these generous souls.

Connoisseurs of unusual churches will be well rewarded by a short detour to **Southrey**, a remote hamlet set beside the River Witham. Built of timber by the parishioners themselves in 1898, St John the Divine is painted brilliant white outside and sky blue within. Resembling some Mission station in the Australian outback, this quaint little church stands on a plinth incorporating gravestones from Bardney Abbey.

NETTLEHAM
4 miles NE of Lincoln off A46 or A158

This sizeable village lies between two Roman roads, Ermine Street (A46) and

THE PLOUGH

1 The Green, Nettleham, Lincolnshire LN2 2NR
Tel: 01522 750275

For more than a hundred years, the premises that now house **The Plough** served as a butcher's shop. The shop opened in 1825 and it wasn't until 1931 that the building was bought by the brewers Bateman who still own this attractive hostelry overlooking the village green.

Inside, the low sloping ceiling, old beams and the pew bench seating around two sides all contribute to the traditional atmosphere. Paul and Linda Clarke took over here in 1988 and they have made the inn very much a social centre for the village. Darts and crib matches are regular events and those pub visitors who detest juke boxes will be pleased to know that The Plough is a music-free area.

At the time of writing, food is not available but Paul and Linda have plans to create a restaurant on the first floor with seating for 50 diners. They intend to serve traditional English pub food and the restaurant may well be up and running by the time you read this. Meanwhile, The Plough is a friendly and relaxing place in which to sample some well-maintained ales, amongst them Bateman's XB cask ale and a guest ale which changes on a regular basis.

another running eastwards to Wragby (A158). Nettleham was once a far more important place. Edward I came here in 1301 and the village witnessed the first installation of a Prince of Wales, later Edward II. The king and his son stayed at the Nettleham palace of the Bishop of Lincoln. This sumptuous mansion was almost completely destroyed 250 years later during the 1536 uprising against Henry VIII. Only some lumpy earthworks remain. At the heart of the village,

Nettleham's village green is much smaller than it used to be but what remains includes some attractive 17th and 18th century cottages.

HEIGHINGTON
4 miles SE of Lincoln off B1188 or B1190

Heighington is a village of narrow winding streets and attractive stone houses, with the towers of Lincoln Cathedral visible from the top of the

THE BUTCHER & BEAST

High Street, Heighington, Lincs. LN4 1JS
Tel: 01522 790386

A pub with a long and interesting history, **The Butcher & Beast** is located in the village of Heighington, off the B1188 two miles east of Lincoln. Paul Kirby took over here as landlord in April 1999 after having been chef for the previous three years. His culinary skills have ensured that this most agreeable of hostelries has built up quite a reputation for its food as well as its beer

You can eat anywhere you can find a seat, (the pub is often packed out), but if you want a table in the 28-cover restaurant it's advisable to book. The lunchtime bar menu and blackboard specials, and the evening à la carte, all provide top quality eating, from the soup of the day, or Crispy Coated

Lobster Tails amongst the starters; home made Fisherman's Pie, fillet, rump or sirloin steaks, or vegetarian Amorini and Stilton Bake, as main courses; along with a tempting selection of delicious desserts. Other options include Gammon Steak glazed with brown sugar and served with pineapple or a fried egg, Whole Trout with Almonds, grilled or pan fried, and an appetising Leek and Mushroom Crumble. The 3-course Sunday lunch brings a choice of three roasts, as well as a Cold Meat Platter. The regular bill of fare is supplemented by a selection of daily specials and a particularly popular item on the menu is Paul's special "Pie of the Week" - Steak & Ale perhaps, or Steak & Stout. Everything on the menu is freshly prepared to order.

Among the ales are a number from Lincolnshire brewer Bateman's, Bateman's XB and Triple X, plus 3 guest ales which change each month. Paul also provides outside bars for local events. Behind the pub is a terrific garden with a delightful little "secret" - an almost hidden stream with a population of ducks. Hanging baskets and plant troughs make a further colourful display and it is no surprise to find that the pub has won awards for its blooms.

village. The chapel here has a rather odd history. It dates back to medieval times but by the early 1600s had fallen into disrepair. A local man, Thomas Garrett, paid for its restoration but its rôle changed once again in Victorian times when it was adapted to form part of the village school.

GAINSBOROUGH
15 miles NW of Lincoln on A156

Britain's most inland port, Gainsborough is located at the highest navigable point on the River Trent for seagoing vessels. During the 17th and 18th centuries, particularly, the town prospered greatly and although many of the lofty warehouses lining the river bank have been demolished, enough remain to give some idea of its flourishing past.

The town's most famous building is the enchanting **Gainsborough Old Hall**, one of the most striking architectural gems in the county. The Hall was built in the 1470s by Sir Thomas Burgh, a Yorkist supporter in the Wars of the Roses. Sir Thomas later entertained Richard III in the Great Hall with its vast arched roof. The kitchens also remain virtually unchanged since those days. A century or so later, around 1597, a London merchant, William Hickman, extended the building in Elizabethan style. Then, in 1720, the Hickman abandoned their now "old-fashioned" mansion for a new house at nearby Thonock and the Old Hall was badly neglected. In subsequent years, it served a whole range of purposes - a theatre, public house, linen factory, and Congregational chapel before ending up as flatlets in the 1940s. A rescue group, the Friends of the Old Hall, was formed in 1952. They acquired the lease and restored the fabric which was surprisingly little damaged. The Hall is generally considered one of the best preserved medieval manor

HEMSWELL COURT

Lancaster Green, Hemswell Cliff,
Lincolnshire DN21 5TQ
Tel: 01427 668508 Fax: 01427 667335

One of the premier venues in Lincolnshire for weddings, banquets and conferences, **Hemswell Court** has an interesting history. It was formerly the officers mess for RAF Hemswell which is now Caenby Corner Estate. The estate was first used in 1916 as a night landing ground for the Royal Flying Corps. It became a busy airfield during World War II, and between 1958 and

1963 became a base for American Thor missiles. The RAF departed in 1975 and a decade passed before it was sold to a developer. The estate now contains an enormous variety of businesses - antique centres, retail shops, an air museum and even a manufacturer of concrete gnomes!

Hemswell Court, which overlooks spacious lawns and gardens, can accommodate up to 200 guests for functions of every kind. It also contains two bridal suites and en-suite accommodation for

up to a further 30 people, including one double room on the ground floor. Hemswell Court has been created by Shaun Lees who also operates the nearby Restaurant & Coffee Shop(Caenby Corner Estate), which offers a wide selection of traditional home cooking, with the chef's special Steak Pie a popular favourite. A Carvery and Salad Bar are available every day, there's a daily special, and vegetarian dishes are served on request. Hemswell Court is open every day of the year for pre-booked functions except for Christmas Day, Boxing Day and New Year's Day.

THE CLAMART CAFÉ & BAR

7 Shelford Street, Scunthorpe, Lincs. DN15 6NU
Tel: 01724 281707

Immediately after its opening in 2000, the owners of **The Clamart Café & Bar,** Brian Williams and Howard Frapwell found they had a major success on their hands. Managed by Howard's daughter Rebecca, The Clamart immediately established itself as a stylish and popular venue. One of its attractions is the eye-catching use of the spacious interior, reminiscent of a Victorian street with various separate areas such as the Balcony Bar and the "piazza"-style seating on the ground floor. The décor is equally striking with trees in tubs, lots of flowers and elegant cast iron tables.

Food is served in the separate restaurant area, every day from noon until 2pm, with a Carvery on Sundays when it's essential to book. In addition to all the usual beverages, the Clamart serves two real ales, Tetley's and Boddington's. Also under the same roof is an excellent Thai restaurant, the Stima Gardens, which is open every evening, Tuesday to Saturday, from 6pm until last orders around 10pm. The Clamart is open all day, Monday to Saturday, and on Sundays from noon. Children are welcome until 8pm. (Please note that credit cards are not accepted). Another attraction at The Clamart is the Sportman's Bar which has a pool table, large screen television and fruit machines.

THE CROSBY HOTEL

Normanby Road, Scunthorpe
Lincolnshire DN15 6BQ
Tel: 01724 843830

An impressive Edwardian building dating back to 1910, **The Crosby Hotel** occupies a spacious corner site just a short walk from the town centre. When partners Ian and Diane Charles, and William Hendry, took over here in October 2000, the hostelry had fallen on hard times but as the result of a lot of time, money and energy they have put this grand old inn back on the map. Already, the Crosby seems to become busier day by day.

A major element of the partners' success is the quality food they serve every day right up until 10.30pm - a wide choice that ranges from a tasty sandwich to a hearty steak. There are non-smoking areas and the inn has a children's licence. To accompany your meal, there's an extensive selection of beverages, including one real ale, Marston's Pedigree, which will soon be joined by others. Another attraction here is the regular entertainment. There's karaoke on Wednesday and Thursday evenings from 7.30pm, a Disco featuring pre-1990s music on Friday and Saturday evenings, and the week is rounded off by a Pop Quiz on Sunday evening. The partners have already transformed this welcoming old inn but, they say, "There's much, much more to come!"

houses in the country. Today, it is run jointly by Lincolnshire County Council and English Heritage, and is open most days throughout the year.

Gainsborough also boasts an outstanding church. Beautifully set in its own grounds in the centre of the town, **All Saints** is a magnificent example of a Georgian classical "city" church. The interior, with its massive columns, box pews and gallery, is richly decorated in gold and turquoise. This glorious building is open during daylight hours, tours are available and there's even a cafeteria and gift shop.

Another notable building is **Marshall's Britannia Works** in Beaumont Street, a proud reminder of Gainsborough's once thriving engineering industry. Built around 1850, the quarter-of-a-mile long frontage bears an impressive figure of Britannia herself.

Gainsborough is believed to have provided material for George Eliot's *The Mill on the Floss*. The now-demolished Ashcroft Mill on the River Trent was the model for Tulliver's mill and the *eagre*, or **tidal bore**, that precipitates the tragic climax of the novel is clearly based on the surge that happens at Gainsborough. This usually takes place about 50 minutes after high tide at Grimsby and the bore can be anything between 8ft and 13ft high.

SCUNTHORPE

Up until the 1850s the main activity around Scunthorpe was the maintaining of rabbit warrens - the local breed with their silvery coats being much in demand with furriers. Then a local landowner, Rowland Winn, discovered that the poor local soil lightly covered vast deposits of ironstone. Scunthorpe's rapid rise to becoming a major steel town was under way. Today, the Corus plant produces

more than 4 million tonnes of liquid steel, from a 690 hectare site which contains 90 miles of railways.

On selected summer weekends, the **Appleby Frodingham Railway Preservation Society** runs 2 hour railtours around the plant. Pulled by a restored steam locomotive, the fully guided tour takes in all aspects of iron and steel making and includes a glimpse of red hot steel being rolled in the mills.

More of Scunthorpe's industrial and social heritage is on display at the **North Lincolnshire Museum & Art Gallery**, with exhibits that include an ironmonger's cottage. The town has also created a Heritage Trail which takes visitors through three of the parks created by Victorian benefactors - Scunthorpe is proud of its parks and gardens and has claimed the title of "The Industrial Garden Town of rural North Lincolnshire". The Trail also includes **Brumby Hall**, an attractive 17th century manor house, now a nursing home, and Brumby Woods, one of very few remnants of truly ancient woodland in the region.

AROUND SCUNTHORPE

NORMANBY
4 miles N of Scunthorpe off B1430

Normanby Hall was built in 1825 for the Sheffield family and extended in 1906. The interior is decorated in Regency style, and displays include eight rooms that reflect the changes made down the years, as well as two costume galleries. The 300-acre Park has plenty to see and enjoy, including a deer park, duck ponds, an ice house in the middle of the miniature railway circuit, a Victorian laundry and a walled garden. The **Normanby Hall Farming Museum** majors on rural life in the age of the heavy horse, and among the exhibits illuminating the workings of a 19th century country estate are traditional agricultural equipment and transport, and country crafts. Near the park gates, some picturesque estate cottages bear witness to the Sheffield family's reputation as good landlords. Rents were low and job security was good, so perhaps the only drawback was that the Sheffield family restricted the number of public houses they would allow on their lands.

A mile or so northwest of the Hall, St Andrew's Church in the agreeable village of Burton-on-Stather contains an impressive range of memorials to the Sheffield family, the oldest of which dates back to the 1300s.

ALKBOROUGH
11 miles N of Scunthorpe off A1077

A scenic walk leads from Burton to Alkborough, where the medieval maze known as **Julian's Bower** is a perplexing talking point. Not a maze made of hedges, but a pattern cut in the turf, it occupies a beautiful location on a clifftop overlooking the River Trent. The design of the maze is reproduced in the porch of the 11th century village church, and again in a window high above the altar.

HORKSTOW
10 miles NE of Scunthorpe on B1204

The Humber Bridge isn't Lincolnshire's only bridge of distinction. About 2 miles west of Horkstow stands a suspension bridge which is also remarkable in its own small way. **Horkstow Bridge** was designed and built by Sir John Rennie in 1844 to cross the River Ancholme, serving the brick kilns which once operated here. With its arched stone supports and wooden decking, Horkstow is probably unique and is certainly one of the world's oldest suspension bridges.

THE GEORGE INN

Market Place, Winterton, Lincs. DN15 9PT
Tel: 01724 732270

A handsome Georgian building of attractive grey stone, **The George Inn** was once a coaching inn and has all the charm and character of a traditional hostelry. Real fires and a welcoming atmosphere add to the appeal. Mine hosts, John and Sue, took over here in 2000 and have completely refurbished the first floor restaurant which re-opened at Easter 2001.

The restaurant is non-smoking, seats 25, and customers can choose either from the regular menu or from the blackboard specials. Children are welcome in the restaurant. Food is also available in the downstairs lounge where the wide range of beverages, (including two real ales, Stones and Tetley's),

is supplemented by a very extensive collection of miniatures on display. John and Sue are especially proud of their staff, a friendly team that comprises Maureen, Barbara, Bessie, Jackie and Ann, plus the accomplished chef Stephanie Morrison. The George has a secluded Beer Garden where barbecues are occasionally held in summer.

Entertainments include a general knowledge Quiz every Monday evening, a Pop quiz on the second Wednesday in the month, and live entertainment on the last Friday in the month, all of these events starting at 8.30pm. The inn is open Monday to Friday from 3pm; Saturday from 11.30am; Sunday from noon. There is ample car parking.

BARTON-UPON-HUMBER
10 miles NE of Scunthorpe off A15

Today, Barton is dominated by the colossal south tower of the Humber Bridge, connecting Lincolnshire with East Yorkshire. This has been a major crossing point for more than a thousand years. The Domesday Book recorded a ferry here and the community was then the largest town in north Lincolnshire. In the 1770s, Daniel Defoe gave a vivid description of

his passage across the Humber *"in an open boat in which we had about fifteen horses, and ten or twelve cows, mingled with about seventeen or eighteen passengers, we were about four hours tossing about on the Humber before we could get into the harbour at Hull"*. (The river at this point is only about 2½ miles wide).

Defoe dismissed Barton itself as *"a town noted for nothing that I know of"*. This is rather unfair since Barton had then, and still does, a renowned church, **St Peter's**,

THE WHEATSHEAF

3 Holydyke, Barton upon Humber, Lincs. DN18 5PS
Tel: 01652 633175

A former coaching inn, **The Wheatsheaf** looks very appealing with its whitewashed walls and tubs of flowers. The inside is just as inviting, breathing the authentic atmosphere of an olde-worlde hostelry, complete with real ales from the cask and hearty, wholesome food. The real ales include the difficult-

to-find Stone's Bitter, John Smith's Cask, Theakston's Best Bitter, and a guest beer that changes each week.

The fare on offer ranges from main courses such as Sirloin Steak, deep fried Haddock or a Curry of the Day, to salads and sandwiches, all freshly prepared from the very best ingredients and served with seasonal vegetables. Available every lunchtime and evening, the meals are very reasonably priced, representing good value for money, and there are also special deals for pensioners. Sunday lunch is especially popular, ideal for families since children's portions are avaialble.

Mine hosts at The Wheatsheaf are Malcolm and Sarah Eayres, a welcoming couple who have maintained the inn's traditional character serving good food and fine ales. Sarah knows the pub well since she worked here for 7 years, became manager and is now joint tenant with her husband. Together, they have made the pub well known for its charity work, raising considerable sums for good causes.

Barton itself grew up around the ancient river ferry which for several hundred years, right up until 1981, transported passengers across the Humber to Hull and East Yorkshire, a role which has now been assumed by the mighty Humber Bridge which soars above the town. There are viewing areas at each end of the bridge which can also be crossed on foot if you have a head for heights. Close to the foot of the bridge are two important Nature Reserves, both open to the public: Barton Clay Pits, a 5-mile area along the river bank, and Far Ings which is home to more than 50 nesting bird species, 230 varieties of wild flowers, and hundreds of different kinds of moth.

with a remarkable Saxon tower, some 70ft high. The church was deconsecrated in 1967 and is now in the care of English Heritage. An exhibition is open daily between 2pm and 4pm.

Barton's surviving church, St Mary's was originally a satellite of St Peter's, and a considerable part of its fabric pre-dates 1300. An interesting brass commemorates Simon Seman, wine merchant, alderman and Sheriff of London, who died in 1433. He is shown, almost lifesize, standing on two wine barrels.

The heart of the town still has some pleasant streets - Fleetgate, Bargate, Beck Hill and Priestgate, all distinguished by mainly Georgian and early Victorian buildings.

Baysgarth House, now a museum, is an 18th century mansion with a collection of 18th and 19th century English and Oriental pottery, a section on country crafts and an industrial museum in the stable block. The surrounding park has a picnic area, play area and various recreational facilities.

Barton has two notable sons of whom it is proud: Sir Isaac Pitman was the schoolmaster here in the 1830s and later devised the system of shorthand that bears his name; Chad Varah, founder of the Samaritans, was also born here.

Just to the north of Barton, on the banks of the Humber, is an observation area for viewing the mighty **Humber Bridge**. Opened in 1981, this is Europe's longest single-span suspension bridge with an overall length of 2,428yds (2,220m). This means that for more than a third of a mile only four concrete pillars, two on each bank, are preserving you from a watery death. From these huge pylons, 510ft (155m) high, gossamer cables of thin-wired steel support a gently curving roadway. Both sets of pylons rise vertically, but because of the curvature of

the earth they actually lean away from each other by several inches. The bridge is particularly striking at night when the vast structure is floodlit.

Around the bridge are important nature reserves. **Barton Clay Pits** cover a five-mile area along the river bank and offer a haven for wildlife and recreation for sporty humans. **Far Ings**, with hides and waymarked trails, is home to more than 230 species of wild flowers, 50 nesting bird species and hundreds of different sorts of moths.

BARROW-ON-HUMBER
12 miles NE of Scunthorpe on A1077

Barrow-in-Humber was still a thriving market town when a 4-year-old lad named John Harrison arrived here with his family in 1697. He was later apprenticed as a carpenter but his consuming interest was in making clocks and watches. In 1735 he won the Board of Longitude's huge prize of £20,000 for inventing a ship's chronometer that would pinpoint a ship's longitude. Disgracefully, Harrison had to wait almost 40 years before the Board paid up. The story of his achievement was told in the recent bestseller and film, *Longitude*. Harrison is buried in Hampstead, but Barrow's Church of the Holy Trinity has a portrait of the inventor, and a sundial made by his brother James stands in the churchyard.

About a mile to the north of the village, a picnic site by the A1077 on the way to Barton-on-Humber provides a great view of Humber shipping, the great bridge and the outline of Hull across the estuary.

ELSHAM
10 miles E of Scunthorpe off A15

A popular venue for family days-out, **Elsham Hall Country and Wildlife Park** surrounds an 18th century mansion, the home of Captain and Mrs Elwes. They opened the park in 1970 *"to promote enjoyment of the countryside and wildlife, and an appreciation of the arts and rural crafts"*. The attractions on offer include a small zoo, children's farm, butterfly garden, carp feeding jetty, arboretum, garden centre, craft centre and workshops, café, and even a theatre which also hosts weddings, medieval banquets and conferences.

WRAWBY
8 miles E of Scunthorpe on A18

The elegant **Wrawby Postmill** is a landmark that can be seen for miles around. Built in 1760, and beautifully restored in 1964, it is the last surviving postmill in the area. The mill is open to visitors on Bank Holiday Mondays and on the last Sundays in June and July, from 2pm to 5pm.

BRIGG
7 miles E of Scunthorpe on A10

King John was not universally liked but one of his more popular deeds was the granting of a charter (in 1205) which permitted this modest little town to hold an annual festivity on the 5th day of August. **Brigg Fair**, along with Widdecombe and Scarborough, has joined the trio of "Best Known Fairs in England", its celebrity enhanced by a traditional song, (twice recorded by Percy Grainger), and the haunting tone poem, *Brigg Fair*, composed by Frederick Delius in 1907. Almost 800 years later, the fair still attracts horse traders from around the country, along with all the usual fun of the fair.

King John's son, Henry III, also showed favour to the town. He granted the loyal burghers of Brigg the right to hold a weekly market on Thursdays - a right they still exercise to the full. Each week, the

ARTIES MILL

Wressle Road, Castlethorpe, Brigg,
Lincolnshire DN20 9LF
Tel: 01652 652094 Fax: 01652 657107
website: www.artiesmill.co.uk

Conveniently located on the A18 about a mile west of Brigg, **Arties Mill** is one of Lincolnshire's most interesting locations for good food, drink and accommodation. The Mill was originally built 1790 and was still working right up to the 1960s. Sadly, its sails have been dismantled but the Mill owners, Janet and Stephen McGrath, have preserved many interesting features of the old building. The Mill interior and the adjoining grain sheds have been attractively converted into bars, restaurants and function rooms

The Lounge Bar, with seating for up to 80 people, serves tasty bar meals daily from 11.30am to 10pm, while the Carvery Restaurant (booking advisable) is open every weekend evening and on

Sunday between noon and 8pm. The Conservatory, Function Room and the Upstairs Round Room are all used for private functions or meetings for groups of anything up to 115 seated, or 130 buffet style. A separate modern building, The Lodge, offers a wide range of accommodation with family, twin and double rooms all available. There are 25 rooms altogether and all but three of them are equipped with en suite facilities, colour TV, direct dial telephone, trouser press and hospitality tray. A full English Breakfast is served in the dining room every day between 7am and 9am.

OLIVERS GUEST HOUSE

Church Street, Scawby, nr Brigg,
Lincolnshire DN20 9AH
Tel: 01652 650446
e-mail: eileen_harrison@lineone.net

The attractive village of Scawby is just minutes from Exit 4 of the M180 and provides an excellent base for exploring north Lincolnshire and the Wolds. The place to stay here is undoubtedly **Olivers Guest House**, a charming whitewashed house which is believed to be more than 300 years old. In its time, the building has served as a butcher's shop and a post office, but since 1982 Olivers has been offering quality bed & breakfast accommodation. Eileen Harrison arrived here in 1999 and has continued the tradition of friendly, welcoming hospitality.

Guests have the use of a very comfortable lounge and can also enjoy the spacious, well-maintained garden. There are just 3 guest bedrooms, 2 twins and a double, all of them very tastefully furnished and decorated in traditional style. The rooms are well-equipped and provided with extra facilities such as trouser-presses. A hearty English breakfast is served in the attractive dining room - vegetarian and other dietary preferences are catered for. Eileen is also happy to provide an evening meal if required. Scawby village boasts a church with an unusual dedication to St Hibald in which there are some fine memorials to the Nelthorpe family who still live in nearby Scawby Hall. This lovely old Jacobean mansion is private but can be seen from the lane north of the church.

THE HORSE & CART

185 Scawby Road, Scawby Brook,
Brigg, Lincolnshire DN20 9JX
Tel: 01652 652150

A free house, **The Horse & Cart** offers its patrons an excellent choice of beverages, including real ale from the local brewery, "Tom Woods", plus four more genuine brews as well as a guest ale which is changed regularly. The inn is also well known for its outstanding food, served at very reasonable prices. Chef Chris Wilkinson received a Highly Commended award in the British Meat Steak Pie of the Year 2001 competition for his succulent Steak & Mushroom Pie

with sherry gravy, topped with walnut pastry. Chris also offers a selection of other pies, (Lamb & Mint, for example, or Vegetarian Quorn & Mushroom), along with fish dishes such as fresh Grimsby haddock, and vegetarian options. Meals are served in the spacious lounge/restaurant which has a verandah outside, a veritable sun trap with pleasant views across the fields. There's also a children's play area.

Carol and Paul Brown, both of them Lincolnshire born and bred, took over here in November 2000. A friendly and welcoming couple with a young daughter who is a great favourite with customers, they have made the Horse & Cart a popular venue for locals and visitors alike, especially at weekends when live music is added to the inn's regular attractions.

market place is crammed with around 100 stalls. During the summer months, a farmers' market is also held on the 4th Saturday of each month. A pedestrianised town centre, combined with ample parking nearby, has made Brigg's markets some of the busiest in north Lincolnshire.

Many visitors to Brigg, including the architecture guru Nikolaus Pevsner, have commented that some of the town's most interesting buildings are its pubs. Pevsner picked out for special mention the Lord Nelson, with its broad Regency bow window, the Dying Gladiator, remarkable for the *"gory realism"* of its pub sign, and the Black Bull which boasts *"a vigorous Edwardian pub front"*.

SCAWBY
3 miles W of Brigg on B1207

This attractive village, with its stone and brick buildings set amongst trees, has grown up around Scawby Hall (private)

whose extensive park stretches away to the north. The Jacobean Hall can be seen from a lane that leads from the church and the church itself contains monuments to the Hall's owners, the Nelthorpe family. The memorials date from 1640 to 1830. Just across the road from the church, John Wesley is said to have preached in the long barn with a pantiled roof.

KIRTON-IN-LINDSEY
8 miles S of Scunthorpe on B1398 & B1206

Mount Pleasant Mill is a fully operational four-sailed mill dating from 1875. Restored in 1991, it is once again a working mill and still grinding corn. Visitors can look around the mill, buy the freshly milled flour in the shop, and enjoy refreshments in the tea shop. The mill is open daily throughout August, (except Mondays); at other times on weekends and Bank Holidays only.

RISTORANTE IL MULINO

Market Place, Kirton in Lindsey, Lincolnshire DN21 4LZ
Tel: 01652 648370 website: www.ilmulino.co.uk

Connoisseurs of good food and wine should make their way to the Market Place of this pleasant little town and look out for the Italian flag fluttering over the **Ristorante Il Mulino**.

Established in 1998 by Luigi and Nicola Scatola whose family hail originally from Sicily, the restaurant offers an outstanding choice of authentic Italian cuisine, prepared and cooked by Luigi's brother-in-law, executive chef Abrielo Di Stefano. Nothing frozen finds its way into

Abrielo's kitchen, only prime quality local produce delivered fresh each day. No pizzas dishes either, but an appetising selection of fish, meat and pasta dishes, served with some imaginative sauces, and all at very competitive prices. Vegetarians are also well-catered for. The wines, naturally, all come from Italian vineyards and perfectly complement Abrielo's range of dishes.

The restaurant is housed in a building, thought to be about 200 years old, where the low beamed ceilings, a central fountain, classical statuary, crisp tablecloths and napkins, and the elegant decor all help to create a very special atmosphere. Upstairs, there's a small lounge where diners can enjoy a pre-dinner or after dinner drink, comfortable in the knowledge that there's no rush - once your table is booked, it's yours for the evening. For special occasions, a first floor function room is available with covers for up to 35 guests. Ristorante Il Mulino is open each evening from Tuesday to Saturday and also caters for weddings, Christenings etc. and small parties.

HAXEY
18 miles SW of Scunthorpe on A161

Haxey is the site of a nature reserve, but is best known for the **Haxey Hood Game**, launched around 2.30 on the afternoon of Twelfth Night in front of the parish church. Three hundred men divided into four teams compete to push a leather 'hood' into the pub of their team's choice. The game apparently started in the 12th or 13th century when a lady lost her hood

and a number of village men scrambled to retrieve it. The strongest man caught the hood but was too shy to hand it back, and was labelled a fool by the lady, while the man who eventually handed it over was declared a lord. The lady suggested that the scene should be re-enacted each year, and gave a plot of land for the purpose. The "sway" of men struggle across the fields working the hood towards the appropriate pubs and always staying within the sway - no open running. When

THE ROYAL OAK

8 Church Street, Kirton in Lindsey, Lincs. DN21 4PN
Tel: 01652 648407 Fax: 01652 640224

Just across the road from Kirton's imposing church with its massive Norman tower, **The Royal Oak** is a lively and sociable hostelry with a history of hospitality going back to the days of stage coach travel.

Mine hosts at this welcoming free house are Tony and Marilyn Bell. Tony, from Yorkshire, used to be with RAF Air Communications; Marilyn, from Wales, was formerly a local care worker. Since they arrived here in May 1999, they have made the Royal Oak a real centre of local life. The Pigeon Club fly their birds from here, the Ramblers Club has made the inn their headquarters, and the pub also sponsors the local Junior Football Club. There's karaoke on Wednesday evenings, a disco on Friday and live entertainment every Saturday. Elvis Presley fans will be fascinated by the collection of Elvis memorabilia in one of the two bars, both are which look very inviting with their open fires, beamed

ceilings and bow windows with leaded lights. There's a pool and games area at one end; the Sportsmans Bar at the other.

The Royal Oak's chef, Klara, is an accomplished cook whose menu, along with traditional English favourites, includes some appetising dishes imported from her native Germany: wonderful Wiener Schnitzels, for example, and strudels to die for. Her famous red cabbage is always popular, especially when it accompanies the Sunday Roast Lunch which offers a choice of 4 different roasts. To complement Klara's wonderful cooking, the inn stocks a wide selection of beverages, including a permanent real ales, Barnsley Bitter, and a guest ale which changes regularly and has featured the intriguingly named Old Leg Over amongst its choices.

This spacious old inn also has 5 guest bedrooms, available all year round. There's a family room with an en suite shower, and 1 double, 1 twin, and 2 singles, all of which have full facilities. Within easy reach of the M180 and the historic City of Lincoln with its manifold attractions, The Royal Oak provides an excellent base for exploring this unspoilt corner of the county.

the sway reaches the winning pub, the landlord touches the hood to declare the game over, and free drinks paid for by a collection end the day in time-honoured style. Rather an elaborate build-up to a drinking session, but just one of the quaint traditions that make English country life so colourful.

EPWORTH
12 miles SW of Scunthorpe on A161

This small town, the southern "capital" of the Isle of Axholme, is a hallowed place for Methodists from all over the world. From 1696 until his death in 1735 the Revd Samuel Wesley was Rector here. John Wesley was born at the **Old Rectory** on June 17th, 1703: his brother Charles on December 18th, 1707. Two years later, inflamed by one of the Rector's outspoken sermons, local people set fire to the Rectory. The house was rebuilt incorporating ribs and keels from ships

broken up in the nearby River Trent. The house still stands today, a charming Queen Anne building. Several of its rooms have been refurnished in period style and some of the brothers' possessions are on display. There are also collections of portraits and prints, and you can even stay for bed and breakfast.

St Andrew's Church, where Samuel Wesley was minister, is a short walk from the town centre. His table tomb stands near the southeast door and it was from this vantage point that John would address his followers after he had been refused access to the church. Inside, the 12th century font in which both John and Charles were baptized can still be seen.

The best way to follow the footsteps of the Wesleys is to join the Wesley Trail which has information boards placed at various locations connected with the family. A pamphlet giving full details is available from the Old Rectory.

AULD SOUTH YORKSHIRE

Trent Side, Keadby,
Lincolnshire DN17 3EF
Tel/Fax: 01724 783518

For some 200 years, the **Auld South Yorkshire** inn has been offering hospitality to travellers although its name comes from the days when the South Yorkshire Railway used to serve this village alongside the River Trent. Keadby was then a port of some significance but it's now a peaceful place with more traffic on the canal and River Trent than on the road.

Joanne and Kevin Doughty arrived here in November 2000

and have quickly established a reputation for serving quality food and real ales. Food is served seven days a week with the whole menu of traditional pub fare available throughout the day. Joanne, who has many years of experience in the licensed trade, is the chef and her menu offers a good choice of dishes including steaks, locally caught fresh fish, and some wonderful home made pies and desserts. John Smith's is the permanent real ale with a selection of guest beers which change regularly.

This is a lively pub with pool, darts and even its own football team, a quiz night on Fridays and live music once a month. Accommodation is also available: there are 5 guest bedrooms - 2 family, 2 doubles and a single, all comfortably furnished and available all year round.

SANDTOFT
10 miles W of Scunthorpe off A161 or Exit 2 of M180

On a wartime airfield on the Isle of Axholme, **Sandtoft Transport Centre** is home to Britain's largest single collection of trolleybuses and motorbuses. Started in 1969 by a small and enthusiastic group of volunteers, the collection includes vehicles dating from 1927 to 1985, including magnificent 6-wheeled double-decker trolleybuses and a fascinating one-and-a-half decker from Aachen in Germany. A wired circuit outside the depot allows visitors to ride in these splendid silent giants. Children can enjoy a ride on the steam and electric hauled miniature railway, and "drive" a trolley or motorbus on a simulator. A nostalgic film is shown in the Ritz Lecture Theatre and other attractions include a children's adventure playground, exhibition area and souvenir shop.

4 Nottingham and South Nottinghamshire

As any local lad will be happy to tell you, Nottingham used to be called 'Snotingham' after the unfortunately named Snot, chief of a 6th century Anglo-Saxon tribe. But there was a settlement here long before then. In Celtic times it was known as Tigguocobauc, 'the house of caves', an appropriate name since this ancient people lived in the caves that occur naturally in the soft local sandstone. When the Vikings arrived in England in 878, they recognised Nottingham's importance by making it one of the five boroughs of the 'Danelaw' - the area of Middle England they controlled. There was more significant development in Norman times when the famous Castle that features so prominently in the Robin Hood legends was built.

Trent Bridge, Nottingham

Rich deposits of coal in the Trent Valley brought further prosperity and provided the funds for building Wollaton Hall, a superb Elizabethan mansion on the edge of the town. Then the Industrial Revolution saw the mechanisation of the lace and hosiery industries, and the scale of coal mining operations expanded dramatically. The grimy legacy of all this industrial activity was memorably recorded in the classic 1960 film *Saturday Night & Sunday Morning*.

Early 21st century Nottingham is a much cleaner place: the once soot-blackened Lace Market has been spruced up and Maid Marian Way, once described as *"the ugliest street in Britain"* has been smothered with flowers, shrubs and bushes.

The glory of the central part of the county is Southwell Minster, a uniquely graceful building which is perhaps the least well-known cathedral in the country. Southwell itself is small, with a population of less than 7000, but is a delightful town with many fine buildings and a picturesque old coaching inn where Charles I spent his last night of freedom. There's a strong connection too with Lord Byron who as a young man stayed with his mother at Burgage House during school and university vacations. The town is also where the Bramley apple originated and the local dish, Southwell Galette, is well worth tasting.

Surrounding this appealing little town is a maze of country lanes and scattered ancient villages. Laxton, in the heart of the county, is notable for still maintaining its medieval open field system of farming and the special court that manages its affairs. Bleasby is associated with the founder of the Salvation Army, William Booth, who lived there as a boy; and part of the county's industrial heritage is preserved at Calverton where a curate in Elizabethan times, William Lee, invented the stocking knitting frame in 1589.

With its historic castle, magnificent parish church and a host of fine buildings, Newark is an immensely likeable place. In medieval times, the town thrived as a centre for the wool trade, benefiting from its position on the Great North Road and beside the River Trent.

Robin Hood Statue, Nottingham Castle

The Civil War brought great suffering but, apart from the Castle, surprisingly little damage to the town's buildings. Although Newark itself was a Royalist stronghold, the local gentry supported Cromwell so there were many skirmishes. In fact, there were few places in southeast Nottinghamshire that did escape the ravages of the bitter struggle between king and Parliament.

South of Newark lies the Vale of Belvoir, an unspoilt pastoral landscape dotted with the spires of village churches and overlooked by the mighty towers and turrets of Belvoir Castle, just across the border in Lincolnshire. The Vale has always been lightly populated but no fewer than three Archbishops of Canterbury were born here, (including the martyr Thomas Cranmer), as well as the great novelist, Samuel Butler, and the naval hero, Earl Howe.

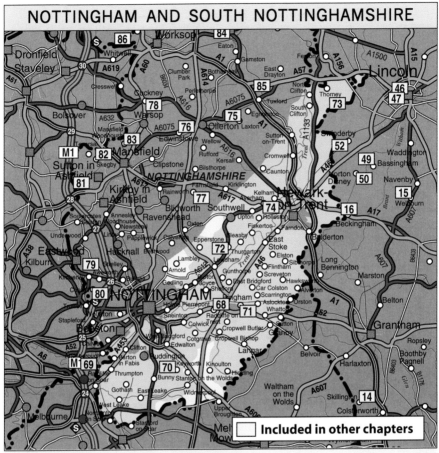

NOTTINGHAM AND SOUTH NOTTINGHAMSHIRE

☐ **Included in other chapters**

© MAPS IN MINUTES ™ 2001   © Crown Copyright, Ordnance Survey 2001

PLACES TO STAY, EAT, DRINK AND SHOP

68	The Trent Hotel, Radcliffe-on-Trent	Pub with Food	Page 106
69	Eaton Farm, Long Eaton	Pub and Restaurant	Page 108
70	The Salutation, Keyworth	Pub with Food	Page 113
71	The Moot House, Bingham	Pub with Food	Page 113
72	Coach & Horses, Thurgarton	Pub with Food	Page 122
73	Bottle & Glass, Harby, nr Lincoln	Pub with Food	Page 127
74	Manna Herbs, Averham, nr Newark	Bed and Breakfast	Page 129

NOTTINGHAM

A lively city of some 300,000 inhabitants, Nottingham offers a vast choice of shops, restaurants (more than 200 of them), cinemas, art galleries, two theatres, a world-class concert hall, and a host of other visitor attractions. The city also boasts a leading University, a major medical centre and a legendary football team, Nottingham Forest. The self-proclaimed "Queen of the Midlands", Nottingham is known worldwide because of the legendary Robin Hood and his persecutor, the villainous Sheriff of Nottingham. Others associate the city with Boots the Chemist, Players cigarettes (whose packets carry a picture of Nottingham Castle), Raleigh cycles and motor-cycles, and with the ice skaters Torvill and Dean - their world-beating performances led directly to the siting in Nottingham of the **National Ice Centre**.

A good place to begin exploring the city is in the **Old Market Square**, known to locals as "Slab Square" and believed to be largest market square in the country. Although no market has been held here since the 1920s, the vast expanse of the square still lies at the centre of Nottingham life. At its eastern end stands the dignified **Council House** with its porticoed frontage and a dome that is a replica of St Paul's in London. Part of the stately ground floor with its lofty ceilings and neo-classical architecture now houses some prestigious shops.

Until the Council House was built, the Market Square was the setting for the famous Nottingham Goose Fair which began in medieval times and gained its name from the large flocks of geese that were sold here around Michaelmas. Mentioned in a charter dated 1284, the Goose Fair still takes place in early October but has grown so much it is now held at Forest Fields on the edge of the city.

A short walk from the Market Square, in the appropriately named Maid Marian Way, **The Tales of Robin Hood** tells the story of the celebrated outlaw through a series of historically accurate displays depicting scenes such as Robin's imprisonment by the Sheriff of Nottingham to feasting in Sherwood Forest. After a tour by chair ride visitors can then explore the history of

Council House, Old Market

Tales of Robin Hood

the legend and also learn about the detective work undertaken in the 1930s in an attempt to authenticate the legend.

A further couple of minutes walk brings you to the entrance to **Nottingham Castle** which commands an imposing position on a rocky outcrop high above the city centre. However, those looking for the famous castle which features so frequently in the tales of Robin Hood will be sorely disappointed as the present buildings date from after the English Civil War and precious little remains of the original medieval fortification.

The original castle was built soon after the Battle of Hastings by William Peveril as part of William I's general fortification of many strategically important sites. Its elevated position, overlooking the city and the River Trent, made Nottingham Castle one of the foremost castles in Norman England and it played host to many important visitors. Of a typical Norman motte and bailey design, the stone walls are thought to have been added in the early 12th century and it was further fortified by Henry II. Nottingham Castle's heyday came in the 14th and 15th centuries however, when not only was King David II of Scotland held prisoner

here for a while around 1346 but, in the mid-1400s, Edward IV proclaimed himself king from Nottingham Castle. Later his brother, Richard III, rode out from here to the Battle of Bosworth field and his death.

For some reason, the Tudors shunned the castle which gradually fell into disrepair until Charles I came to Nottingham in 1642 and raised his standard, marking the beginning of the Civil War. Unfortunately, the king found little support for his cause in the city, (only 30 citizens joined his troops), and so he moved on to Shrewsbury, leaving Nottingham and its castle in the hands of the Parliamentarians. During the course of the war, the Royalists made several attempts to recapture the castle but Cromwell's supporters held out. After the fighting was over the castle building was rendered uninhabitable and was finally demolished in 1674 by the Duke of Newcastle who then built his own palace on the site.

Today, that palace is home to the **Castle Museum and Art Gallery** (free on weekdays). Some remains of the original castle still stand, most notably the 13th century gatehouse, though much restored, and parts of the moat and outer bailey are visible. The museum, when it was opened by the Prince of Wales in 1878, was the first municipal art gallery in the country outside London. Today, the collection is particularly noted for its fine selection of Victorian paintings. The museum also has an outstanding collection of silverware and ceramics.

Alongside the Castle Museum is the **Sherwood Foresters Regimental**

Robin Hood Statute, Nottingham Castle

castle. It is through this passageway that some two dozen conspirators crept to capture Roger de Mortimer, the lover of Queen Isabella. When her husband, Edward II was murdered, Isabella had allowed de Mortimer to effectively rule in place of her18-year-old son, Edward III. De Mortimer's presumption was later punished by death. Edward III was in the castle at the time of de Mortimer's capture and is believed to have known about, and encouraged, the plot.

Also at the base of Castle Rock and housed in a terrace of four 17th century cottages is the **Brewhouse Yard Museum**. Depicting the life of the people of the city up to the 1990s, the museum has accurately furnished rooms as well as a series of reconstructions that includes a Victorian kitchen and shop window displays of the 1920s.

Museum, which continues the castle's connections with the military. The regiment was first raised in 1741 and among the many displays there is an area dedicated to the Nottingham flying ace of World War I, Captain Albert Ball, VC. He died in 1917, at the age of 20, having shot down 43 enemy aircraft. A statue erected to his memory stands in the castle grounds.

At the base of Castle Rock lies the famous **Trip to Jerusalem Inn** where the crusaders are said to have stopped for a pint before setting off on their long journey to the Holy Land. Dating back to around 1189, it claims to be the oldest pub in England, a claim hotly contested by other hostelries it must be said. Set back into the sandstone rock, the building was once the brewhouse for the castle and from here travellers to the Holy Land bought their ale. In the pub's cellars is **Mortimer's Hole**, a cave hewn out of the sandstone rock which leads to the

Just around the corner, the **Museum of Costume and Textiles** (free) in Castle Gate contains a fine collection of costumes from 1790 to the mid-20th century, all displayed in period rooms. There are also many other exhibits on show including tapestries; knitted, woven, and printed textiles; and fashion accessories through the ages. The museum is housed in a terrace of brick houses that was constructed in 1788 by Cornelius Launder, a former High Sheriff. Castle Gate is an interesting street in itself and well worth a second look. The entrance to the museum has one of the finest examples of an 18th century doorcase and fanlight to be seen in the area.

Further down Castle Gate is **Newdigate**

House, built in a refined fashion in 1680 and distinguished by a wrought iron screen and gates dating from the early 1700s. The house now forms part of the United Services Club but between 1705 and 1711 it was the home of Marshal Tallard, commander of the defeated French army at the Battle of Blenheim in 1704.

Trip to Jerusalem Inn

Nearby, in Castle Road, is a charming medieval building that is home to the **Lace Centre** (free). As well as holding lace-making demonstrations, the Centre stocks a vast selection of high quality lace available for purchase. A remarkably well-preserved example of a timber framed house of around 1450, the building was moved from its original site on Middle Pavement in 1968. Continuing the textiles theme, not far away and set in the heart of Nottingham's historic and recently revitalized Lace Market, is the **Museum of Nottingham Lace**, occupying a restored chapel in High Pavement. Here the story of Nottingham's famous industry is told, from the days when it was a cottage craft through to mechanisation and the days of the great textile factories. Visitors can see some of the giant machines that produced the delicate material and also various types of lace being made.

Across the road from the Museum, in the impressive Shire Hall, the **Galleries of Justice** provides an unusual and interesting insight into justice 19th century style. "Condemned", a major crime and punishment experience, allows visitors to put themselves in the place of an accused in the harsh days around 1833. Cramped cells, capital punishment, and the possibility of transportation to the New World were the lot of a hapless criminal in those days and their discomfort is made very real by the restored period settings.

Also in High Pavement is Nottingham's largest parish church, **St Mary's**, which is also probably the city's oldest as it appears to have been founded in Saxon times. However, today's church dates from the 15th century though there are some 19th and early 20th century additions which include windows by a series of renowned stained glass makers. Also inside is a Bishop's Throne carved in 1890 when it was thought that the church would become the cathedral for the diocese of Southwell.

Another short walk brings you to the **Caves of Nottingham**, a popular attraction which lies beneath the Broadmarsh Centre, one of the city's major shopping precincts. The city is built on sandstone and throughout Nottingham's history the rock has been tunnelled to provide first shelter and then hiding places. More than 400 man-made caves run beneath the city streets. Now, thanks to local voluntary groups, these caves have been saved for future generations. The most spectacular cave in the system, the Pillar Cave, was carved out back in 1250 and contains remnants of the country's only underground tannery. The caves were commonly used as pub cellars: the constant temperature being ideal for the storage of beer and wine. More recently, they served as air raid shelters during the blitz of World War II and one of the caves has been left as a memorial to those desperate times.

In Nottingham, as in many other industrial towns, the late 18th century saw the building of canals to serve the expanding populations and aid the transportation of goods. In 1796, the **Nottingham Canal** was completed, linking the town with many of the country's arterial waterways. Almost 15 miles in length and rising by a series of 20 locks some 130 feet, the canal ran from the River Trent, through the centre of Nottingham, to the Cromford Canal at Langley Mill, in neighbouring Derbyshire. Today only some 7 miles and three locks are left but this does include the stretch through the city. A walk along the banks of the canal may not be one of the county's most scenic trails but it does give a very good insight into the life of Nottingham in the last century.

Along the Nottingham Canal, and still with its own basin found under an arch for easy loading and unloading, is the **Canal Museum.** Dating from the mid-19th century, this four storey building was the warehouse for one of the largest firms of canal carriers, Fellows, Morton, and Clayton. The firm went into liquidation in 1948 and this magnificent building has been restored and refurbished to house many displays and models illustrating the history of the Trent Valley. The story,

from rise to decline, of the country's network of canals and navigable waterways is also told and includes a reconstruction of an area of the warehouse as it would have appeared in its heyday.

On the edge of The Park, a former royal hunting ground that was developed for housing in 1827, stands the Roman Catholic **Cathedral of St Barnabas.** Built in 1841 by Pugin, the exterior is rather severe although the spire is very fanciful. Inside, much of Pugin's original decoration has been replaced though his stained glass windows remain in the aisle. The cathedral has an interesting literary connection since it was here that the author Graham Greene was inducted into the Catholic religion.

AROUND NOTTINGHAM

WOLLATON
2 miles W of Nottingham on the A609

Built in creamy white Ancaster stone, **Wollaton Hall** (free on weekdays) is one of the most attractive and elaborate Elizabethan mansions in the Midlands. Set in a spacious park, the house was built in the 1580s to the designs of Robert Smythson, who also designed Hardwick Hall in Derbyshire. His client was Francis Willoughby whose family had made a fortune from the local coal mines. The Elizabethan passion for symmetry is extravagantly displayed on the magnficent front façade with its matching classical columns, busts of philosophers and mythological characters, and flamboyant gables.

The Hall was sold to Nottingham City Council in 1924 and only three rooms have been restored to their former grandeur: the great hall, the entrance hall, and a beautiful salon.

The building is also home to the **Natural History Museum** which is based on the collection of Francis Willoughby, a noted naturalist of the mid-1600s, while some of the Hall's outbuildings have been transformed into the Nottingham Industrial Museum where the city's major industries are all represented. There are bicycles, from boneshakers and penny-farthings through to Raleigh and Humber models, and the progression to the motorcycle is given space in the form of the Brough machines of the 1920s and 1930s. (It was whilst riding a Brough motorcycle that TE Lawrence had his fatal crash in 1935). Textiles, and particularly stocking frames and knitting machines, can be found here as can machinery from the pharmaceutical industry. Finally, the local coal mines are also represented and there is a particularly fine example of a horse winding gin from 1844 on display in the courtyard.

The park surrounding the Hall is one of the city's great amenities. The 525 acres are contained within a 7-mile long wall, providing security for the herds of deer that roam here as they have for more than 400 years.

Martin's Pond, thought to be the first nature reserve opened in a city, was probably a medieval fishpond belonging to Wollaton Hall. In the surrounding land, over 150 species of flowering plants and 70 species of birds have been recorded. Nearby Harrison's Plantation, which is also managed by the Nottinghamshire Wildlife Trust, is an area of mixed woodland planted sometime in the 1700s.

STRELLEY
4 miles NW of Nottingham off the A6002

Though the village lies close to the centre of Nottingham, Strelley still retains several cottages originally built for workers on the Strelley Hall estate. The

manor of Strelley goes back to Norman times and was once held by Ralph Edge who, on three occasions, was elected Lord Mayor of Nottingham in the 17th century. The village church, dating from the 13th century, has some outstandingly fine monuments to the local de Strelley family, the original lords of the manor, whilst its well preserved 15th century rood screen is exceptionally tall and slender.

BULWELL
3 miles NW of Nottingham on the B682

Originally the whole area surrounding the village was covered by forest and it is probable that the settlement took its name from a spring in the old woodland. However, a local legend tells the story of the naming of the village rather differently. Apparently, an enraged bull gored a rock here and released a stream of sparkling spring water.

Those familiar with the film version of Alan Sillitoe's story *The Ragman's Daughter*, will recognise Bulwell as the movie's location. One building that stands out is Strelley House, which dates from 1667 and was founded as a free school by George Strelley. The first governor of the school was William Byron (later the 3rd Lord Byron) and at first the intake was limited to 30 boys. Above the porch can be seen a carved stone panel which contains the Strelley coat of arms.

BESTWOOD
6 miles N of Nottingham off the A60

Bestwood was a favourite hunting ground of Charles II who often stayed here with Nell Gwynne. One local story tells of a wager the king struck with Nell, saying she could have all the land she could ride around before breakfast. Nell, not known for being an early riser, made an exception on this occasion. The next morning, she rose at dawn and rode

around the countryside dropping
handkerchiefs along the way. Arriving
back before breakfast, Nell claimed her
winnings and Charles kept his side of the
bargain. Whether or not the story is true,
the king certainly gave Nell substantial
landholdings in the area.

Nell's illegitimate son by the king was
created the 1st Duke of St Albans and it
was a direct descendant of his, the 10th
Duke, who built the present Bestwood
Lodge. Begun in 1862, the lodge is a
grand house with flying buttresses, gables,
and chimneys, and its best feature is
undoubtedly the loft entrance tower with
its high pyramidal roof.

Part of the old royal hunting park is
now **Bestwood Country Park** whose 450
acres offer many differing landscapes.
Here you'll also find the **Bestwood
Pumping Station**, erected in the early
1870s. The Duke only gave his permission
for it to be built after the architect
solemnly promised that it would look
nothing like a pumping station. With its
150ft tower, cooling pond disguised as an
ornamental lake, and surrounded by
beautifully maintained gardens, the
station certainly lives up to the architect's
promise.

ARNOLD
3 miles N of Nottingham on the B684

On the outskirts of Nottingham, this once
separate town is now a suburb of the
expanding city. Like many towns and
villages around Nottingham, Arnold was
very much part of the local lace and
hosiery industry and, in 1860, the firm I
and R Morley built their factory here. Still
standing today, though the company
ceased operation in 1963, Morley's
Hosiery Factory is a fine example of mid-
Victorian industrial architecture. Two
storeys high, with eight bays and a large
central clock, it has an elaborate
extension of three storeys added in 1885.

GEDLING
3 miles NE of Nottingham off the A612

Another village that has been absorbed
into the city, Gedling dates back to before
the days of the Norman Conquest when it
was known as Ghellinge. It has a fine
church with a magnificent steeple which
has been soaring above the landscape for
some 700 years.

Though coal was been mined in the
village since the Middle Ages it was the
sinking of two shafts in Bell field in 1900,
as well as the earlier arrival of the railway
in 1846, which turned Gedling from a
rural village into a bustling suburb.
Gedling colliery did not last long as it was
one of the first pits to be closed, in 1933,
when much of the mining industry of
Nottinghamshire was cut back.

SNEINTON
1 mile E of Nottingham on the A612

Sneinton's main claim to fame is as the
birthplace, in 1829, of William Booth, the
founder of the Salvation Army. The small
terraced house where he and his family
lived until 1831 is still standing in
Notintone Place, fronted now by a statue
of the great man. The family home has
become the **William Booth Birthplace
Museum**: entry to the house is free but by
appointment only.

After his father's early death, Booth's
mother was forced to move to Goosegate,
Nottingham where she ran a shop selling
toys and sewing materials and it was
whilst living in this deprived area that
Booth first became aware of the appalling
conditions in which the urban working
classes lived. He was only 16 when he
gave his first sermon in a house in Kid.

In 1849, Booth left Nottingham for
London where he became a Methodist
minister. But, finding the church
structures too constraining, he established
in 1865 the Christian Missions which, in

1878, was renamed the Salvation Army. During the next 10 years, the movement spread to all corners of the world, including America, Australia, and South Africa. The Army is still mobilised, with more than 1000 local corps in the UK involved in both social and evangelistic work. Its missing persons bureau traces anything up to 5000 people each year.

Sneinton stands on one of the several hills that make up the city. Sneinton's hill is crowned by a distinctive landmark: **Green's Mill** (free), a five storey brick tower mill dating from 1807. Now beautifully restored after becoming derelict earlier this century, as well as suffering from fire damage in 1947, the mill is back in working order and flour milled here is on sale in the shop. The mill was built by George Green, a prosperous Nottingham baker, but it was his son, also called George, who made even more of a mark. Without any formal education after the age of nine, George went on to become one of country's leading scientists and mathematicians. Although George died in 1841, at the age of 48, many of his techniques are still applied today.

COLWICK
2 miles E of Nottingham on the A612

A large area of some 250 acre around old gravel workings has been converted into **Colwick Country Park**, where, as well as expanses of water offering facilities for sailing, rowing, and fishing, there is also a nature reserve. This country park was once part of the estate surrounding the 18th century Colwick Hall, now a hotel, but originally the home of the Byron family. Nearby is Nottingham's popular race-course.

HOLME PIERREPONT
3 miles E of Nottingham off the A52

Although Holme has been in the hands of the Pierrepont family since 1284, the present **Holme Pierrepont Hall** dates from the early 1500s and is regarded as one of the best examples of a brick built house in the county. Opening times are restricted but the hall is well worth a visit. Some of the ground floor rooms been restored to their original state and furnished in the style of the early 17th century, and the Upper Lodging still has superb ceiling timbers dating from the 1400s.

Also worthy of a visit is **St Edmond's Church**, situated adjacent to the hall. Inside are several interesting Pierrepont family monuments, including a 14th century brass to an unknown lady, and the church retains some features of the original 13th century building.

These days, Holme Pierrepont is more widely known as the home of the **National Water Sports Centre** (free, except during special events). Built to Olympic standards, the Centre boasts a full size rowing course and a wild water slalom course, all man-made from the pasture and quarries which once dominated the area.

RADCLIFFE ON TRENT
3 miles E of Nottingham on the A52

Old Radcliffe on Trent developed around a Roman crossing over the river; later, a Saxon manor was founded here; and during the 18th century it became an estate village for nearby Holme Pierrepoint. In Victorian times, it became a satellite of Nottingham whose citizens built comfortable villas on the wooded banks of the Trent. Radcliffe still has something of the atmosphere of those days, with a winding main street and plenty of trees. Its church too is Victorian,

THE TRENT HOTEL

64 Shelford Road, Radcliffe-on-Trent,
Nottinghamshire NG12 1AW
Tel: 0115 911 3395

Built as a spacious private residence well over a century ago, **The Trent Hotel** is an impressive building, architecturally interesting and standing in lovely grounds. Many of the old features have been retained, such as the tiled fireplaces and beamed roofs, and mine hosts, Marianne and Tony, who took over here in the December 2000 have also been careful to maintain the inn's appeal as a community pub and a base for local sports clubs. There's a quiz every Thursday evening, (with free chips for everyone!), and occasional live entertainment on Saturday.

Outside, there's a beautifully presented, and extensive, beer garden where Marianne and Tony will be introducing table service for summer 2002 and even installed two outdoor heaters to ensure their customers' comfort. Marianne is a part-time lecturer to students with learning difficulties and one of her current priorities is to provide disabled access and toilets at the hotel. The Trent is also popular because of its appetising food, served every lunchtime and evening except Sunday when meals are served between noon and 5pm. Children are welcome here; there's plenty of parking space, and all major credit cards are accepted.

with a saddleback roof; a striking, lofty interior, and an interesting brass recording the death of Anne Ballard in 1626. She is depicted wearing a long dress and a ruff while kneeling at a desk. Outside, the graveyard contains some elegantly carved slate headstones.

WEST BRIDGFORD
2 miles S of Nottingham on the A60

This town, now very much a suburb of Nottingham, lies across the River Trent from the rest of the city and is home to the famous **Trent Bridge** test and county cricket ground as well as the home of Nottingham Forest Football Club.

EDWALTON
3 miles S of Nottingham on the A606

The village takes its name from a Saxon settler, Eadweald, who was responsible for reclaiming the surrounding land from marshes. Though the village has grown in size, because of its close proximity to the centre of Nottingham, the main street still retains some village charm.

Edwalton is a place well worth visiting for anyone interested in flowers and gardening as is it the home of Wheatcrofts, the internationally renowned rose growers.

BEESTON

Lying on the southwest outskirts of Nottingham, Beeston is famous as the home of **Boots the Chemist**. Jesse Boot was born in 1850 and left school at the age of 13 to work in his mother's herbalist shop in the centre of Nottingham. She had started the business to supplement her husband's meagre income as a farm labourer. Following his death, when Jesse was only 10 years old, the shop became the mainstay of the family. Jesse quickly learnt the trade and in 1888 he set up the Boots Pure Drug Company.

In a business where quacks and charlatans abounded, Boot's emphasis on the purity of his drugs and medicines, (and his competitive prices), attracted customers everywhere and by 1896 the company had a chain of over 60 shops. It was at his wife's suggestion that Jesse expanded the lines in the shops to include jewellery, stationery, books, and art. In 1920 the business was sold to an American company only to be bought back by Jesse's son during the depression in 1933. A great benefactor to the city and surrounding area, Jesse was knighted in 1903, created a baronet in 1917, and finally raised to the peerage as Lord Trent in 1929, two years before his death.

Beeston is, essentially, an industrial town and, as well as being home to the Boots factory, it was also home to the Humber bicycle factory from 1880. At first employing only 80 staff, by 1900 the workforce had risen to 1800. Humber began production of, first, motorcycles and then motorcars in 1903. The company moved its manufacturing base to Coventry in 1908 but the early Humber trademark can still be seen on the old factory building.

AROUND BEESTON

CLIFTON
2 miles SE of Beeston on the A453

At first sight this village near the River Trent seems swamped by modern development but the character of the old village can be found in and around the green. The manor of Clifton was held by the family of that name from the 13th century up until 1953 when they gave up the hall to what is now Nottingham Trent University.

Along the banks of the River Trent is Clifton Grove, a wooded cliff above the riverbank, where visitors can stroll in the footsteps of Paul Morel and Clare Dawes, characters in D.H. Lawrence's *Sons and Lovers*. This stretch of the River Trent was also the setting for a tragic love story. In 1471, a young squire called Henry Bateman went to the Crusades with his master. When he returned, he discovered that his sweetheart Margaret had fallen for another man and married him. The heartbroken lover threw himself into the Trent from Clifton Grove. Some time later, Margaret herself took the same way out, presumably in remorse for her

BARTON-IN-FABIS
2 miles S of Beeston off the A453

The village of Barton-in-Fabis (originally Barton-in-the-Beans) is a charming little place with strong connections to the Sitwell and Sacheverell families. The church is dominated by their memorials and stands close to the site of the old Hall. In the early 1960s, Sir Osbert Sitwell made a sentimental tour of the area and the rather disappointing results are recorded in his book *Tales My Father Taught Me* (1962). *"The three days"* he recalled, *"were a series of triumphant anti-climaxes. It rained all the time…At one place we visited the house had just been pulled down"*.

However, he was pleased to see that the brick dovecote at Barton was still standing.

Built in 1677 for William Sacheverell, this is the only octagonal dovecote in the county and half of the original 1,200 nesting boxes survive to this day.

THRUMPTON
3 miles S of Beeston off the A453

This quiet village lies right on the border with Derbyshire and, though it has seen

EATON FARM

Wilsthorpe Road, Long Eaton,
Nottinghamshire NG10 4AW
Tel: 0115 946 2613
website: www.coringbossman.co.uk

Eaton Farm takes its name from the extensive farm that once covered hundreds of acres and was renowned for the quality of horses bred there. Over the years, much of that land has been devoured by housing estates and the M1 motorway, but Eaton Farm remains as an oasis - known as an excellent watering-hole and also highly regarded for the quality of the food on offer. The Eaton Farm pub/restaurant was constructed in 1990, an attractive building with walls of rich red brick and a pantiled roof. The interior is equally smart with lots of wood panelling, exposed beams and rafters, pine furniture, stained glass features and lots of bygone artefacts, amongst them a vintage bicycle hanging from the roof.

The outstanding food here is available every day from noon until 10pm, (9pm on Sunday), and the various menus between them cater for every palate and purse. The bar menu offers jacket potatoes,

burgers, sandwiches, baguettes and main courses such as vegetable & cheese pie, gammon steak and breaded plaice. In the 100-seater restaurant the extensive menu opens with a good choice of starters - home made soup, Oriental Prawns and Game Terrine amongst them. Main courses include Lemon Battered Whitby Scampi, steaks, chicken dishes and a vegetarian Caesar Bake - broccoli and asparagus bound in a creamy Brie sauce topped with sliced potatoes. Salads, light bites, pasta dishes and several Chef's Specials add to the choice. Children have their own, unusually extensive, menu which provides very good value for money. To round off your meal there's a hard-to-resist selection of hot and cold desserts, Lemon Squidgy perhaps, or an appetising Fruits of the Forest Tart. And to complement your meal there's a very wide range of beverages available that includes wine by the bottle, large or standard glass, 2 real ales (Banks Bitter & Marston's Pedigree), and all the popular beers and spirits. Eaton Farm's restaurant is understandably popular so bookings are essential on Saturday evenings and Sunday lunchtime.

During the summer months, weather permitting, Eaton Farm holds barbecues every Friday and Saturday evening from 6pm in the beautifully maintained gardens where you can also enjoy your refreshments during the rest of week. Another popular attraction at the pub is the monthly karaoke, held on a Saturday evening and starting at 7.30pm.

Eaton Farm accepts all major credit cards, apart from Diners, and has extensive parking space.

many changes, including the building of new houses for commuters to nearby Nottingham and Derby, there is still a village spirit here. Originally called Turmodeston, the small settlement once lay inside the present park of Thrumpton Hall. In the 17th century, John Emerton enclosed the park and new cottages were built around the church where some can still be seen today. The H-shaped hall, with Flemish gables, has inside such wonders as a balustrade carved with acanthus scrolls, richly carved doors, and some fine wall panelling dating back to the days of Charles II. The 8th Lord Byron inherited the house through marriage and some relics of the poet Byron are displayed here.

During the 19th century, Lucy, Lady Byron, lived at the hall for most of her 88 years and since she owned virtually the whole village ruled it with a firm but genial hand. She restored the village church and, since she loved religious music, selected her staff on the basis of their singing voices. The Thrumpton choir was much in demand and often sang at Southwell Minster.

CHILWELL
1 mile SW of Beeston on the A6005

Chilwell has a rather sad claim to fame as the site of one of the worst disasters to occur in England during World War I. Then as now, Chilwell was the site of a huge ordnance depot and it was here that a massive explosion took place in March, 1918. One hundred and forty-one people were killed.

ATTENBOROUGH
2 miles SW of Beeston off the A6005

This compact village has strong links with Oliver Cromwell and the Parliamentary cause of the 17th century. In 1611, Henry Ireton was born at Ireton House and later became one of the most senior officers in the Parliamentary army. He fought at Edgehill and Naseby, and also took part in the siege of Bristol. In 1646 he married Bridget, Cromwell's daughter. Ireton was appointed as one of the judges who tried and sentenced Charles I. Remaining loyal to Cromwell, he had just assumed the office of Lord Deputy of Ireland when he was struck down by the plague in 1651. He was buried in Westminster Abbey but after the Restoration in 1660 his body, along with that of Cromwell, was taken to the gallows at Tyburn. Here it was put on public display before being beheaded and then buried beneath the gallows.

The christening records of several members of the Ireton family, including those of Ireton's daughter, (Cromwell's granddaughter), are preserved in the village church.

Bearing the name of Attenborough, it's appropriate that the village was the first in Nottinghamshire to have a Nature Reserve. It was opened in 1966 and the 200-acre site contains 120 acres of lakes and some 40 islands.

STAPLEFORD
2 miles W of Beeston off the A52

In Stapleford churchyard can be found the best preserved Saxon carving in the county in the form of a 10ft high cross shaft. Dating from the late 11th century, the intricate carving depicts an eagle standing on a serpent - said to be the symbol of St Luke. The church, which dates mainly from the 13th and 14th centuries, has many war memorials to lost heroes. The village was once a thriving centre for framework knitting and terraced cottages built specifically for the workers can still be seen in Nottingham Road.

One other feature of Stapleford worthy of a look is the **Hemlockstone**, a massive redstone boulder standing 30 feet high and weighing around 200 tons situated opposite Bramcote Park. Geologists believe the rock was probably deposited here by glacial action, whilst wind erosion has contributed to its brooding appearance. Its geological make up consists of sandstone, cemented by the mineral barite which is found in large quantities throughout the Stapleford and Bramcote Hills.

The village school was renamed the Arthur Mee Centre in memory of the writer who grew up in the town and was educated at the school. Born in 1875, Mee left school at 14 to work for the *Nottingham Evening Post* before moving to London and finding his niche writing for children. His works include the *Children's Bible*, the *Children's Encyclopaedia*, and the *Children's Shakespeare* but it is probably for *The King's England*, a series of guide books which ran to some 80 volumes, that Mee is best remembered.

RUDDINGTON

This historic village, whose name is derived from the Saxon word Rudda - meaning headman - was once the home of many hosiery workers and several of their cottages still remain. In 1829, a factory and frameworkers cottages were built around a courtyard in Chapel Street. Later, a school was built and this is now occupied by the **Ruddington Framework Knitters' Museum** which depicts community life through several reconstructed shops and an Edwardian schoolroom. Of the 25 hand frames seen here today, most are fully operational and there is an opportunity to buy samples made at the museum.

The industry reached its height in 1880, with the staggering number of 20,000 frames operating in Nottingham, Derbyshire, and Lincolnshire. As well as the knitting frames on show, the museum

also has other machinery of specific importance to the village and to the hosiery industry. Regular demonstrations are given using the working exhibits. Visitors can try out their own weaving skills on one of the collection of circular sock machines.

Not far away is the **Ruddington Village Museum**, housed in the old village school building of 1852. Concentrating on the everyday life of the villagers, the museum has reconstructions of several shops and craftsmen's workshops including an Edwardian fish and chip shop. As well as having one of the school rooms restored to look as it once did, there is also a room devoted to a collection of farming implements.

AROUND RUDDINGTON

GOTHAM
3 miles SW of Ruddington off the A453

The name is actually pronounced 'Goat'm' and the village should not be confused with the home of the caped crusader, Batman. However, the village is remembered as the home of the Wise Men. King John had decreed that he wished to build a hunting lodge here in the village. Naturally displeased at having to give up their land to the king's whims, the villagers devised a plan. They decided that the best way to dissuade the royal presence was to feign madness. When the king's messengers entered the village, the inhabitants reacted in such a peculiar way that the men returned to His Majesty with the suggestion that the mad men of Gotham should be left well alone. Such were the odd tales of their bizarre acts that Dr Andrew Borde published the *Merrie Tales of the Mad Men of Gotham* in the 16th century. There are many bizarre stories but one of the finest is kept alive in the name of the village pub - The Cuckoo Bush. A group of villagers, captivated by the song of a cuckoo, decided to capture the bird by encircling the bush in which it was sitting by a fence. Unfortunately, the men did not think to build a roof so the cuckoo simply flew away.

RATCLIFFE ON SOAR
6 miles SW of Ruddington off the A453

The tiny village of Ratcliffe on Soar has a pretty little church, with an eye-catching blackened spire, and a handsome manor farmhouse set picturesquely on the meadow banks of the River Soar. Although a massive power station looms over everything and the railway clatters by, this charming village is still definitely worth a visit.

Holy Trinity Church, with its broach spire and four pinnacles, houses some splendid tombs belonging to the Sacheverells. A Ralph, three Henrys, and their wives lie here under the watchful gaze of the cooling towers. Here too, Sir Osbert found fault with his ancestors' resting places, having apparently discovered the church under water when he came to pay his respects!

WEST LEAKE
4 miles SW of Ruddington off the A6006

Recorded in the Domesday Book as Leche, this surprisingly rural village has two Roman tracks on its boundaries as well as evidence of Roman occupation. The remains of the fish pools which stood near the medieval manor house can still be made out though the house ceased to be the home of the lord of the manor in 1750.

NORMANTON ON SOAR
7 miles SW of Ruddington off the A6006

Lying in the valley of the River Soar,

which at this point marks the county boundary with Leicestershire, the village is centred around its charming, early-13th century St James' Church. Fortunately the building has been completely restored following a devastating fire in 1986 and its tall, broached spire, considered the best example in England, has been returned to its former elegance.

BUNNY
2 miles S of Ruddington on the A60

This pretty village has a wealth of lovely architecture and owes much of its charm to the eccentricities of its one-time squire, Sir Thomas Parkyns (1663-1741). A man obsessed with the sport of wrestling, Sir Thomas employed two full time professionals to spar with him at Bunny Hall. He also organised an annual tournament in the village to promote local wrestling talent and this event continued for nearly 70 years after his death. In St Mary's Church, which was designed by Sir Thomas, his memorial graphically illustrates his commitment to the sport. It depicts the squire standing victorious over his defeated opponent on a wrestling mat, while Old Father Time stands by, perhaps as referee.

Another of Sir Thomas' hobbies was collecting stone coffins which he provided free to those of his tenants in need of one. During his long lifetime he rebuilt much of the village to his own designs, provided a school, gave his tenants free medical and legal advice, and also found time to write a Latin Grammar and a book on wrestling, *Cornish Hugg Wrestling*.

EAST LEAKE
4 miles S of Ruddington off the A60

Like its neighbour, West Leake, the village name is derived from the Anglo-Saxon word Leche, meaning water meadow, and both villages lie on the banks of a tributary of the River Soar. The village church, which was mentioned in the Domesday Survey of 1086, was extensively restored in the 19th century but has retained its prize possession, a Vamp Horn or *shawm*. This extraordinary instrument is some 8 feet long and only five others are known to exist. Invented in 1670 by Samuel Morland, the horn was used by the bass singer to lead the choir from the gallery.

STANFORD ON SOAR
7 miles S of Ruddington off the A6006

Built as an estate village in 1839, Stanford lies at the southernmost point of Nottinghamshire where the River Soar, the King's Brook river, and the Grand Union Canal all blend together. Here also lies the disused track of the Great Central Railway that once ran from Nottingham to Marylebone. The church interior has some lovely decorative stencilling and many monuments to the Dashwood family

WIDMERPOOL
5 miles SE of Ruddington off the A606

This village is widely regarded as one of Nottinghamshire's oldest settlements, already in existence during Roman times. The village's present appearance owes much to the Robinson family, prosperous mill owners from Nottingham. It was they who built the great Victorian Widmerpool Hall (private) in 1872, landscaped the park with plantations of evergreens, and spent lavishly on rebuilding the village church, struck by lightning in 1836, and now hidden away amongst the trees.

WILLOUGHBY-ON-THE-WOLDS
6 miles SE of Ruddington off the A46

Willoughby lies close to the county border with Leicestershire so it is not

uncommon to see the huntsmen of the Quorn riding through the parish. The Quorn Hunt also meets in the village several times in the season and is often joined by Prince Charles.

This is an ancient village, its name being derived from the Danish word Wilgebi - meaning village of the willows. Close by lies the Roman road, Fosse Way, and a Roman settlement, Vernemetum, has been found near the site of an Anglo-Saxon burial ground.

STANTON ON THE WOLDS
4 miles SE of Ruddington off the A606

This rural village, which was until the 1960s home to seven dairy farms, has few really old buildings though the village dates back to Norman times. In the late 18th century, Stanton was hit by a freak storm in which giant hailstones rained down on the cottages and smashed their roofs. The ancient village Church of All Saints did, however, survive and it can be found standing alone in a field and reached by a footpath. Dating from the 11th century, the church, one of the smallest in south Nottinghamshire, is built mostly of boulders some of which, undoubtedly, were purloined from the nearby Fosse Way.

KEYWORTH
3 miles E of Ruddington off the A606

In the heart of south Nottinghamshire's farming country this, until very recently, small village prides itself on having produced no fewer than 30 professional cricketers, one of whom went on to be capped for England. The village too has had its share of scandals and one local legend tells of a tenant farmer who was visited by the rector who had a complaint to discuss. The farmer was not very agreeable to the criticism and soundly horse-whipped the clergyman before sending him on his way. This whip is still in existence though the nature of the complaint the rector was making is unknown.

BINGHAM

The unofficial "capital" of the Vale of Belvoir, Bingham is an ancient medieval market town which grew up around the church. After passing through a period of depression in the 19th century, the town is once again thriving. The area around the market square has been smartened up and the octagonal **Butter Cross** with its Victorian tiles and inscriptions provides an attractive focus here. Most of the buildings around the market place are also Victorian but All Saints' Church is medieval, dating from the 13th century though, again, there are many Victorian

THE SALUTATION

Main Street, Keyworth,
Nottinghamshire NG12 5AD
Tel: 0115 937 2465

If you are a devotee of ITV's reborn soap opera Crossroads, you will find **The Salutation** strangely familiar. All the pub and bar scenes for the popular serial are filmed at this charming old hostelry which dates back to the mid-1700s. It was built then as an alehouse and blacksmith's, a common and very practical combination of businesses in those days. The interior of The Salutation still retains a wonderful olde worlde atmosphere, full of character and charm.

Mine hosts, Graham and Debbie, are a friendly and welcoming couple with some 13 years experience at inns across the East Midlands. Debbie is in charge of the kitchen and offers both a regular menu and specials board, as well as a kiddies' menu. Amongst her specialities are the succulent Lamb and

"Boozy Beef" dishes. Customers can enjoy their meals anywhere in the beamed rooms, which have designated non-smoking areas or, in good weather, outside in the beer garden or on the patio. The choice of beverages includes 3 real ales, along with a wide range of popular brews, spirits and wines. For additional entertainment there's a pool table, quiz and internet machines, a piano, a disco on the first Friday of each month, and barbecues during the summer. The pub has ample off road parking and all major credit cards are accepted apart from American Express and Diners.

THE MOOT HOUSE

Bowland Road, Bingham, Nottinghamshire NG13 8RW
Tel: 01949 837146

A smart modern building of glowing red brick, **The Moot House** is very much a family-run business. There's Geoff and Jayne Heywood, Jayne's sister Amanda, and their mother, Eileen Fletcher. Jayne is a cook with flair and dishes such as her homemade Steak & Guinness Pie have made The Moot House a popular dining venue. Jayne also offers some appetising vegetarian dishes and her across the board menu is available every weekday lunchtime and evening; Saturdays from noon until 6pm; and on Sundays from noon until 4pm. Beverages include real ales and this lively hostelry also offers Bingo on Wednesday, a quiz on Thursday; live singers on Saturday and a monthly karaoke evening.

additions and decorations.

Bingham was the third Nottinghamshire town to provide an Archbishop of Canterbury. George Abbot's tenure of office was almost as unremarkable as that of Thomas Secker of Sibthorpe except for one unfortunate accident in 1621. Abbot was out shooting deer with a crossbow when he missed and killed a gamekeeper instead.

Other celebrities connected with the town include the Rev. Richard Wren, vicar of the parish and father of Sir Christopher; and Edward VII's mistress, Lily Langtry, who rather strangely is commemorated on the chancel screen in the church. In fact, she was a clergyman's daughter and often stayed at Bingham Rectory. When the parish commissioned a modern screen depicting the town's history, the artist Frank Miles, who also happened to be the son of the vicar, included the famous courtesan.

AROUND BINGHAM

COTGRAVE
4 miles SW of Bingham off the A46

The discovery of an Anglo-Saxon burial ground on Mill Hill, Cotgrave's highest point, confirms that there has been a settlement here for many centuries. The excavation team uncovered the skeletons of nearly 100 people including some 13 children and the remains have been dated to around the mid to late 6th century.

Close to the burial ground stood the village's old post mill, itself the site of an unsolved mystery. One of the millers disappeared without trace after having been accused of pilfering corn. Rumours in the 19th century suggested that a body had been discovered in the mill foundations and, despite believing that

this could be the remains of the missing miller, the villagers kept quiet and the rumour was never investigated. During an excavation of the post mill site in the 1970s the skeleton of a male was uncovered which showed injuries that suggested that the unfortunate man was killed by a blow to the head. Whether or not this was all that remained of the missing miller has never been established.

Cotgrave is probably most well known as the home of Cotgrave Colliery which opened in 1964 and was a showplace mine for a number of years. The promise of work here for the next 100 years brought many miners from other coalfields to the village and also generated a huge expansion and building programme. Unfortunately, major geological faults made it impossible to mine the huge reserves and the colliery is now closed.

KINOULTON
6 miles S of Bingham off the A46

The village, on the edge of the wolds, stands on high ground and from this vantage point there are views over the Vale of Belvoir to Belvoir Castle. Today, Kinoulton is a large commuter village but it has a long and interesting past. In the 12th century, there was a castle here, its commanding position being ideal since it was also close to the Fosse Way. Archbishop Cranmer had a palace nearby and, to the west of the village, lies the spring which brought the village to prominence in Georgian times as a spa with curative properties. Later, the arrival of the Grantham Canal ushered in a period of mild prosperity. (The canal still passes through the village and provides some pleasant walking).

Standing beside the canal, Kinoulton's **Church of St Luke** was a gift of the squire, the Earl of Gainsborough, in the

1760s. The earl felt the old church was too near what was then a major thoroughfare, the Fosse Way. The slate headstones in the old churchyard have some fine inscriptions but not all of the stones have survived. Some were "borrowed" by the local baker to line his oven, a piece of re-cycling that was exposed when a customer noticed that his loaf was imprinted with the words *"In loving memory"*.

HICKLING
7 miles S of Bingham off the A606

Lying on the western edge of the Vale of Belvoir, this agricultural village was the site of a busy basin on the Grantham Canal. Building work on the basin finished in 1797 and the canal, which carried coal, building materials, and agricultural goods, was in constant use until the 1930s when it began to fall into disrepair. Recently cleared, Hickling Basin is once again attracting people, this time visitors who come to see the resident flocks of wildfowl.

UPPER BROUGHTON
9 miles S of Bingham on the A606

At Upper Broughton the A606 twists in a double dog-leg turn before straightening out and passing into Leicestershire half a mile down the road. The village used to be called Broughton Sulney, but this name is now only used for ecclesiastical purposes. This alternative name stems from Norman times when the village and surrounding land was owned by Aluredus de Sulnei.

In the centre of the village are two greens. In springtime, one of them is a riot of golden daffodils, amongst them a species that is named after the village. On the second green can be seen the remains of a cross which is thought to have been placed here to commemorate the end of the Black Death.

COLSTON BASSETT
4 miles S of Bingham off the A46

For centuries this small village was the property of the Bassett family and later the Hackers and the Goldings. Between them they planted the many trees that shade the winding lanes, built a noble manor house, landscaped the gracious park, and in 1892 added a striking if rather over-elaborate church. The cumulative effect is to make Colston Bassett one of the most picturesque villages in the Vale of Belvoir.

At one time the village was large enough to sustain its own weekly market and the partly medieval **Market Cross** can still be seen. Since 1933, the Cross has been owned by the National Trust - the first property it acquired in Nottinghamshire. The Cross stands near the old post office, itself a picture postcard building that used to feature in GPO advertisements during the 1960s.

On the outskirts of the village stand the forlorn ruins of the former village church which has been abandoned since 1892.

CROPWELL BISHOP
3 miles SW of Bingham off the A46

Much of the furniture from Colston Bassett's old church was moved to Cropwell Bishop and installed in St Giles' Church. St Giles is the oldest building in this sizeable village and dates back to around 1215.

The village lies close to the old Roman road, the Fosse Way, now the A46. The coaching inns of Cropwell Bishop are said to have given shelter to highwayman Dick Turpin whilst he was plundering the coaches using the busy thoroughfare.

In modern times, the village has prospered from gypsum works. Two of the works' bottle kilns still stand alongside the Grantham Canal.

CROPWELL BUTLER
2 miles SW of Bingham off the A46

Mentioned in the Domesday Book, Cropwell Butler is often twinned with its neighbour, Tithby since that is where its parish Church of the Holy Trinity stands. A quiet and rural place, Cropwell Butler does, however, have one son, Thomas Smith, who achieved a certain celebrity. Born in 1621, Thomas was the son of a small landowner in Cropwell Butler and later went on to found a group of banks which are now part of the National Westminster. The NatWest branch in South Parade, Nottingham is still referred to as Smith's Bank Branch.

LANGAR
3 miles S of Bingham off the A52

"Really, the English do not deserve great men", declared George Bernard Shaw. "They allowed Butler to die practically unknown". He was referring to Samuel Butler, author of *The Way of All Flesh*, who was born in the elegant Georgian rectory at Langar on December 4, 1834. A trenchant satirist, Butler mocked the pomposity and exposed the hypocrisy of the Victorian middle classes. No wonder they didn't much care for him. Langar itself appears in his major work as Battersby-on-the-Hill and the portraits of its residents are far from flattering. Even so, with the centenary of Butler's death in 1902 fast approaching, perhaps it is time for the village to commemorate one of its most famous residents in some way.

This small rural village in the heart of the Vale was also the home of Admiral Richard, Earl Howe (1726-99), "Black Dick of Lanagar". Richard achieved national fame on the Glorious 1st of June, 1794, at the Battle of Ushant where his victory included the capture of seven French ships of the line. The Admiral himself merits only a modest plaque in **St**

Andrew's Church, but other generations of the Howe family; their predecessors, the Scropes, as well as the Chaworths from nearby Wiverton Hall, are all celebrated by an extraordinary gathering of monuments. The most splendid is a 4-poster free-standing alabaster monument to Thomas, Lord Scrope, who died in 1609, and his wife: according to Pevsner *"the figures are good enough to be in Westminster Abbey"*.

To the south of Langar, the former airfield is surrounded by an unsightly industrial estate which nevertheless contains the **Wild Flower Farm Visitors Centre,** part of a commercial nursery, where visitors are able to explore the wild flower meadows and see a wide variety of species in their natural habitat.

GRANBY
4 miles SE of Bingham off the A52

This small, once self-sufficient village is still proud that its name was adopted by the Dukes of Rutland, of nearby Belvoir Castle, as the courtesy title of their eldest son. It was John, son of the 3rd Duke, who brought most lustre to the name as Commander in Chief of the British forces in Germany in the mid-1700s. The Marquis was immensely popular with his troops, many of whom followed an old tradition on leaving the Army and became publicans. Which explains why so many hostelries up and down the country are named *The Marquis of Granby* - including naturally the inn at Granby itself.

SUTTON
4 miles E of Bingham off the A52

This little hamlet, which is sometimes called Sutton-cum-Granby, has been in existence for over 1000 years and remains remarkably unspoilt. Now overlooked by Belvoir Castle, Sutton once had its very own castle. This was not a grand stone affair but rather a fortified homestead with a moat to which villagers could retire and seek shelter in troubled times. Traces of the moat can still be seen in the fields. The fortified house no longer exists but Sutton can boast one of the smallest chapels in the country. Measuring just 18ft square and with its door opening straight onto the village's main street, Sutton Chapel was built in 1860.

WHATTON
3 miles E of Bingham off the A52

The Norman St John's Church was restored in the 1860s under the direction of Thomas Butler, rector of Langar, and the stained glass windows, including some crafted by William Morris to the designs of Burne-Jones, were added later that century. The font, which is dated 1662, replaced one that had been damaged during the Commonwealth. This church was used by Thomas Cranmer and his family until he left the area to take up his studies at Cambridge. A memorial to his father, Thomas Cranmer senior, who died in 1502, can be found inside.

ASLOCKTON
2 miles E of Bingham off the A52

This village is now separated from its neighbour, Whatton, by the main Nottingham to Grantham railway line, though the footpaths linking the two can still be walked today. This was the village in which Thomas Cranmer was born and spent his early years. Born in 1489, he attended the parish church at Whatton and also a local grammar school, possibly at Southwell, before leaving at the age of 14 to continue his education at Cambridge. It was in 1533 that Henry VIII proposed this obscure theologian and academic as Archbishop of Canterbury, an appointment which had to be approved by the Pope - the last time Rome had any

say over who should be Primate of All England.

One of Cranmer's first duties on gaining his appointment was to pronounce the marriage between Henry VIII and Catherine of Aragon null and void. During the course of his 23 years in office, Cranmer also pronounced invalid Henry's marriage to Anne Boleyn and granted him a divorce from Anne of Cleves. Loyal to his monarch throughout, Cranmer aided Henry in effecting the break of the Church in England from Rome. He was also responsible for drafting much of the Common Prayer book that was used right up until the 1970s when it was replaced by a modern language version. Following the death of Henry VIII, Cranmer was convicted of treason under Mary I and burnt at the stake in 1556.

Though not built until the late 19th century, Aslockton Church is appropriately dedicated to St Thomas whilst the village school also bears the name of its most famous resident. **Cranmer's Mound**, to the east of the church, is a high Norman motte some 15 feet high which is clearly visible from the footpath to Orston. Further along this same footpath can be seen the site of the manor house where Cranmer was born.

SOUTHWELL

Southwell is undoubtedly one of England's most beguiling towns, miraculously preserved from developers and with scarcely an ugly building to be seen. From whichever direction you approach, it is the twin towers of **Southwell Minster** that first catch the eye. With their pyramidal "Rhenish Caps", these towers are unique in this country although they would look perfectly in place anywhere in the Rhineland. James VI of Scotland was mightily impressed by Southwell when he passed through the town in 1603 en route to his coronation as James I: *"By my blude"* he is said to have exclaimed, *"this kirk shall justle with York or Durham or any other kirk in Chistendom"*.

Southwell Minster

Perhaps the least well-known of English cathedrals, Southwell's history goes back to 956 when Oskytel, Archbishop of York, established a church here. The present building was erected in three phases. The nave, transept and western towers are the oldest part, completed around 1150; the east end was built around 1240, and the superb Chapter House around 1290.

Octagonal in design, the **Chapter House** has been hailed as the pinnacle of the Decorated period of architecture - *"among chapter houses as the rose amongst flowers"*. The architectural historian, Nikolaus Pevsner devoted a whole book, *The Leaves of Southwell*, to the incredible wealth of stone carvings of foliage decorating the arcades above the Canons' seats.

The word most often applied to the cathedral is "serene" and, as one visitor put it, *"Other churches may be older, a few may be larger, but none are more beautiful"*.

There is no space here to detail all the cathedral's other treasures but the striking eagle lectern in the choir has an interesting story attached to it. The lectern was originally installed at Newstead Abbey. However, during the widespread looting at the time of the Dissolution, the monks threw the lectern into the lake, intending to retrieve it later. 'Later' turned out to be 200 years later, in 1750 in fact. Half a century after that the 5th Lord Byron presented the lectern to the Minster.

The cathedral stands in a delightful precinct, surrounded by attractive buildings.

To the south stand the ruins of the palace of the archbishops of York built in the 14th and 15th centuries. Parts of the old palace, closest to the minster's south doorway, have been incorporated into the present Bishop's Palace.

At the east end of the minster is **Vicar's Court**, a charming group of five Queen Anne house built for the Vicars Choral around 1702. Just across the road from the minster is a picturesque old coaching inn, the 16th century Saracen's Head. Charles I spent his last hours of freedom before his final surrender in this delightful half-timbered building. At that time the inn was known as the King's Head: the name was changed after Charles's execution.

Just to the north of the Saracen's Head is Burgage Manor (private), a handsome Georgian pile where the young Lord Byron stayed with his mother between 1803 and 1807 whilst on holiday from Harrow and Cambridge. He joined the local theatrical group and it was his friends in the town who convinced him to publish his first set of poems. Under the title *Hours of Idleness*, the book was published by Ridges of Newark and brought great acclaim to the young poet.

Southwell can also be credited as the birthplace of the Bramley apple. The story goes that in the early 19th century, two ladies planted some apple pips in their cottage garden in the nearby village of Easthorpe. Nature took its course and one of the seedlings grew into a tree. By this time, Matthew Bramley owned the cottage and the quality of the tree's fruit began to excite public interest.

Mr Henry Merryweather, a local nurseryman, persuaded Bramley to let him take a cutting, which he consequently propagated with enormous success. Permission had been granted on the condition that the apples took Mr Bramley's name and not the two ladies'! **The Bramley Apple Exhibition** (free) in Halam Road explains the full history and development of this famous fruit. Whilst in the town visitors should also look out for Southwell Galette, a scrumptious pastry confection of hazelnuts, sultanas, and, of course, Bramley apples.

The disused railway line from Southwell to Mansfield, opened in 1871, is now an attractive footpath known as the **Farnsfield to Southwell Trail**. As well as the varied plant and wildlife that can be found along the 4½ mile walk, there is also plenty of industrial archaeological interest including the Farnsfield Waterworks of 1910, a late 18th century cotton mill, and Greet Lily Mill, a corn mill on the banks of the River Greet.

Norwood Park (by appointment only) is the only one of the four original parks around Southwell that remains today. The property of the Archbishops of York, the park remained in the possession of the Church until 1778. A house was built here in Cromwell's day but the present building dates from 1763. Open to visitors during the summer months, the house has a very lived in feel and, as well as many 17th and 18th century family portraits, there is also a fine collection of china.

The surrounding parkland was laid out in the 18th century at the same time as the ice house and temple were built, and the lime avenue planted. However, the park is much older and it is believed that some of the surviving fishponds are the same as those mentioned in the Domesday Book.

AROUND SOUTHWELL

OXTON
4 miles SW of Southwell on the B6386

A charming village near the edge of Sherwood Forest and surrounded by parkland, Oxton has a goodly number of 17th and 18th century houses and cottages. The Sherbrooke family have been the lords of the manor here since the 16th century and Oxton still retains the feel of an estate village even though the hall was demolished in 1957. An oddity is to be found in a yard opposite the Green

Dragon Inn. Here stands the tomb of Robert Sherbrooke who died in 1710. The unusual location is explained by the fact that Sherbrooke was a Quaker and this was the site of their meeting house.

Other Sherbrookes were buried in more orthodox fashion in the family vault beneath the nave of the village Church of St Peter and St Paul. Their family hatchments adorn the interior along with a splendid Royal Arms of George II. A third 'I' was added after the accession of George III. The church has its foundations in Saxon times though the chancel is Norman and the nave and tower date from the 14th century. In 1986, the work to add two more church bells, bringing the total to six, was finished; the oldest bell, which is still very much in use, dates from 1638.

The uncovering of **Oldox Camp**, one of the largest and best preserved Iron Age hill forts in Nottinghamshire, to the north of the village suggests that this was the original site of Oxton. Extending over some 3 acres, the fort is surrounded by a single ditch and bank, except at the entrance to the fort where the defences are doubled.

CALVERTON
6 miles SW of Southwell off the B6386

The charming cottages in this industrial village date back to the early 19th century and were once the homes of framework knitters. Carefully restored by the Nottinghamshire Building Preservation Trust, the cottages originally formed three sides of a rectangle, though one side is now missing. Unusually, the large windows which provided the light for the knitters are found on the ground floor instead of the more usual upper storey.

It was a curate of Calverton, William Lee, who invented the stocking knitting frame in 1589. According to an old story,

his invention was the result of an unsuccessful love affair. Whenever William visited the girl he wanted to marry she *"always took care to be busily employed in knitting…He vowed to devote his further leisure to devising an invention that should effectually supersede her favourite employment of knitting"*. Lee succeeded in creating an immensely complicated machine that could produce top quality work between 10 and 15 times as quickly as the fastest hand knitters. To develop it further he sought the patronage of Elizabeth I but the queen refused to encourage something that would mean great job losses for her loyal subjects.

After being refused a patent by Elizabeth I, Lee travelled to France and gained the promise of support from Henry of Navarre. Unfortunately, Henry was assassinated before any promises were made good and it is believed that Lee died in Paris in 1610. Lee's brother, James, brought the frame back to London where the hosiery industry first developed before it settled in the Midlands later in the 17th century.

Also at Calverton is **Patchings**, formerly known as Painters' Paradise, a series of gardens that have been designed with the artist in mind. Here, amongst the rolling hills of north Nottinghamshire, is a perfect reconstruction of Claude Monet's garden at Giverney, complete with the elegant little bridge and the pool of water lilies that he painted so often. Attractive gazebo studios are dotted around the 50 acres of grounds, each designed to provide a picturesque view. An impressive building of Norwegian spruce - one of the largest wooden structures in England - offers further facilities for artists and visitors: studios, workshop and dark room as well as a licensed restaurant.

EPPERSTONE
5 miles SW of Southwell off the A6097

This attractive village, protected by a conservation order, was once described as *"one of the daintiest little villages in the county"*. Pevsner considered it *"uncommonly pleasing"*. The church stands high on a hill, overlooking the unspoilt old inn and the lane sloping down to a stream. Some elegant Georgian and Victorian houses, some earlier cottages and a tall brick dovecote all add to the charm.

LAMBLEY
7 miles SW of Southwell off the A612

As its name suggests, Lambley was the place where lambs were reared and the fields around the village are still home to grazing sheep and lambs. Though close to both Southwell and Nottingham, Lambley's air of rural peace and tranquillity derives from its position at the bottom of a valley formed by branches of the Cocker Beck, a tributary of the River Trent.

An ancient settlement, after the Norman Conquest the manor of Lambley was granted to the Cromwell family and, in 1394, Ralph Lord Cromwell was born in the village. Ralph went on to become Lord Treasurer of England in the time of Henry VI and he also had the distinction of presenting to Parliament a statement of the narional wealth which is regarded as the first Budget. Though he acquired great wealth, Ralph did not forget his birthplace. In his will he made provision for the rebuilding of the village church. That was in 1450 and the church has remained virtually unaltered ever since. After Ralph's death, the Cromwell manor fell into disrepair and today the site on which the house stood is occupied by the Rectory.

Right up until the early 19th century, Lambley remained very much a rural community but then the framework knitting industry took over. Though many of the typical long windows have either been altered or bricked up, the cottages where the knitters worked long, hard hours can still be seen.

BURTON JOYCE
8 miles SW of Southwell on the A612

As at Lambley, Burton Joyce's church is separated from the village by a busy road. Inside the church is a striking 14th century effigy of Sir Robert de Jorz de Bertune whose family name also provides the village name. Later, this village on the banks of the River Trent came into the possession of the Earls of Carnarvon. The Carnarvon Reading Room is named after the 5th Earl, who is better known as the discoverer of the Tomb of Tutankhamen.

LOWDHAM
5 miles S of Southwell on the A6097

Known locally as the village which ran away from the church, Lowdham acquired this unusual nickname after the construction of a dual carriageway in the 1930s. Dividing the village in two, the carriageway left the church on one side with much of the rest of the village on the other.

Founded in the late 12th century, the impressive Church of St Mary the Virgin houses a fine effigy of Sir Jon de Ludham, a knight whose son fought with Edward III at the Battle of Crecy.

THURGARTON
4 miles S of Southwell off the A612

This picturesque village, surrounded by low hills, is one of the most ancient settlements in Nottinghamshire, deriving its name comes from the old Norse name

COACH & HORSES

Main Street, Thurgarton,
Nottinghamshire NG14 7GY
Tel: 01636 830257

The Coach & Horses is an appropriate name for this charming old coaching inn that stands on the former turnpike road between Nottingham and Southwell, now the A612. Built in the 1700s, the inn has gradually been extended over the years by incorporating neighbouring cottages but the atmosphere remains delightfully olde worlde throughout. Some of the ceiling beams are inscribed with injunctions such as Call frequently, drink moderately, part friendly.

Mine hosts, Donna and Brennan, took over here in the spring of 2001 after many years experience in the catering and licensed trades. Brennan is the cook, offering appetising home made dishes every weekday lunchtime and evening, and from noon until 7pm on Sunday. (The inn is open all day, every day, for drinks). Brennan's speciality is seafood but there's a wide choice of other dishes, either from the regular menu or from those listed on the blackboard. No fewer than 6 real ales are always on tap, along with 2 guest ales and an extensive selection of other popular beverages. In good weather you can enjoy your refreshment in the small beer garden and patio outside. All the usual pub games are available and Monday is quiz night when everyone is welcome to take part. There's ample off road parking at the rear and all major credit cards are accepted apart from Diners.

Thorgeirr. Following the Norman Conquest, William I granted the manor of Thurgarton, along with 34 others in Nottinghamshire, to Walter d'Ayncourt. It was Walter's second son, Roger, who, in the mid-12th century, founded Thurgarton Priory for the Augustinian order. Originally, it rivalled Southwell Minster in size and splendour but today only the magnificent west tower and doorway remain.

In 1538, Henry VIII closed the priory, granting the buildings to his cup-bearer, William Cooper, and the land to Trinity College, Cambridge. The priory church fell into disrepair, with many of the villagers making use of the stone and timber in their own houses, and it was not until 1854 that the church was restored by the Milward family. Some of the priory's other stone buildings were replaced by a Georgian house and, in 1884, when the diocese of Southwell was founded the priory became the residence of the bishop. The house is now owned by Boots plc, who have a research centre here.

Thurgarton has a very pleasant cricket ground which is overlooked by both the church and the priory. Though not a large place, the village can still turn out a couple of teams and regularly plays host to teams from other villages.

A couple of miles south of the village, **Ferry Farm Country Park** provides an ideal location for a family outing. The Park extends over a 20-acre site adjoining the River Trent and is home to lots of friendly animals that children can pet and feed. There's also an activity play area; assault course; shop and restaurant.

SHELFORD
8 miles S of Southwell off the A6097

The name Shelford means the place of the shallow ford so, presumably, there was once a ford here across the River Trent which flows in a horseshoe bend around the village. Though now a quiet and tranquil place, in the winter of 1644 Shelford was the site of a particularly fierce battle. Royalist soldiers, taking shelter in the church tower, were smoked out by the Parliamentarian army who set fire to straw at the tower's base. During the same weekend, some 140 men were slaughtered by Cromwell's men at the manor house which was subsequently burnt to the ground.

The Royalist troops were commanded by Shelford's Lord of the Manor, Philip Stanhope, a member of the illustrious family who later became Earls of Chesterfield. There are some fine memorials to the Stanhopes in the village church, including one by Nollekens.

EAST BRIDGFORD
7 miles S of Southwell off the A6097

The village is situated on a ridge overlooking a crossing of the River Trent and the edge of Sherwood Forest beyond. The village Church of St Peter is believed to stand on one of the earliest Christian sites in Nottinghamshire. There was already a church here in the 9th century since it is known to have been plundered by the Danes when they came up the river to Nottingham.

From the 1700s until 1936 gypsum was extensively mined in the village. The Satin Spar, as it was known, was of such a fine quality that it was exported to North America. At one time there were several craftsmen in the village making ornaments from the spar and examples of their work have been exhibited in London.

BLEASBY
3 miles S of Southwell off the A612

This attractive village near the River Trent offers a full range of leisure pursuits both

from the river bank and on the water itself. The village is a real blend of the old and new. The oldest building is the 14th century farmhouse, Manor Farm, which also has a very fine 18th century square Dovecote. Built of brick and with a tiled roof, the dovecote has, halfway up, a projecting brick ledge to prevent rats from getting into the cote through the flight holes.

The founder of the Salvation Army, William Booth, spent some years in the village as a young boy when his family lived at Old Farm. Booth's sister, Mary, was baptised in the village Church of St Mary the Virgin.

GUNTHORPE
6 miles S of Southwell off the A6097

The manor of Gunthorpe is mentioned in the Domesday Book and was granted by William the Conqueror, along with others in the area, to one of his faithful noblemen, Roger de Busli. This ancient village owes its existence to the ford here across the River Trent. During the 1st century the Romans used the ford when travelling between their fort at Margidunum in the east to the lead mines of Derbyshire.

FISKERTON
3 miles SE of Southwell off the A612

Another attractive village, Fiskerton lies on the banks of the River Trent, a location which played an important part in its prosperity during the 19th century. Not only was Fiskerton a hive of activity with a lace factory and a firm making stove polish, blackening, and ink, but it was also busy with river traffic and there were warehouses and wharves along the banks.

Fiskerton was also the place where the troops coming from Southwell crossed the River Trent in 1487 on their way to the final battle of the Wars of the Roses at East Stoke. Today, the village is much more peaceful; a walk along the riverbank provides the opportunity to see a heron or even a kingfisher whilst Southwell racecourse lies on the village border.

ROLLESTON
3 miles E of Southwell off the A617

Holy Trinity Church is certainly one of the county's finest churches and is also the source of a great treasure: a portion of the original paper register covering the years 1584 to 1615. An interesting and historic document completed by the vicar of the time, Robert Leband, it gives the local gossip as well as the price of corn and notes of local events. A curiosity in the church is a fragment of a Saxon cross, built into the wall and scratched with the words *Radulfus me fe*, (Radulfus made me). It is one of very few surviving Saxon works in England to bear its author's signature.

Kate Greenaway, the author and illustrator of many children's books spent much of her childhood at Rolleston and she often referred to the time she spent in the village as a source of inspiration.

UPTON
2 miles E of Southwell on the A612

Upton boasts a couple of very good pubs and its nine-pinnacled church is worthy of a visit too. A famous son of the village was James Tenant, the man who cut the world renowned Koh-I-Noor diamond. But, perhaps, the most impressive building here is Upton Hall, a stylish Grecian villa with a central dome and elegant colonnade, built in the early 1800s. The hall is now the headquarters of the **British Horological Institute** and, inside, visitors can see the National Exhibition of Time - a fascinating display of clocks, watches, and other horological pieces.

When Francis West (who later became Bishop West) first came to Upton as its new vicar it was in the severe winter of 1947. With postwar fuel shortages, many people would retire to bed early and the new vicar was no exception, particularly as the vicarage was not only large but draughty. Francis West used the time to read through some 17th century account books he discovered in an ancient parish chest. The vicar later published an edited version, *Rude Forefathers*, which tells the fascinating story of everyday life in Upton in the years leading up to and following the Civil War.

KIRKLINGTON
3 miles N of Southwell on the A617

Kirklington's church is partly Norman and anyone venturing inside will see that the pulpit has some small holes in its side that have been plugged with more recent wood. The explanation for this odd feature is that in the early 1800s, Kirklington's sporting rector would use the pulpit as a portable screen when he went duck shooting. He would fire at the ducks through the holes in the pulpit's sides!

KERSALL
6 miles N of Southwell on the A616

From the A616 Newark to Ollerton road, a lane leads steeply down the hillside to this secluded village set beside a stream known as The Beck. Although the settlement is believed to be an ancient one, it does not have – and never has had, a church.

NEWARK-ON-TRENT

John Wesley considered Newark one of the most elegant towns in England; more recently the Council for British Archaeology included it in their list of the best 50 towns in the country; and in 1968 Newark town centre was designated as one of the first Conservation Areas. Its medieval street plan remains intact, complete with a fine market square which is still busy every day of the week, except Tuesdays, with a market of one kind or another - plus a Farmer's Market once a month.

The square is lined with handsome houses and inns. The most remarkable of them is the 14th century former White Hart Inn which has a magnificent frontage adorned with 24 plaster figures of angels and saints. Close by are the Saracen's Head where Sir Walter Scott often stayed, and the Clinton Arms, the preferred lodging of W.E. Gladstone during his 14 years as Newark's Member of Parliament.

Dominating one side of the square is the noble Georgian **Town Hall**, built in 1777 and recently fully restored. It now houses the town's civic plate and regalia, and an art gallery displaying works by Stanley Spencer, William Nicholson and notable local artists.

The grandest building of all though is the **Church of St Mary Magdalene**, by common consent the finest parish church in the county. Its slender, elegant spire soars above the town and serves as a landmark for miles along the Trent Valley. The church dates back to the early 12th century though all that survives of that structure is the crypt which now houses the treasury. Much of the building seen today dates from the 14th, 15th, and 16th centuries and its exterior is a fascinating blend of carvings and tracery. The interior is spacious and airy, and the treasures on display include a huge brass commemorating Alan Fleming, a Newark merchant who died in 1373; a dazzling Comper reredos of 1937; a splendid east window depicting Mary Magdalene; a Victorian mosaic reproducing Van Eyck's

Adoration of the Lamb; and fragments of a painted "Dance of Death" from around 1500.

Newark's recorded history goes back to Roman times when the legionaries established a base here to guard the first upstream crossing of the River Trent. One of their major arterial roads, Fosse Way, passes close by on its way to Lincoln.

Saxons and Danes continued the settlement, the latter leaving a legacy of street names ending in –gate, from *gata*, the Danish word for street.

When the Normans arrived, they replaced the wooden castle with one of stone. The present building is mostly 12th century and for some 300 years it was owned by the powerful Bishops of Lincoln. Then in 1483, ownership of the castle was transferred to the Crown and leased out to a succession of noblemen.

The castle's most glorious days occurred during the Civil War. The people of Newark were fiercely loyal to Charles I and endured 3 separate sieges before finally surrendering to Cromwell's troops. Parliament ordered the "slighting" of the castle, rendering it militarily useless, but left the demolition work to the townspeople. Understandably, they showed little enthusiasm for the task of demolishing the 8ft thick walls. As a result, the ruins are quite substantial, especially the mighty gateway that Pevsner called *"the biggest and most elaborate of its period (1170-75) in England"*. It was here that King John, devastated by the loss of his treasure while crossing the Wash, came to die in 1216. The castle crypt and an intimidating beehive dungeon have also survived. Guided tours of the castle, (and the town), are available and its history is colourfully interpreted at the **Gilstrap Centre**. This lies within the Castle Grounds which, with its gardens and Victorian bandstand, is a popular venue for special events as well as a pleasant spot for a picnic.

Newark possesses several other reminders of the Civil War. As a defensive measure, two small forts were built to guard this strategic crossing over the River Trent. The King's Sconce, to the northeast, has since disappeared but its twin, the **Queen's Sconce**, still lies to the southeast. Named after Queen Henrietta Maria, who brought supplies into the town after the first siege in 1643, this square earthwork has a bastion in each corner and a hollow in the middle.

In the town centre, on Kirk Gate, are **Henrietta Maria's Lodgings**, where according to legend the queen stayed in 1643. Travelling from Bridlington to the king's headquarters at Oxford, the queen was bringing with her men and arms from the continent. She had paid for them by selling off some of the Crown Jewels.

Nearby is the **Governor's House** where the governors of Newark lived during the Civil War and also the place where Charles I quarrelled with Prince Rupert after the prince had lost Bristol to Parliament. This wonderful timber framed building was restored in the late 19th century and during the work a medieval wall and some beam paintings were revealed along with some graffiti dating from 1757.

With such a wealth of history inside its boundaries, Newark naturally has its fair share of museums. **Newark Museum** (free) is housed in a former school which dates back to 1529 and the history of the town is traced from the Stone Age to the 19th century. A large Anglo-Saxon cemetery, discovered in Millgate, is also on display.

Occupying a former riverside warehouse, the **Millgate Folk Museum** (free) concentrates on everyday life in the 19th and 20th centuries. The exhibits include an interesting array of shops and shop fronts, and there is also a

reconstruction of an early 20th-century terraced house. The Mezzanine Gallery within the museum hosts temporary exhibitions featuring the work of local artists, designers and photographers.

On the outskirts of the town, at **Beacon Hill**, one of the greatest victories over the Roundheads took place, in 1644, when Prince Rupert arrived to lift the second of Newark's sieges. Under Sir John Meldrum, the Parliamentarians lost more arms and equipment than during any other engagement of the Civil War.

Just east of the town, close to the A1, lies the **Newark Air Museum**, one of the largest privately managed collections in the country. Opened in the 1960s, the museum has more than 50 aircraft and cockpit sections on display. Visitors can see jet fighters, bombers, and helicopters which span the history of aviation as well as a great deal of aviation memorabilia, relics, and uniforms on display in the Exhibition Hall.

AROUND NEWARK-ON-TRENT

CROMWELL
5 miles N of Newark off the A1

The large 17th century rectory in the village is now home to the **Vina Cooke Museum of Dolls and Bygone Childhood**. Appealing to adults and children alike, there are all manner of children's toys on display but perhaps the most interesting are the handmade dolls depicting royalty, stars of stage and screen, and famous historical characters.

SUTTON ON TRENT
7 miles N of Newark off the B1164

One of the largest Trentside villages, Sutton was once famous for basket-making, fishermen's baskets in particular. It has a fine church, first established in Saxon times, and noted for its Mering Chapel. Dating from the early 1500s, the chapel was brought here from the village of Mering on the other side of the Trent. Mering has since vanished completely into the watery lowlands surrounding the Trent. The superb **Mering Chapel,** however, contains a distinguished memorial in Purbeck marble to Sir William Mering. The tomb is separated from the aisle by a very rare oak screen crafted around 1510. Sir William's family, like his village, is extinct.

SOUTH CLIFTON
12 miles N of Newark off the A1133

This pleasant village along the banks of the River Trent still has the remains of an old wharf where the coal from Derbyshire and Yorkshire was unloaded before being distributed throughout the surrounding area. The river here is still much used though the local fishermen now have to contend with water-skiers travelling up and down.

On the village green stands a young oak tree, planted in 1981, along with a plaque commemorating the achievements of a local farmer, Dusty Hare, who has lived in the parish all his life, scored the highest number (7000) of points in Rugby Union Football and was honoured with an MBE in 1989.

NORTH CLIFTON
13 miles N of Newark off the A1133

The village, like its neighbour South Clifton, also lies on the east side of the Trent, close to the border with Lincolnshire. The two villages are, however, quite separate, but they share the same church, dedicated to St George the Martyr, which lies between them and has an imposing 15th century tower.

An unusual attraction here is the **Pureland Meditation Centre and Japanese Garden** which offers a haven of peace for all ages who wish to come and experience the benefits of relaxation and meditation. Buddha Maitreya, a former Zen monk from Japan, has devoted the last 20 years to creating the delightful Japanese with its large central pond, bridges, and a small pagoda where visitors can relax and meditate among an abundance of flourishing plants and trees. The garden is open every afternoon, except Mondays, between April and October.

THORNEY
14 miles N of Newark off the A57

In 1805, this once peaceful little village was the site of a dreadful murder. A local labourer, Thomas Temporell, also known locally as Tom Otter, was forced to marry a local girl whom, it was claimed, he had made pregnant. Tom was so upset by the

BOTTLE & GLASS
High Street, Harby, nr Lincoln, Nottinghamshire NG23 7EB
Tel: 01522 703438

Although only a few miles from Lincoln, the **Bottle & Glass** is known as the "Hidden Pub", tucked away as it is on a country lane. It's well worth seeking out for its welcoming atmosphere, good food and well-maintained ales including 2 real brews. Mine hosts, Kevin and Liz Bendell, are both from Nottinghamshire and they have made this a popular venue. They both share the cooking, with food available every lunchtime and evening except Monday. Their home made steak pies are specially recommended. Other attractions include a smart patio area, monthly quizzes and karaokes, and a large off road parking area.

accusations and the enforced marriage that, in a frenzy, he murdered his bride on their wedding night. The story goes that he then took her body and left it on the steps of a public house in Saxilby, Lincolnshire. Caught and tried, Tom was sentenced to death with the extra penalty of gibbeting, (the practice of hanging the offender's body in chains at the scene of their crime).

Small though it is, Thorney possesses a huge and magnificent church, built in 1849 by the Nevile family of nearby Thorney Hall (now demolished). Constructed in the Norman style, the church contains a wealth of superb stone carvings, both inside and out. Amongst them are no fewer than 17 fearsome dragons' heads.

TUXFORD
12 miles NW of Newark on the A1

This pleasant little town used to have its own market and, because of its position on the Great North Road, prospered greatly during the days of stage coach travel. A devastating fire in 1702 destroyed most of the town, and the rebuilding produced some attractive Georgian buildings. Amongst the buildings that did survive are the pleasing little Grammar School with its hipped roof and dormer windows, founded in 1669, and the medieval Church of St Nicholas. The church contains some interesting memorials to the White family and a striking font of 1673 standing beneath a magnificent hanging canopy.

CAUNTON
7 miles NW of Newark off the A616

The village Church of St Andrew was rebuilt by the Normans at the beginning of the 13th century but by the 1800s the building had fallen into such a state of disrepair that the altar, a wooden box,

was only used as a resting place for the hat and gloves of visiting curates. Restored in 1869, the church contains many monuments to the Hole family, Lords of the Manor here since Elizabethan times.

The best known member of the Hole family was Samuel Reynolds Hole who became known as the Rose King - a title bestowed on him by Tennyson. Before becoming Dean of Rochester, Hole lived at Caunton Manor as the squire and vicar and it was here that he began his extensive study of roses. By 1851, Samuel recorded that he had over 1000 rose trees in more than 400 varieties, a collection which was to make him the most famous amateur rose grower of all.

KELHAM
3 miles W of Newark on the A617

Originally an estate village serving Kelham Hall, the village farms were amongst the first to grow sugar beet when it was introduced to England during World War I. A lane still leads from the village to the huge sugar beet factory a mile or so to the west. Kelham Hall, now council offices, is the third manor house to be built on the site. The first was the "Kelum Hall" where Charles I was briefly imprisoned. That building was destroyed by fire in 1690. Another mansion was built for the Sutton family, Lords of the Manor of Kelham. That too went up in flames, in 1857. The present building was designed by George Gilbert Scott and opinions are sharply divided over the merits of its red-brick towers, pinnacles, gables and Gothic windows.

Like the Hall, Kelham's bridge over the Trent also suffered misfortune: during the frightful winter of 1881 ice packs floating down the river demolished the old wooden structure.

AVERHAM
4 miles W of Newark on the A617

Pronounced locally as "Airam", this pleasant village is somewhat overshadowed by the nearby power station at Staythorpe. But there's a picturesque corner off the main road where the Norman church and Georgian rectory form an appealing little group on the edge of the Trent. In the rectory grounds stands the remarkable **Robin Hood Theatre**, established by a former Rector and built by a local carpenter. The Rev. Cyril Walker opened it in 1913 as a private theatre for opera lovers. It has a fully equipped stage and orchestra pit, and boasted the rare amenity of being lit by electricity. The late, great Sir Donald Wolfit, a local man born at nearby Balderton, gave his first performances here. The theatre went through a rocky period in the 1960s and closed for several years but it is now operating successfully again offering a variety of shows and plays throughout the year.

FARNDON
4 miles SW of Newark-on-Trent off the A46

Another riverside village, Farndon boasts some handsome Georgian houses, a church with Saxon and Norman details, good fishing and a busy marina. During the 1930s, when the aerodromes at Syerston and Newton were under construction, sand and gravel were needed for the building of the runways. Both were taken from the banks of the River Trent here leaving the pits which now form the basis of the marina.

EAST STOKE
4 miles SW of Newark-on-Trent on the A46

The village is the site of the last great conflict of the War of the Roses: the Battle

MANNA HERBS
Manor Cottage, Church Lane, Averham, Newark, Nottinghamshire NG23 5RB
Tel: 01636 704437
e-mail: valeriewillcocks@hotmail.com

Manna Herbs must surely be unique. Where else would you find stylish bed and breakfast accommodation provided in an historic building, standing in a courtyard amidst a colourful display of herbs. Guests also have access to the cottage herb garden, which has been created by Professor Arthur and Mrs Valerie Willcocks over the last 16 years and is used for charity fund-raising events.

The barn conversion is beautifully decorated and can accommodate up to 8 guests. The residents' lounge is recorded in the 1851 Religious Census as a Methodist Chapel and is now a peaceful, relaxing area. Television, (including Sky-TV), radio, tape and CD player along with a large selection of CDs are all available. Telephone charges are at BT rates and e-mail and fax facilities are free. Leading off from the lounge is a bedroom area, bathroom, dining area and kitchenette. Breakfast at Manna Herbs is definitely something special and offers a huge choice. In addition to the usual array of cereals and juices it also includes fresh fruit, croissants, freshly ground coffee, herbal teas, coddled eggs, smoked eggs and more. Evening meals are also available. The barn floor and much of the furniture at Manna Herbs is English Oak and the facility is therefore unsuitable for smokers.

of Stoke Fields that took place here on 16th June 1487. The battle saw the army of Henry VII defeat the Yorkists and the pretender Lambert Simnel in a bloody conflict that lasted for three hours and resulted in 7,000 deaths. The defeated army fled across the meadows to the river which is known locally to this day as the Red Gutter. Many of those who died in battle lie in Deadman's Field nearby, and local farmers have occasionally uncovered swords and other relics from the battle when ploughing their fields.

Though the battle site is the main attraction in the village, East Stoke has a history that goes back to the days of the Roman occupation. **The Fosse Way**, which divides the village in two, was originally part of the great Roman road from Bath to Lincoln and East Stoke is thought to be the site of the Roman fort of Ad Pontem.

The village inn, the Pauncefote Arms, is named after Lord Pauncefote who died in 1902 and is buried in the churchyard here. His Lordship was, astonishingly, the very first British Ambassador to the United States. Indeed, he was the first Ambassador from any nation since the States did not recognise the title until 1893; before then, the senior diplomat was known as the Minister.

ELSTON
5 miles SW of Newark-on-Trent off the A46

This rural village was once well-known for the local trade of skep-making, or basket-making, using specially grown willows, but the craft has all but died out.

Evidence of early dwellers in the area has been found in the form of Stone Age flint and Roman pottery - not surprising as the village lies close to Fosse Way. However, little of Elston's early history has been documented though there has been one famous family living here. Elston Hall was owned by the Darwin family from 1680 until as recently as 1952

and this was where Erasmus Darwin was born in 1731. Erasmus was a polymath - inventor, doctor of medicine, poet, philosopher, prophet and founder of the Lunar Society. He envisioned the development of aeroplanes, motor cars and submarines, invented a typewriter and a rudimentary "speaking machine". His fame has been eclipsed by that of his grandson, Charles, who formulated the theory of evolution. Rather uncharitably, Charles has been recorded as claiming that his theory owed nothing to the work of his pioneering grandfather.

Elston church contains an impressive array of monuments to various members of the Darwin family.

A curious building on the outskirts of the village is the deserted **Elston Chapel**, a quaint little building with a Norman doorway and many other Norman and medieval features. Its origins have been shrouded in mystery but recent research has suggested that the building was the chapel to the hospital of St Leonard that once existed in this locality.

FLINTHAM
5 miles SW of Newark-on-Trent off the A46

Little has changed in this quiet village over the years. At one time, all the cottages in the village were owned by the occupants of Flintham Hall, but Flintham's life as an estate village is now a thing of the past. The privately-owned **Flintham Museum** preserves some of those bygone days, re-creating rural life through the eyes of a village shopkeeper complete with vintage décor and authentic old-style packaging and artifacts. Opening times are restricted: for more details, telephone 01636 525111.

Flintham Hall (private) is a grand Victorian manor house with a huge conservatory resembling the Crystal Palace which dominates the main village street. Parts of Flintham Hall date back to the 17th century but it was greatly extended in the 1800s and now presents a Victorian appearance. It is still very much a family home.

SCREVETON
7 miles SW of Newark-on-Trent off the A46

The ancient village, whose name means farm belonging to the sheriff, has a delightful, small 13th century church which lies in a secluded position some way from the village. Reached by a footpath, the Church of St Wilfrid is home to a fine alabaster tomb of Richard Whalley who is depicted with his three wives and 25 children at his feet.

CAR COLSTON
8 miles SW of Newark-on-Trent off the A46

Now a conservation area, this village is fortunate in that it has remained unspoiled by modern development. Of particular interest here are the village's two greens which both date from the reign of Elizabeth I.

At that time individual strips of land were cultivated by the villagers and the typical ridge and furrow appearance can still be made out. In 1598, the parish was enclosed, the land being turned into the fenced fields that became the norm, but the land in the middle of the village was left open so that the villagers could graze their cattle. The Large Green, at 16½ acres, is the largest in the county and, at the other end of the village lies Little Green (a mere 5½ acres).

There are several interesting houses in the village but **Old Hall Farm**, which dates from 1812, is probably the one that receives most attention. The interest is generated, not so much by the building itself but because it was the home of Robert Thoroton, who in 1677 published his *Antiquities of Nottinghamshire*. The first major history of the county, the work was

updated in the late 18th century by John Throsby and remains today one of the prime sources for local historians.

SCARRINGTON
8 miles S of Newark-on-Trent off the A52

The main attraction of this small village is not a grand house or a splendid village church but a remarkable man-made edifice. A pile of around 50,000 horseshoes towers 17 feet high and was built by the former blacksmith, Mr Flinders. Over the years, souvenir hunters have taken the odd shoe here and there, with the result that the monument is bending over very slightly at the top.

However, the obelisk which Mr Flinders began in 1945, stands rock solid though all he used to bond the shoes was his skill and a great deal of luck! At one time it was coveted by an American visitor who wished to buy it and transport it to the United States.

SIBTHORPE
5 miles S of Newark-on-Trent off the A46

All that remains above ground of a priests' college, founded here in the 14th century, is the parish church and a **Dovecote** (NT). Found in the middle of a field and some 60 feet high, this circular stone building has a conical tiled roof and provide nesting places for more than 1,200 birds.

Of the three Archbishops of Canterbury born in Nottinghamshire, Thomas Cranmer is by far the most well known, but Sibthorpe was the childhood home of Thomas Secker who was Archbishop from 1758-68. Despite holding the position for a decade, Secker appears to have done nothing of any note.

HAWKSWORTH
6 miles S of Newark-on-Trent off the A46

One of a number of attractive villages in

the Vale of Belvoir, Hawksworth is well worth a detour. The 16th century stone manor house still has its mid-17th century dovecote and the church is much older than it first appears. The base of the tower was constructed in the 13th century of stone but the upper storeys were added during the 1600s. Inside is part of an intricately carved Saxon cross and in the tower's south wall is a Norman tympanum.

ORSTON
8 miles S of Newark-on-Trent off the A52

The village is typical of many in this area of Nottinghamshire and, down the years, it has managed to maintain its rural character. Back in medieval times, Orston had one of the finest gypsum workings in the country though all that remains today of the Royal Plaster Works is a partially filled in pit in the centre of the village and some overgrown ponds on the outskirts.

Just outside the village is the site of a mill and records show that there was a mill here as long ago as 1216. However, in 1916, the last mill on the site was dismantled and shipped half way round the world to New Zealand where it achieved a certain amount of fame as that country's first working windmill.

ALVERTON
7 miles S of Newark-on-Trent off the A52

A small hamlet of just a handful of houses, Alverton's tiny population is augmented by two resident ghosts. The first has been seen in the old Church of England schoolhouse, which is now a private residence, and is believed to be

the ghost of a teacher who was murdered at the school.

Alverton's second ghost, an elderly lady dressed in Victorian clothes, has been sighted at one of the hamlet's larger houses. The lady is believed to be Mary Brown, a sewing maid to Queen Victoria, who gave up her job after the death of her sister-in-law. Mary moved back to her brother's house to act as housekeeper to him and his four children and, by all accounts, she proved to be a formidable woman. She ruled the house with a rod of iron. In later years, when noises were heard on the upper floors, it was said that "Aunt Polly was on the warpath again!"

BALDERTON
2 miles SE of Newark-on-Trent on the A1

Effectively a suburb of Newark, this once rural village expanded greatly during the twentieth century and now has several industries, shops, schools, and housing estates. However, many of the village's original old buildings can still be seen including the toll house which stands as a reminder to the days of stage coach traffic along the Great North Road.

The crooked spire of **St Giles' Church** rises high above the main crossroads in the village. The fine, decorated Norman doorway, which dates from the 13th century, is much visited by architects and its plague plaque and numerous memorials to battles, both home and abroad, tell of the events which affected the lives of the villagers.

On the northern edge of the village, close to the railway bridge, a plaque on a semi-detached gabled house records the birth here of Sir Donald Wolfit in 1902.

5 Sherwood Forest and North Nottinghamshire

Now officially designated as "Robin Hood Country", the tract of land running north from Nottingham is an attractive mix of woodland and rolling hills. It was once part of a great mass of forest land covering much of central England, stretching from Nottingham in the south to Worksop in the north and from the Peak District to the Trent Valley in the east.

It seems likely that it was William the Conqueror who designated Sherwood as a Royal Forest, an administrative term for the private hunting ground of the king. The land was not only thickly wooded but also included areas of rough heathland as well as arable land, meadow land, small towns, and villages. The Norman kings were passionate about their hunting and, to guard their royal forests, there were a set of rigidly upheld laws, to con-

Sherwood Forest, Birklands

serve the game (known as the venison) and vegetation (known as the vert). No one, even those with a private estate within the royal forest, was allowed to kill or hunt protected animals, graze domestic animals in the forest, fell trees, or make clearings within the boundaries without the express permission of the king or one of his chief foresters. It is little wonder then, that with such strict rules imposed upon them, that the people turned to the likes of Robin Hood and others who defied the laws and lived off the king's deer.

To the north of the forest is the area known as The Dukeries which is scenically one of the most attractive parts of the county. Here in the 18th century, no fewer than 4 different Dukes acquired huge estates: Rufford, Welbeck, Clumber, and Thoresby. All their great houses are now put to different uses but the glorious parks they created, especially at Clumber, make this a delightful area to visit.

The area around Mansfield was once the industrial heart of Nottingham-shire, its landscape dominated by pit-head wheels and chimneys, and the serried ranks of miners' terraced houses. Much of that industrial legacy is still evident but there are some surprisingly attractive enclaves to be found, like the village of Linby, for example.

Ironically, this down-to-earth area of the county is also closely associated with one of England's most romantic writers, George, 6th Lord Byron, the poet described by a contemporary as *"mad, bad and dangerous to know"*. The family estate was at Newstead Abbey but Byron only lived there for a few years - he was too poor to pay for its upkeep. However, after his death in Greece, his body was brought back to Newstead and buried in the nearby town of Hucknall.

A writer even more closely involved with the area is D.H. Lawrence who was born at Eastwood in 1885. Lawrence's novels give a true insight into the lives of those living in a colliery town at the beginning of the 20th century and al-though he claimed to detest his home town, his works often reveal a nostalgic affection for the sights and smells of this former mining area.

North Nottinghamshire is "Pilgrim Fathers' Country"since it was here that the unorthodox worship of Richard Clyfton inspired such men as William Brewster of Scrooby, and William Bradford of Austerfield, later Governor of New England. The best introduction to their story is to follow the "Mayflower Trail", devised by Bassetlaw District Council, which follows a circular route starting from Worksop.

Also in Worksop is the unusual National Trust property, Mr Straw's House, a time-capsule from the 1920s where nothing has altered in the subsequent 80 years. Retford and Blyth are both attractive old market towns: the former with some fine Georgian building; the latter boasting one of the most monumental Norman churches in the country. Another ecclesiastical site of note is Mattersey Priory - little remains of the 12th century monastery but the riverside location is enchant-ing.

Walking in the Forest

There are lovely gardens at Morton Hall, near Retford, and Hodsock Priory near Blyth; country parks at Langold and Clumber; and right on the border with Derbyshire, Cresswell Crags, where our ancestors inhabited the dark mysterious caves some 70,000 years ago.

Though most of Bassetlaw is rural, there are reminders of the industrial past in the great sweep of the Chesterfield Canal as it slices through the centre and, at North Leverton, the grand sight of the only working windmill in the county.

SHERWOOD FOREST & NORTH NOTTINGHAMSHIRE

Included in other chapters

© MAPS IN MINUTES ™ 2001   © Crown Copyright, Ordnance Survey 2001

PLACES TO STAY, EAT, DRINK AND SHOP

CROSSHILL HOUSE

Laxton, Newark, Nottinghamshire NG22 0NT
Tel: 01777 871953 Mobile: 07971 864446
e-mail:Roberta@crosshillhouse.freeserve.co.uk
website: www.crosshillhouse.com

An attractive building occupying a picturesque position in an unspoilt village, **Crosshill House** stands in ¾ of an acre of its own grounds and offers not just outstanding bed & breakfast accommodation but also a comprehensive range of health and beauty treatments. The owners, Roberta and Robert Gray have created this peaceful and healthy environment as an ideal place for visitors to unwind, enjoy being pampered and escape from the stresses and strains of everyday life. For those who are staying overnight, there are 2 delightful guest bedrooms, both of them beautifully appointed to a high standard, including en suite facilities. The rooms sleep either 2 or 3 guests and a cuddly toy sits waiting on each bed to help visitors relax! (Please note that Crosshill House is a non-smoking establishment throughout).

At breakfast time there's a choice of either a Full English, continental or healthy option meal, and vegetarian requirements can also be catered for. Light healthy lunches are available to those having treatment but not evening meals. However, a short stroll across the village green will bring you to the Dovecote Inn which serves excellent food

and stands right next door to the Visitors' Centre.

Roberta's health and beauty treatments are available to guests and non-residents alike. Highly qualified in a whole range of treatments, Roberta's "menu" includes a wondrous variety of massages - aromatherapy, Swedish, G5, (a deep massage using specialised equipment to break down fatty deposits and to relieve aches and tension), gommage, self heating mud and others. Roberta is also well-versed in Thalasso therapy - the use of sea water to treat a wide variety of skin conditions and muscular aches. Thalasso facials, eye treatments, waxing, hand and foot care, anti-cellulite treatment and reflexology are amongst the many treatments available. Roberta is also qualified to provide sports massage and injury treatment.

Refreshed and invigorated by your treatment, you can take either a guided walk through the surrounding countryside, or follow one of the long or short routes described in leaflets available here. Details of jogging routes are also to hand and cycle hire is also available.

Popular attractions within easy reach include the Sherwood Forest Country Park, the Sherwood Forest Fun Park, and the Sherwood Forest Farm Park, all at Edwinstowe about 7 miles to the west, Southwell Cathedral and the White Post Modern Farm Centre to the south, while over to the east is the impressive cathedral city of Lincoln.

OLLERTON

Not to be confused with the more workaday town of New Ollerton, Old Ollerton is a delightfully preserved cluster of old houses, a charming Georgian coaching inn covered in creeper, and a church set beside the River Maun. Straddling the river is **Ollerton Water Mill**, more than 300 years old. Visitors are welcome to wander around the ancient building with its huge water wheel, browse in the Exhibition Area, watch a short video illustrating the age-old milling process, or sample the refreshments in the tea room.

The name of the village was originally Alreton, or Allerton, meaning farm among the alders, and the trees still grow here along the banks of the River Maun. The village lay on the road from London to York (though now it is bypassed) and also on the roads from Newark to Worksop and Lincoln to Mansfield. As a consequence, Ollerton developed as a meeting place for Sherwood Forest officials and the inns became staging posts during the coaching era.

Over the centuries the village was owned by several families including the Markhams. Staunch Catholics, the Markhams, along with their servants, were persecuted in the 16th century and their private hidden chapel can still be found in the roof of the present Ollerton Hall. The hall, which came into the hands of the Savile family in 1746, is now derelict.

AROUND OLLERTON

WELLOW
1 miles SE of Ollerton on the A616

This pretty conservation village is located on the site of an early settlement and was once fortified by an earthwork and, on the western side, by Gorge Dyke. The remains of the earthwork can still be seen and villagers have retained the right to graze their cattle on enclosed land. On the village green stands the tallest permanent **Maypole** in England - 60ft high, colourfully striped like a barber's pole, and with a cockerel perched on the top. Because earlier wooden poles rotted away, were stolen or got knocked down, this one is made of steel and firmly fixed in place. It was erected to commemorate Elizabeth II's Silver Jubilee in 1976 and forms the focus for the May Day festivities held on the Spring Bank Holiday Monday. The jollities include dancing around the Maypole and the crowning of a May Queen.

Other notable features of this surprising village include a ducking-stool; part of the old stocks; and a 17th century case clock in the 12th century parish Church of St Swithin. The clock face was made locally to commemorate the coronation of Elizabeth II in 1953. Each year on the 19th September, the three church bells, which are between 300 and 400 years old, are rung in memory of a certain Lady Walden. Some 200 years ago she was paying a visit to Wellow and became lost in a local wood. Following the sound of the church bells, Lady Walden eventually found her way to the village and, such was her relief, that she left money for the bells to be rung each year on that day.

LAXTON
4 miles E of Ollerton off the A6075

Laxton is unique since it is the only place in the country that has managed to retain its open field farming system. Devised in the Middle Ages, this system was generally abandoned in the 18th and 19th centuries when the enclosure of agricultural land took place. The fields have been strip farmed here for about

1,200 years and the system ensured that farmers had an equal share of both good and poor land. A farmer could hold as many as 100 strips, representing about 30 acres. In the 1600s the strips were, on average, about half an acre in size but, with the advent of more efficient means of ploughing, this increased to three-quarters of an acre. The familiar three year crop rotation also ensured productive use of the land.

Another unique feature of this fascinating village is the magnificent **Dovecote Inn** which is owned (but not run) by the Queen. Here, a form of manorial government that has survived from medieval times still continues. Each winter, villagers gather at the inn each winter to appoint a jury which is then responsible for inspecting the fallow fields in the next cycle. The jurors tour the fields left fallow for the past year then adjourn for lunch back at the Dovecote. During the afternoon they then discuss any offences committed by farmers. A week later comes the Court meeting.

The 18th century was a great time of rebuilding in Laxton and many of the houses display the patterned brickwork that was typical of this period. The still visible stonework around the bottom of some buildings suggests that the foundations were of much older timber framed constructions.

Just north of the village, along a lane close to the church, is another fascinating aspect of Laxton's medieval history. This is the Norman motte, or **Castle Mound**, which lies almost hidden beneath the trees. At the beginning of the 12th century, the stewardship of Sherwood Forest moved to Laxton and the village became the administrative centre for the forest. As a consequence, the motte and bailey castle was one of the biggest in this part of the country. Although no ruined keep or crumbling walls exist today, the castle earthworks are still the largest and best preserved in the county.

EGMANTON
5 miles E of Ollerton off the A1

Reached by quiet winding lanes, Egmanton is little visited these days but during the Middle Ages a local woman claimed to have had a vision of the Virgin Mary. The Shrine of Our Lady of Egmanton became a major place of pilgrimage right up until the Reformation.

The cult was revived in 1896 by the 7th Duke of Newcastle who commissioned Sir Ninian Comper to completely restore and redecorate the church. The result is an exuberant recreation of a medieval church with all its colour and graven images. The exterior is really quite modest but the interior is resplendent and inspiriting, with the light from many tapers and candles helping to create a mesmerising atmosphere.

The church is rich with other splendours too - an elaborately decorated and gilded organ, painted panels and pulpit, and many other religious objects. The shrine, which can be found on the north side of the chancel, houses the figure of the Virgin, surrounded by flowers and candles and protected by a canopy.

RUFFORD
2 miles S of Ollerton off the A614

Rufford Abbey was founded in 1148 by Gilbert de Gant as a daughter house to Rievaulx Abbey. During the Dissolution it suffered the fate of many religious houses and came into the hands of the 6th Earl of Shrewsbury, fourth husband of the redoubtable Bess of Hardwick. The Earl pulled down most of the abbey and built a grand Elizabethan mansion. All that remains of the abbey is a vaulted crypt, said to be haunted by the ghost of a giant monk with a skull-like face. According to the parish register for Edwinstowe, a man died of fright after catching sight of this unholy visitor!

In 1626, the house descended to the Savile family who, together with their descendants, the Earls of Scarborough, lived here until 1938 when they sold the estate to the County Council.

The abbey's stable block now houses an impressive craft centre while the restored 18th century Orangery hosts modern sculpture exhibitions.

The grounds of the abbey, now the **Rufford Country Park**, are well worth a visit. In addition to the nine formal gardens near the house, there also some hides where birdwatchers can overlook a portion of the lake which has been designated a bird sanctuary. In the grounds too stands an 18th century corn mill, now home to a display of Nottinghamshire history, and two icehouses dating from the mid-1800s. As well as the majestic Lime Avenue, there is also the Broad Ride, at the southern end of which are several animal graves. Most were pets belonging to the family at the house but one grave is that of the racehorse Cremorne, the 1872 Derby winner.

BILSTHORPE
4 miles S of Ollerton off the A614

The hall where, during the Civil War, Charles I is reputed to have hidden in a cupboard still exists but is now incorporated into a farm that stands opposite the village church.

Bilsthorpe remained a quiet farming community, as it had been for many centuries, right up until 1922 when a coal mine was sunk in the village by Stanton Ironworks. An explosion at the mine with a subsequent loss of life brought the vicar and the mine manager into a dispute over compensation. The manager, unwilling to pay out, built a wooden church away from the main part of the village and near the temporary accommodation provided for the mine workers. Bilsthorpe continued to have two churches up until the nationalisation of the coal mines when the wooden church became the church hall.

EDWINSTOWE

Lying at the heart of Sherwood Forest, the life of the village is still dominated by the forest, as it has been since the 7th century.

Sherwood Forest

Edwin, King of Northumbria, who gave the village its name, died in the Battle of Hatfield in 632 and the village developed around the church built on the spot where he was slain. In 1912 a cross was erected to mark his grave by the Duke of Portland. From then on until the time of the Domesday Survey, Edwinstowe remained small. Following the Norman Conquest, the village found itself within the boundaries of the royal hunting forest of Sherwood and it became subject to the stringent laws of the verderers. Dating from the 12th century, the **Church of St Mary** was the first stone building in Edwinstowe and according to legend it was here that the marriage took place between Robin Hood and Maid Marian. Buried in the graveyard here is Dr Cobham Brewer whose *Dictionary of Phrase & Fable*, first published in 1870 and still in print, is possibly the most readable reference book ever compiled.

A little way up the road leading northwards out of Edwinstowe is the **Sherwood Forest Visitor Centre**. Sherwood, the 'Shire Wood', was once a great woodland mass stretching from Nottingham to Worksop. Although only relatively small pockets of the original forest remain today, it is still possible to become lost amongst the trees. Whether or not Robin and his Merry Men ever did frolic in the greenshawe is, however, debatable. Arguments still rage as to which particular historical figure gave rise to the legend of the famous outlaw. Records from the 12th century suggest a number of possible candidates, including the Earl of Huntingdon.

During the 15th century, several references to the outlaw can be found in the writings of two Scottish historians. In 1521 a third Scotsman, John Major, wrote *"About the time of King Richard I, according to my estimate, the famous English robbers*

ROBIN HOOD FARM

Rufford Road, Edwinstowe, Nottinghamshire NG21 9JA
Tel: 01623 824367/825435/825322

Located in the heart of Robin Hood Country and adjacent to the South Forest Leisure Complex, **Robin Hood Farm** offers top quality bed and breakfast accommodation in a 200-year-old farmhouse. When Duncan and Una Hodgson bought the property a few years ago it was in a very sorry state. They have converted it bit by bit, installed modern amenities, competely redecorated and furnished all the rooms, and the house now boasts an AA 3-diamond classification. There are 3 guest bedrooms - 1 double en suite; 1 twin and 1 family room. All the rooms have excellent furnishings and are supplied with those little extras that make your stay a rather special one. No wonder that many of

the Hodgson's bookings are from repeat visitors. Children are welcome; reasonably sized pets are accepted; and there are discounts for longer stays.

The house stands in magnificent gardens and children will find plenty to amuse them in the well-equipped play area. A generous breakfast is included in the tariff and although evening meals are not provided, there is a very good pub, (also named after Robin Hood), just across the road, and plenty of other eating places in the neighbourhood. Other attractions nearby include Rufford Park and the Sherwood Forest Country Park.

Robert Hood and Little John were lurking in their woods, preying on the goods of the wealthy." However, none of the historians gave any clues as to the sources of their writings. By the 16th century, there were two conflicting stories emerging as to the birthplace of Robin, one suggesting Kirklees whilst the other suggested Locksley.

Tracing the stories of Robin Hood is a difficult task as the tales, which have been told for over 600 years, were spoken rather than written since few local people could read and write. One of the earliest known stories of the outlaw's exploits can be found on a piece of parchment which dates from the mid-15th century but it was not until William Caxton set up his printing press in London in 1477 that cheaper books could be produced. From then on, the story of Robin Hood, his merry band of men, Guy of Gisborne, and the evil Sheriff of Nottingham has inspired countless books and at least a dozen major films. Amongst others, the medieval outlaw has been portrayed by Douglas Fairbanks, Kevin Costner and Sean Connery.

Undeterred by the vague foundations upon which the legend is built, visitors still flock to see the great hollow tree which the outlaws purportedly used as a meeting place and as a cache for their supplies. The **Major Oak** is located about 10 minutes walk along the main track in the heart of the forest and presents a rather forlorn appearance. Its 30ft girth and branches 260ft in circumference are now supported by massive wooden crutches and iron corsets. There is no

denying that the tree is at least 500 years old, and some sources claim its age to be nearer to 1000 years. Despite its decayed appearance the tree is still alive thanks to careful preservation. Recent tests have established that some parts of the tree have successfully taken to grafting and there are hopes that at some stage a whole colony of minor oaks may be produced.

The visitor centre also houses a display of characters from the Robin Hood stories, with appropriate scenes of merry making. This theme has also been successfully translated to the city of Nottingham in the Tales of Robin Hood exhibition.

Another impressive attraction in Edwinstowe is the **Sherwood Forest Fun Park** which can be found to the north of the A6075 Mansfield to Ollerton road. This family-run funfair contains a variety of popular fairground rides, including dodgems, a ghost train, and a giant Astroglide. The park is open daily, 10.00 to dusk between mid-March and mid-October, and admission is free.

Not far from Edwinstowe, off the A6075, is the **Sherwood Pines Forest**

The Major Oak, Sherwood Forest

Farm Park, a naturalist and animal lover's delight. Enjoying a peaceful setting in a secluded valley on the edge of Sherwood Forest, the Farm Park boasts no fewer than 30 rare and threatened species of farm animal and is beautifully laid out, with ornamental ponds and three wildfowl lakes. A peaceful spot to relax can be found by visitors even on the busiest of days. The pets' corner and the aviary of exotic birds is always a delight. There is so much to see and do here that it is every bit a fun day out for the adults as for the younger family members. Youngsters will appreciate the adventure playground and everyone can enjoy playing spot the baby wallabies in their mums' pouches, while wandering round the scenic farmland.

A couple of miles south-east of Edwinstowe is **Vicar Water Country Park.** Open daily throughout the year, from dawn to dusk, the Park covers 80

hectares of attractive countryside, complete with a large lake, and provides excellent walking, fishing, cycling and horse-riding. Footpaths and bridleways link the Park to the Sherwood Pines Forest Farm Park; the Timberland Trail; the Maun Valley Way and the Robin Hood Way. The Visitor Centre has ample information about the area and also a café.

AROUND EDWINSTOWE

FARNSFIELD
7 miles S of Ollerton off the A614

Close to the crossroads of the A614/A617 near Farnsfield are two popular family attractions. **White Post Modern Farm Centre** is a working farm with more than 4000 animals, amongst them llamas, deer, owls, piglets, chicks and even mice.

THE WARWICK ARMS

Main Street, Farnsfield, Newark,
Nottinghamshire NG22 8EP
Tel: 01623 882360
e-mail: nicolapublican@aol.com

There's been a pub on this site since the early 1800s but the present **Warwick Arms** is an attractive modern building with glowing red brick walls and a pantiled roof. Inside, the dining room with its high arched ceiling with its pine cladding and French doors leading to the beer garden provides an elegant setting for the quality food on offer. A distinctive feature of the décor is the RAF memorabilia displayed around the rooms - paintings, prints and artefacts celebrating local heroes. The wine list also carries the Farnsfield Pledge, a poem hailing the memory of those "thousands who will never grow old".

The Warwick's landlady, Nicola Morgan, took over here in the spring of 2001 and her outgoing personality quickly ensured the pub's success. Food is available every lunchtime and evening, with a Carvery at Sunday lunchtime. Fresh fish is the speciality here but there's also a good choice of vegetarian and meat dishes, including one for those with very large appetites - the Warwick Belly Buster contains a 60oz steak with 4 eggs, mushrooms, onion rings, peas, chips and a salad garnish. At the other end of the scale, the menu also offers light meals, sandwiches and meals for children. To accompany your meal, there's a well-balanced wine list of vintages from around the world, a choice of 2 real ales and a wide range of other beverages.

There's also a play area and café. Designed for younger children, **Wonderland Pleasure Park & Garden Centre** offers a large tropical house with exotic butterflies and reptiles; a large indoor soft play area; pets' centre; miniature railway; junior rollercoaster and much more. Both attractions are open daily all year round.

In Farnsfield village itself traces of a Roman camp can be found and the ghost of a Roman soldier is reputed to haunt one of the village's pubs. More recently, the village was the birthplace of the explorer, Augustus Charles Gregory. After emigrating to Australia, Gregory became the first person to explore the country's interior. The Royal Geographical Society commissioned an expedition led by him in 1855, a journey during which 5000 miles of the country was mapped. Gregory's respect for the native culture earned him the unofficial title of 'Protector of the Aborigines'.

RAINWORTH
6 miles S of Edwinstowe on the A617

Pronounced 'Renoth' locally, this is a mining village and its development is solely due to the now closed pits. There are, however, two very different places of interest within the village. **Rainworth Water**, a series of lakes and streams, which attracts walkers, naturalists, and fishermen, is also the site of a bird sanctuary founded by the naturalist Joseph Whitaker.

Rainworth's other claim to fame is its fish and chip shop which found itself on the front pages of the national newspapers in the early 1980s as the place where the Black Panther was caught. A local shopkeeper had noticed a man loitering in the area and had contacted the police who kept a watch for the suspicious man on the main street of the village. Suddenly realising that he was being followed, the suspect began shooting at the police, injuring one, but the customers in the chip shop, seeing what was going on, apprehended the man. Though at the time the police did not know the identity of the gunman he later turned out to be the notorious Black Panther who was later convicted of murder.

BLIDWORTH
7 miles S of Edwinstowe on the B6020

A small forest village that changed greatly with the opening of a colliery in the 1920s, Blidworth has changed again following the closure of the pits in the late 1980s. As well as a having a mixture of 1930s miners' homes and early stone cottages, there is also a particularly attractive church. Dating back to 1739, the Church of St Mary of the Purification has some interesting items, including Continental glass and Jacobean panelling. A rather touching monument in the church is one dedicated to a Sherwood ranger called Thomas Leake, who was murdered in the forest in 1598. The stone memorial has some splendid carvings of stags, dogs and the emblems of his office.

The village also has strong associations with the legend of Robin Hood. Maid Marian is reputed to have lived here before her marriage to the outlaw; at Fountaindale are the remains of Friar Tuck's Well; nearby is the site of the portly priest's home where he first met and fought with Robin; and, finally, Will Scarlett is reputedly buried in St Mary's churchyard.

Near the village there are two Forestry Commission areas of woodland which both offer the opportunity for walks and picnics: Blidworth Bottoms and Haywood Oaks, in which some of the largest oak trees in Sherwood can be found.

RAVENSHEAD
8 miles S of Edwinstowe on the A60

Although the name Ravenshead appears in the Domesday Book, the village of Ravenshead is relatively new and dates from 1966 when the three hamlets of Fishpool, Larch Farm, and Kighill merged. Situated by the side of the main road is the Bessie Shepherd Stone which marks the spot where, in 1817, Bessie was murdered as she walked from Mansfield to Papplewick.

Longdale Lane Rural Craft Centre was established in the 1970s and it is the oldest such centre in the country. It's a re-creation of a 19th century village, complete with flagstones and Victorian street lamps. Behind the decorative, period shop fronts a whole host of professional artists can be seen making both traditional and modern objects.

PAPPLEWICK
6 miles NE of Eastwood on the B683

This pretty village, half of which is designated a conservation area, is another of the unexpected rural oases to be found in this industrial part of Nottinghamshire. It still retains many pink stone cottages and the trappings of the industrial age have been almost totally lost. Back in the 18th century, life was very different in this now quiet village: the cotton mills at Papplewick and nearby Linby were notorious for some of the worst excesses of child labour.

Lying at the southern boundary of Sherwood Forest and just south of Newstead Abbey, the village is the starting point for several footpaths leading on to these famous lands. Along one such footpath, walkers, with the permission of the owner, can have a look at a cave known as **Robin Hood's Stable**. It was here that the folk hero is said to have

stabled his horses ready for forays into Nottingham.

Although the grand splendour of Newstead Abbey lies not far away, the village has a most outstanding building of its own, Papplewick Hall (private). It was built around 1790, to a design by the Adam brothers for Frederick Montagu who was at that time Lord of the Treasury.

The village **Church of St James**, hidden away down a country lane, is definitely worth a visit. The tower is 14th century but the rest of the building is a masterpiece of Georgian 'Gothick' architecture. The classical Georgian style is enhanced by a musicians' gallery that runs along the north and west sides, and a striking east window, depicting Faith and Hope, which is a copy of Sir Joshua Reynold's window in New College, Oxford. The squire's pew has survived, complete with its own fireplace. It is said that one particular squire, when he thought the sermon had gone on long enough, would bang on the fire irons as a signal to the vicar to finish his address.

Some of the grandest Victorian buildings were completely utilitarian. **Papplewick Pumping Station**, located to the east of the village, is a perfect example. Built in the late 1800s, its original purpose was to supply water to the expanding city and suburbs of Nottingham. Housing two magnificent beam engines by James Watt and Company and powered by six Lancaster boilers, in its heyday the station could pump 3 million gallons of water a day. Apart from the fascinating machinery, the splendidly decorated Victorian cast iron columns and galleries as well as the stained glass make this one of the more interesting industrial sites to visit. Outside, in front of the red brick engine room is a large cooling pool and the surrounding grounds have been landscaped. Lovingly restored by a dedicated group of enthusiasts, the pumping station is open to the public on Sunday afternoons during the summer.

PERLETHORPE
4 miles NE of Edwinstowe off the A614

Situated in the valley of the River Meden, Perlethorpe lies within the estate of Thoresby Hall, at the eastern end of Thoresby Lake. The first hall was built in the late 17th century for the Earl of Kingston but this was destroyed in 1745 and replaced by a Palladian-style mansion. The hall seen today is a Victorian mansion built by Anthony Salvin in 1864 for the Pierrepont family and is surrounded by the largest park in the county. The Hall itself is now a hotel.

The village church, which was completed in 1876, was built by Salvin at the same time as he was working on the hall. At the beginning of the 20th century Lady Manvers of the great hall took a keen interest in the welfare of the village children and was always informed of any who did not attend Sunday school. She would then visit them and scold those who had failed in their duty. But if a child had been absent because of sickness, she would ensure that hot soup was delivered until the child was well again.

BOTHAMSALL
6 miles NE of Edwinstowe off the A614

Close to Bothamsall the two rivers, the Meden and the Maun, finally merge to become the River Idle. This pretty estate village with its twisting lane has a pleasant church that looks much older than its 150 years. The original church on this site was built in the 14th century, but the only remaining relics are a few monuments, a small brass and the font.

A road to the west of the village leads up to Castle Hill where a ruined outer wall of a castle and an artificial motte formed part of the local defences. No other evidence points to a larger fortification and, as no records exist of a defence to protect this strategic crossing point, the date of the castle can only be guessed to be around the 12th century. However, the views from the hill top are well worth the climb and not only can the plantations which form the Clumber and Thoresby estates be seen but also the neo-Georgian house, Lound Hall, which was built in 1937 at nearby Haughton.

WARSOP
6 miles W of Edwinstowe on the A60

Warsop is really two communities. Market Warsop sits beside the River Meden, while the older settlement of Church Warsop perches on the hilltop on the other side of the river.

Now a large village, the original rural settlement of Church Warsop expanded in the 19th century with the opening of several local collieries and the building of nearby colliery villages. During the General Strike of 1926, some of the miners carried on working and this led to the village being given the nickname of Scab Alley.

Mining has not been the only industry in the area. It was lime from Warsop that was quarried and used in the restoration of Southwell Minster following the Civil War. Today, the scars of the shallow quarrying are barely visible. The areas of humpy ground, noted for their birds and wild flowers, now go by the name of the Hills and Holes.

CUCKNEY
6 miles NW of Edwinstowe on the A60

Five main roads converge on this sizeable village which in medieval times was a marshy island. A large mound in the churchyard is all that is left of Thomas de

THE GREENDALE OAK

Cuckney, Mansfield, Nottinghamshire NG20 9NQ
Tel: 01623 844441/842377

Set in the heart of the village, close to St Mary's Church, **The Greendale Oak** is a charming traditional hostelry with a history stretching back some 300 years. There's an interesting tale attached to its name. In 1724 the Duke of Portland, owner of vast estates around Cuckney, wagered the Earl of Oxford that within his grounds there was an oak tree of such enormous proportions that a carriage and two horses could be driven through it. There was indeed such a tree, known as the Greendale Oak

and with a circumference reputed to be 35ft long. A hole was cut through it, the extracted wood later being used to make a stylish cabinet, and a carriage duly driven through. The Duke had won his bet but the tree, not surprisingly, faded away and only a stump now remains.

This association is just one of the reasons the inn was designated a building of architectural and historic interest. David and Sheila Garner took over here in February 2001 but David has lived in the village for over 50 years so he is well-acquainted with the Greendale Oak both as customer and landlord. Today, the inn specialises in home cooked bar and restaurant meals, with food available every lunchtime and evening. Sunday lunch, with its choice of 4 or 5 different roasts, is especially popular but booking ahead is also strongly advised for Friday and Saturday evenings. To complement your meal, there are always two real ales on tap along with a wide selection of other beers, wines and spirits. The restaurant can cater for up to 60 guests and there's also a private function room ideal for small business conferences, anniversaries and other special occasions.

The Greendale Oak also offers bed and breakfast accommodation, available all year round. There are 5 rooms in all, with a choice of family, double, twin or single, and all the rooms have full heating,

colour television and tea/coffee-making facilities. As we go to press, the addition of en suite facilities for all the rooms is nearing completion. Other amenities include an outside patio area and ample off road parking. All major credit cards are excepted apart from American Express and Diners.

Only half a dozen or so miles from Exit 30 of the M1, the Greendale Oak provides an ideal base for exploring the great houses and parks of the Dukeries or following the footsteps of Robin Hood through nearby Sherwood Forest. The village is also roughly halfway between Sheffield and Nottingham with their manifold urban attractions.

Cuckney's 12th century castle. Because the nearby church was built on the marshes it was necessary in the 1950s to shore it up by building a concrete platform underneath it. In the course of this work the remains of hundreds of skeletons were uncovered. At first it was thought the bones were the grisly relics of some 12th century battle. More recent research has revealed that the remains are much older. They have now been linked to the 7th century Battle of Heathfield between Edwin of Northumbria and Penda of Mercia. An estate village to the country seat of the Dukes of Portland, Welbeck Abbey, Cuckney is made up of farm workers cottages. Along with **Clumber House**, **Thoresby Hall**, and **Rufford Abbey**, **Welbeck Abbey** makes up the four large estates in this area of Nottinghamshire, all owned by Dukes. Naturally, the area become known as The Dukeries. It was the 5th Duke of Portland who began, in 1854, an extensive building programme that turned Welbeck into what is seen today. The most impressive of his additions was the riding school, the second largest in the world, complete with a peat floor and gas jet lighting. The building is now owned by the Ministry of Defence and is used as an Army training college, though the abbey and the grounds have been maintained in perfect condition.

EASTWOOD

"I have always hated it" wrote D.H. Lawrence of the mining town where he was born in 1885. Reviling the *"ugliness of my native village"*, he wished it could be pulled down, *"to the last brick"*. Local people reciprocated his dislike: *"He were nowt but a big soft gel"* said one of his contemporaries many years later when the gawky lad whose mum insisted he

D H Lawrence Birthplace, Eastwood

should never go down the pit had become a writer and painter of international repute.

The Lawrence family home, a two up, two down, terrace house at 8a Victoria Street is now the **D.H. Lawrence Birthplace Museum.** It has been furnished in a late 19th century style with which the Lawrence family would have been familiar. There are also some household items on display which belonged to the family and anyone visiting the museum will see that the house's front window is larger than others in the same street. This is where Mrs Lawrence displayed children's clothes and other linen items which she made and sold to supplement the fluctuating wages brought home by her miner husband.

In 1887, the Lawrence family moved to a larger, end of terrace house in Eastwood which today is known as the Sons and

Lovers Cottage since it featured as the Morels' house, The Bottoms, in Lawrence's novel. This house too is open to the public, though by appointment only, and is also laid out with furnishings and artefacts which are appropriate to the time. Lawrence's father was a miner at the nearby Brinsley Pit and though the family moved house in Eastwood several times, the Lawrences remained short of money. First attending the local school, Lawrence was the first Eastwood boy to gain a scholarship to Nottingham High School where he was a pupil until 1901. Lawrence started his working life as a clerk before undertaking a teacher training course and moving to teach in a school in Croydon.

Though Lawrence had already begun writing, his major novels were not written until after 1912, the year he eloped with his former professor's wife and left England. Drawing heavily on the influences of his upbringing in Eastwood, *Sons and Lovers,* first published in 1913, not only describes the countryside around Eastwood but also portrays many local personalities. The unflattering descriptions of, amongst others, Lawrence senior, caused a great deal of local resentment, a resentment that astonishingly persists to this day in the village.

Lawrence and his wife, Frieda Weekley, returned to England during World War I but they were unable to settle and at one point were detained as suspected German spies. They were soon on their travels once again.

In the early 1920s, Lawrence published *Women in Love* and, a few years later, was diagnosed with tuberculosis, the disease from which he died in 1930. It was whilst he was in Florence, trying unsuccessfully to find a cure for his crippling condition, that Lawrence wrote his most famous novel, *Lady Chatterley's Lover.* First

published in 1928, the full text of the controversial story was not printed until 1960 and, even then, it was the subject of a court case that is almost as famous as the book.

A place of pilgrimage for devotees of Lawrence, Eastwood also attracts those with an interest in railway history. It was at the Sun Inn in the Market Place that a group of "Iron Masters and Coal Owners" gathered on 16th August 1832 to discuss the construction of a railway that would eventually become the mighty Midland Railway. A plaque on the wall of the inn commemorates the seminal meeting.

The railway was formed to compete with the **Erewash Canal**, completed in 1779 and effectively put out of business by the 1870s. Almost a century later, following years of neglect, the canal was cleared and made suitable for use by pleasure craft. The towpath was resurfaced and now provides a pleasant and interesting walk.

Just to the east of Eastwood lies Greasley, once a village in its own right but now almost entirely engulfed by its neighbour. Little is known of Greasley until the 14th century when Nicholas de Cantelupe fortified his manor house adjoining the church. The house became known as Greasley Castle and, today, the traces of the moat and walls can still be seen at Castle Farm.

It was also Nicholas de Cantelupe who, in 1345, founded Greasley Priory for the Carthusian order. The house fell into disrepair after the Dissolution and many of the village buildings have some of the priory's stones embedded in their walls. Each year, in May, a procession of local clergymen, followed by their congregation, walk from the local Roman Catholic church to the priory ruins to hold a service.

Standing on a site where there has been a church for over 1,000 years, St Mary's

Church has, in its parish records of 1603, the marriage of John Robinson. He was a pastor to the Pilgrim Fathers and Robinson also gave a farewell address before the Fathers set sail on the Mayflower.

AROUND EASTWOOD

SOMERCOTES SELSTON
4 miles N of Eastwood on the B600

Mentioned in the Domesday Book as a place with a church and three acres of meadows, like many other village communities in this western area of Nottinghamshire, Somercotes Selston was at that time very much a farming community. But beneath the fertile agricultural land lay coal and leases for coal mining were granted as early as 1206. For centuries the coal mining operation remained small scale but, by the 1850s, Somercotes Selston had taken on many of the aspects of a modern colliery village. The last coal pit in Somercotes Selston closed in 1956 but almost half a century later the village still has a lacklustre air to it.

From the chuchyard of the partly-Norman Church of St Helen there are some splendid views across the neighbouring Derbyshire hills. The graveyard is the last resting place of Dan Boswell, king of the gypsies. For many years newborn gypsy babies were brought to Boswell's gravestone to be baptised and many gypsies made special journeys to the church to pay their respects.

UNDERWOOD
3 miles N of Eastwood on the B600

Coal has been mined in the village and surrounding area since medieval times and Underwood still retains many of the characteristics of a mining community.

In the village can be seen the Elizabethan chimneys of Felley Priory, founded in 1165 and now a private house. Local legend has it that a tunnel ran from this Augustinian foundation to nearby Wansley Hall (now in ruins). Whether this is true or not, the two places are known to have had close associations dating from the Middle Ages.

Jessie Chambers, a friend of D.H. Lawrence and the person believed to have been the inspiration for Miriam in his novel *Sons and Lovers*, taught at Underwood School.

ANNESLEY WOODHOUSE
5 miles NE of Eastwood on the A608

All that remains of old Annesley is the roofless ruin of what D.H. Lawrence described as a *"mouldering church standing high on a bank by the roadside...black and melancholy above the shrinking head of the traveller"*. Another great writer also knew the village well. Annesley Hall was the home of Mary Chaworth, a lady for whom Lord Byron formed an early affection. The poet and the beautiful heiress would often walk up to the breezy summit of Diadem Hill, 578ft high and visible for miles around. The liaison was a little odd since Mary had inherited her great fortune from William Chaworth: William had been killed in a duel by Byron's great uncle, the 5th Lord Byron. Perhaps because of this unfortunate event, Mary did not succumb to the poet's charms. Instead she married John Musters, the sporting squire of Colwick Hall near Nottingham. She died there in 1832 as the result of an attack on the Hall by Reform Bill rioters.

Many of the contents of Annesley's old church were removed to the Victorian All Saints Church, built in 1874 on a hilltop in the new village overlooking the Erewash Valley. Amongst these treasures are an impressive Norman font with interesting carvings, an alabaster figure of a shrouded man, and a small brass of 1595 depicting William Breton, a forester, with his bow and arrows, and faithful dog.

NEWSTEAD
5 miles NE of Eastwood off the A608

A magnificent 13th century ruin attached to a Victorian reworking of a Tudor mansion provides one of the county's most historic houses. **Newstead Abbey** was founded by Henry II around 1170 as part of his atonement for the murder of Thomas à Becket, and sold at the Dissolution of the Monasteries to Sir John Byron who destroyed much of the Abbey and converted other buildings into a mansion. The Newstead estate remained in the Byron family for almost 300 years, its last owner being the celebrated, (and notorious) poet, George Lord Byron.

He inherited the property from his great uncle, the 5th Lord Byron, better known as 'Devil Byron'. As mentioned earlier, the 5th Lord had killed an old family friend in a duel and although he was only convicted of manslaughter, he was obliged to pay huge punitive costs. Ostracised by London society, he retreated to Newstead in malevolent mood. To pay his debts he virtually denuded the estate of its great plantations of oaks. And just to spite his son and expected heir he ordered the slaughter of the deer

herd that had grazed the parkland for generations. As it happened his son died before him and the estate passed to that "brat from Aberdeen" as he referred to his impoverished great nephew who was living there in poverty with his mother.

When the poet arrived at Newstead in 1798, he found that the only room in this huge mansion without a leaking roof was the scullery. The estate was burdened with debts, and so was Byron. He managed to let the estate out for some years but when he finally took up residence in 1808 he was still hard put to make the house even reasonably habitable. In 1817 he gave up the struggle, sold the estate to an old Harrow schoolmate, Col. Thomas Wildman, for £94,000, removed himself to Italy and never saw Newstead again.

Col. Wildman spared no expense in refurbishing and extending the dilapidated house, an undertaking that

Newstead Abbey Wood

took 12 years to complete. The house and grounds that visitors see today is essentially the creation of Thomas Wildman, but the presiding spirit of the house is undeniably that of the wayward poet.

Over the years, many Byron manuscripts, letters, books, pictures and personal relics have found their way back to the Abbey, and both the house and grounds are beautifully maintained by the present owners, the City of Nottingham, to whom the estate was bequeathed in 1931.

The house is open every afternoon from April to September, and the grounds all year round. These include a secret garden; a beautifully carved fountain decorated with fantastic animals; the famous and elaborate memorial to Byron's dog Boatswain, and a large lake where the 5th lord used to re-enact naval battles.

Byron died from a fever while travelling in Greece supporting the patriot's war of independence against the Turks. His body was returned to England but his scandalous reputation for womanizing made a proposed burial in Westminster Abbey unthinkable. Instead, he was interred at Hucknall, a couple of miles south of Newstead Abbey.

LINBY
5 miles NE of Eastwood on the A6011

"One of the prettiest villages on the north side of Nottingham" was Pevsner's rather cautious praise of this small village where a stream runs along the main street with broad grass verges, and enough stone built houses to face down the unfortunate sprawl of 1930s red brick houses near the church.

Situated on the banks of the River Leen, during the late 18th century the riverbank was a busy, bustling place with six cotton mills being powered by the water. The mills were strictly functional but George Robinson, their owner, did not want to be out done by his near neighbours at Newstead Abbey so he added battlements and other ornate features and thus gave Castle Mill its name. Young apprentices were brought in from as far away as London to work in Castle Mill. Housed in small lodges near the mill, the children worked long hours weaving cotton cloth in terrible conditions with minimal food and clothing provided. Brought to work in the mills from a young age, (some were no more than 10 years old), many died early. In Linby churchyard the graves of 42 apprentice children bear witness to Robinson's callous pursuit of profit.

When the 5th Lord Byron dammed the River Leen upstream from Linby, in order to create a lake on his estate, he also played havoc with the water supply to the mills. With a reduction in power, Robinson had to find another reliable power source and in 1786 his sons were the first to apply steam power to a cotton mill when they installed a Boulton and Watt engine.

HUCKNALL
4 miles NE of Eastwood off the A611

An undistinguished little industrial town, Hucknall nevertheless attracts a constant stream of visitors. They come to **St Mary Magdalen Church**, not so much for its 14th century font or for the 27 attractive stained glass windows by Kempe, but to gaze at a simple marble slab set in the floor of the chancel. It bears the inscription:

BYRON, Born January 22nd, 1788,
Died April 19th, 1824.

The inscription is surmounted by a laurel wreath, in classical times the only award to winners in the original Olympic Games. The memorial was presented to the church in 1881 by the King of the

Hellenes in appreciation of Byron's support for the Greeks against their imperial masters, the Turks.

Byron died in Greece where his body was embalmed and transported to England. For several days the body was exhibited at an inn in Nottingham before being buried in the Byron family crypt at Hucknall. Many years later, in 1938, the vicar of Hucknall entered the now closed crypt to challenge a tradition that the poet's body had been removed. He found the lid of the coffin loose and its lead lining cut open.

"Very reverently, I raised the lid, and before my eyes lay the embalmed body of Byron in as perfect condition as when it was placed in the coffin 114 years ago...The serene, almost happy expression on his face made a profound impression on me. The feet and ankles were uncovered, and I was able to establish the fact that his lameness had been that of his right foot".

Hucknall boasts another famous son. Eric Coates, the son of a local doctor, was born here on 27th August 1886. He displayed musical talent at an early age, (he demanded and got his first violin at the age of 6), and became the most celebrated viola player of his generation. But Coates became even more famous as a composer of light music: - his *Sleepy Lagoon* is immediately recognisable to millions as the signature music of BBC Radio's long-running programme *Desert Island Discs*.

KIMBERLEY
3 miles SE of Eastwood on the A610

The town lies on the Robin Hood Way, an 88 mile long footpath devised by the Nottingham Wayfarers' Rambling Club to celebrate its golden jubilee in 1988. Beginning at Nottingham Castle, the path takes in many of the places associated with the legendary hero before reaching

QUEEN'S HEAD

Main Road, Watnall, Nottingham NG16 1HT
Tel: 0115 938 3148 Fax: 0115 938 6774
website: www.queens.head.co.uk

Only a few minutes drive from Exit 26 of the M1, the **Queen's Head** stands alongside the old coaching road to Nottingham. Its first recorded licence dates back to 1801 when it was operating as a coaching inn. Built of the local warm red brick, it's an inviting looking place with flower boxes beneath the windows and picnic tables on the forecourt and in the spacious beer garden. Inside, old beams, settles and a broad semi-circular window seat create a welcoming atmosphere, and so do the friendly staff, one of whom, Ann, notched up 28 years of working here in September 2001.

The landlady of the Queen's Head is Pamela Jones and as she is a vegetarian she has developed a range of meat free traditional and more unusual meals. Meat eaters need not fear; the chef, James Gibbons, ensures that there is always an appetising range of traditional English cuisine includes roast beef or pork dinners, shank of lamb and bangers and mash - served with his special recipe onion gravy. Food is available 12 - 2 daily (3 pm on Sundays) and 6 - 9pm Monday to Friday. Lovers of real ales will be in their element here since there's a choice of no fewer than 6 authentic brews. These change regularly, with some of them supplied by local micro breweries.

its end at St Mary's Church, Edwinstowe, where Robin Hood is said to have married Maid Marian.

AWSWORTH
3 miles SE of Eastwood on the A6096

In order to lay the tracks for the Great Northern Railway line from Derby to Nottingham, a viaduct was needed to carry the railway over the Erewash Canal, the River Erewash, and the Nottingham Canal which all lie close to Awsworth. The resulting construction, built in 1876-7, is still an impressive sight though the line is now disused. One of only two viaducts in England to be made of wrought iron lattice girders, the **Bennerley Viaduct** has 16 spans which are set on pillars 56 feet high.

COSSALL
3 miles SE of Eastwood off the A6096

Now a conservation area, this village draped across a low hill boasts some attractive buildings, notably the picturesque 17th century Willoughby almshouses and a farmhouse which includes part of the original home of the Willoughby family. They were a branch of the Willoughbys of Wollaton, a dynasty that was founded by a wealthy 13th century wool merchant from Nottingham named Ralph Bugge. This rather unfortunate name (which means hobgoblin) was understandably changed

by his descendants to the more acceptable Willoughby; a name taken from the village of Willoughby-on-the-Wolds, on the border with Leicestershire, where Ralph owned a fair acreage of land.

Cossall was another of D.H. Lawrence's haunts and it featured in his novel *The Rainbow* as the village of 'Cossethay', home of the Brangwen family. The fictional character, William Brangwen, is said to have been based on Alfred Burrows, to whose daughter, Louise, Lawrence was engaged for some time. She duly appears as Ursula Brangwen. The Burrows family lived in a cottage, now marked by a plaque, near the charming village church which contains a fine marble tomb of the Willoughbys.

TROWELL
3 miles S of Eastwood off the A6096

Back in 1951 the organizers of the Festival of Britain decided to select a single village to typify the country. From amongst 1600 entrants, and disdaining picture postcard contenders from the Cotswolds or deepest Devonshire, they settled finally on the rather unremarkable village of Trowell. (It did have the useful qualification however of being roughly in the centre of the country). Festival publicity featured photographs of Trowell church with its square medieval tower against a background of tall chimneys and factories.

THE HAVEN

2 Awsworth Lane, Cossall,
Nottinghamshire NG16 2RZ
Tel: 0115 930 7924

The Haven is tucked away in the peaceful little village of Cossall, just a few minutes drive from Exit 26 of the M1. Here, Jill Rhodehouse offers a choice of either bed & breakfast or self-catering

accommodation in beautifully decorated and furnished rooms. B&B guests stay in the main building where there are 4 letting rooms, (1 double en suite; 1 double with wash-basin; 1 twin; 1 single); for those who prefer self-catering there's a self-contained sleeping 2 adults and 2 children. Medium and small dogs are accepted but please note that all the accommodation is non-smoking.

Virtually the only legacy of that temporary fame is the village pub which was renamed The Festival Inn. Today, the village name will only ring a bell with travellers on the M1 who use the Trowell Services area nearby.

First mentioned in the Domesday Book as Torwell, meaning 'the well on the hill', the village was quite a settlement with at least 15 wells and, according to the Norman survey, a priest and half a church. Several of the county's most well known families have been associated with Trowell including the de Trowells, the Willoughby family, and their descendants, the Middletons.

Little changed in this quiet area until the coming of the railways. In 1884, a new station was opened in the village allowing its inhabitants the opportunity to travel more widely. The moors around Trowell had been mined for coal from the 13th century and it was not until 1926 that the Trowell colliery ceased production. The other key industry of the immediate area was iron. The abundance of coal and the nearby River Erewash provided the other materials needed in a forge. As a result, the late 1800s saw the village swamped by an influx of ironworkers from the Black Country. However, village life was not been completely swept away by the industrial age. The oldest building in Trowell is undoubtedly its beautiful St Helen's Church. Parts of the building date from the 13th century, but remains of a previous Anglo-Saxon building were found in the chancel during renovation work.

MANSFIELD

The second largest town in the county, Mansfield stands at the heart of what

were once the great North Nottinghamshire coalfields. That industry has now vanished but Mansfield still has the atmosphere of an industrial town although its economy is now based on a broader spread of varying business.

The most distinctive structure in Mansfield is undoubtedly the great railway viaduct that sweeps through and above the town, carried by 15 huge arches of rough-hewn stone. Built in 1875, it is one of the largest viaducts to be found in an English town and gives some dignity to a community which suffered badly from thoughtless development in the 1960s.

The old market place still hosts markets on Mondays, Thursdays, Fridays, and Saturdays with colourful stalls gathered around the impressive Gothic **Bentinck Monument**. This was erected in 1848 in memory of Lord George Bentinck, the younger son of the Duke of Portland. Bentinck was a long serving Member of Parliament for the town and a great friend of Disraeli. The memorial was raised by public subscription but unfortunately funds ran out before the finishing touch, a statue of Bentinck himself, could be placed in the central space.

Also in the Market Place is the handsome Moot Hall, built for Lady Oxford in 1752 and bearing her arms and an inscription in the pediment. Waverley House, close by, dates from the same period and displays an interesting mixture of architectural styles.

Standing just to the northwest of the market place, **Mansfield Museum** (free) concentrates its collections largely on local interest and includes a model of a Roman villa that once stood at nearby Mansfield Woodhouse. The collection spans the centuries from that early occupation right up to more recent times, with pictures and artefacts relating to the industry of the town and surrounding villages. The adjoining art gallery also carries a local theme and features works by artists of the area including the water-colourist A.S. Buxton, who is well known for his paintings of Mansfield.

Further west, on the outskirts of the town centre stands the Metal Box Factory which grew out of a mustard business established in the 1830s by David Cooper Barringer. In order to keep the mustard dry, the company began to store the powder in metal boxes instead of the traditional wooden crates. By the late 1800s, the market for decorated metal box packaging had grown so great that the company decided to concentrate on the production of the boxes rather than the milling of mustard.

AROUND MANSFIELD

SUTTON IN ASHFIELD
2 miles SW of Mansfield on the A38

This once small village expanded over the years as a result of local coal mining. The modern development has not been kind. However, a few of the original 17th and 18th century cottages can be seen near the Church of St Mary Magdalene. The church contains some Norman work on the west wall, 13th century arcades and a 14th century spire. A tombstone lying beside the path leading to the porch commemorates a certain Ann Burton who achieved the remarkable feat of dying on the 30th February 1836.

THE MINERS ARMS

222 Blackwell Road, Huthwaite, Sutton-in-Ashfield, Nottinghamshire NG17 2RF
Tel: 01623 550087

An old sign on the rear wall of **The Miners Arms** shows its original name - The Arms of the Miner, a legacy from the days when the local coal miners held their meeting here, collected their pay and were held to account for any misdemeanours. The building itself dates back to the late 1700s and is full of character with lots of old beams and a wealth of bygone memorabilia - pewter mugs, bed warming pans and gleaming copper pieces.

A more recent addition is the elegant non-smoking conservatory restaurant overlooking the garden where wholesome home made food is available every weekday lunchtime and evening, and with a popular Carvery on Sundays from noon until 4pm. Paul the chef is noted for his home made Beef & Guinness Pie and on Wednesday evenings there are special Steak Nights with some value for money deals.

The Miners is a family run hostelry with Ann and Brian Eades, their daughter Shelley and son-in-law Scott supported by a dedicated staff. Children are welcome and there's a small play area in the pleasant beer garden at the rear of the inn. Entertainment includes a Quiz on Thursday evenings; karaoke on Fridays, and live entertainment every other Saturday. There's ample off road parking; parties can be catered for; but please note that credit cards are not accepted.

DALESTORTH GUEST HOUSE

Garden Centre & Nursery, Skegby Lane, Skegby,
Sutton-in-Ashfield, Nottinghamshire NG17 3DH
Tel: 01623 551110 (Guest House)
    or 01623 557817 (Garden Centre)
website: www.gardencentresmansfield.co.uk

Hidden away in the tiny village of Skegby, the
Dalestorth Guest House, Garden Centre & Nursery
not only offers quality accommodation in a delightful
Georgian house but also has one of the best garden
centres in the area on its doorstep. The house was
built around 1770 by the Rector of Teversal and
extended in the early 1800s. The mansion has an interesting history, serving for many years as a
"Ladies' Boarding Establishment". In 1976 it was purchased by Philip and Christine Jordan who later
converted it into a guest house offering 13 bedrooms with a mixture of double, twin and single
rooms. A double room with a 4-poster canopy is available for brides and grooms, and all rooms are
equipped with colour television and tea/coffee-making facilities. A hearty English breakfast is included
in the tariff.

The Garden Centre started as a hobby but has developed
into an outstandingly well stocked attraction for gardeners.
Millions of bedding plants, vegetables, herbs, shrubs, roses
and conifers provide a bewildering choice but helpful staff are
always on hand to advise customers on any gardening queries.
The centre also stocks every conceivable kind of gardening
aid, from quality composts to greenhouse glazing clips. Both
the garden centre and the guest house are open every day
except Christmas Day, all year round.

THE WHITE SWAN

34 Station Street, Mansfield Woodhouse,
Nottinghamshire NG19 8BT
Tel: 01623 621259

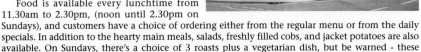

For the last five years or so, **The White Swan**
has been run by the Sterland family - Wendy,
Trevor and their daughter Tina. During that time
they have built up a reputation for warm
hospitality, well-maintained ales and appetising
food at remarkable value for money prices.

Food is available every lunchtime from
11.30am to 2.30pm, (noon until 2.30pm on
Sundays), and customers have a choice of ordering either from the regular menu or from the daily
specials. In addition to the hearty main meals, salads, freshly filled cobs, and jacket potatoes are also
available. On Sundays, there's a choice of 3 roasts plus a vegetarian dish, but be warned - these
lunches are very popular so booking ahead is
recommended. Children are welcome, (they have their
own special dishes), and the dining room has no
smoking areas.

Ales include Mansfield Original, Smooth and Mild,
plus Fosters, Harp and Guinness, along with Strongbow
and Woodpecker ciders. Please note that credit cards
are not accepted. On Friday and Saturday evenings the
Sterlands lay on live entertainment, and on Sunday
evening customers can join in the karaoke
performances. The pub has ample off road parking.

SKEGBY
2 miles W of Mansfield off the A6075

Skegby's church had to be rebuilt in the 1870s because of mining subsidence but some interesting features were salvaged from the old church: some monuments to the Lindley family; a fine east window; and two delightful effigies from the early 1300s showing a Sherwood Forester and his wife. She is dressed in a wimple and long gown; he carries a hunting horn.

The village is lucky in having a particularly fine example of a 14th century cruck cottage though this was not discovered until restoration work was taking place on the building in the 1950s. The village's pinfold, the place where stray animals were held until their owner claimed them, has also been restored and can be found on the Mansfield road.

TEVERSAL
3 miles W of Mansfield off the B6014

A rural oasis in the heart of this former mining district, Teversal stands on a hill looking across to the lovely Elizabethan Hardwick Hall which is actually just over the border in Derbyshire. Teversal village is the fictional home of Lady Chatterley and the woodlands of the Hardwick Hall estate were the meeting place for her and gamekeeper Mellors in D.H. Lawrence's *Lady Chatterley's Lover.*

The village also boasts, according to Pevsner, *"one of the most rewarding village churches in the county".* It has a Norman door, 12th century arcades and a 15th century tower but eclipsing all these are the wonderful 17th century fittings, all marvellously intact. A wealth of colourful hatchments, ornate monuments to the Molyneux and Carnavon families, Lords of the Manor, and original box pews all add to the interest. The Carnavons own family pew has embroidered cushions and is set apart from the lowlier seating by

four spiral columns which give it the appearance of a four-poster bed.

MANSFIELD WOODHOUSE
2 miles N of Mansfield on the A60

Originally a settlement within Sherwood Forest, Mansfield Woodhouse is now virtually a suburb of Mansfield but the core of the village remains remarkably intact and several interesting buildings have survived.

Opposite The Cross, in the heart of the town, stands one of these fine houses, the Georgian Burnaby House. Still retaining many of its original, elegant features the house was obviously built for a prosperous family and, during the mid-1800s, it was occupied by the Duke of Portland's land agent. On the other side of the road stands a stump which is all that remains of the Market Cross, erected here after a great fire in 1304. The village stocks also stood close by and they were once used to detain George Fox, the Quaker Movement founder, after he had preached the gospel to the villagers.

At the bottom of the street stands the oldest building in Mansfield Woodhouse, St Edmund's Church. Most of the original church was lost, along with the parish records, when fire swept through the village in the early 14th century. The present church was built on the same site though it underwent some severe restoration in the 19th century. Standing not far from the church is a manor house known as Woodhouse Castle because of the battlements which were added to the building in the early 1800s. Dating from the 1600s, this was the home of the Digby family and, in particular, of General Sir John Digby, Sheriff of Nottingham, who distinguished himself during the Civil War.

Another building of note is the essentially 18th century Wolfhunt House found just off the High Street. The unusual name is derived from a local tale which suggests that the land on which the house is built once belonged to a man who was employed to frighten away the wolves in Sherwood Forest by blowing a hunting horn.

RETFORD

Retford is actually two communities, East and West Retford, set either side of the River Idle. West Retford is the elder settlement; its twin grew up during the 1100s as a place where tolls could be collected from travellers making the river crossing. Retford has been a market town since 1246 and markets are still held here every Thursday and Saturday.

Retford received a major economic boost in 1766 when the Great North Road was diverted through the town. That was when the Market Square was re-developed and some of the elegant Georgian buildings here, and in Grove Street, still survive from that time. The grand and rather chateau-like Town Hall, however, dates from 1868 and replaced the Georgian hall. Outside the Town Hall can be found the Broad Stone, which is probably the base of an old parish boundary cross. Tradition has it that during the times of the plague in Retford,

in the mid-16th and mid-17th centuries, coins were placed in a pool of vinegar in the hollow in the top of the stone to prevent the disease from spreading whilst trading was taking place at the market.

In the northwestern corner of the square is an archway that leads down to the River Idle. Bearing the inscription "JP Esquire 1841", the archway once led to the gardens of John Parker who lived in a nearby house, now business premises. A close inspection of the garden wall will reveal that it has a hollow curve. This was in order to funnel hot air along the wall to warm the fruit trees grown in its shelter.

Cannon Square is home to one of Retford's more unusual attractions: a Russian cannon. Dating from 1855 and weighing over 2 tons, the cannon was captured by British soldiers at Sebastopol and brought to Retford at the end of the Crimean War. The townsfolk paid for its transportation and, in 1859, after arguments raged about its siting, the cannon was finally placed in the square and named the Earl of Aberdeen after the incumbent Prime Minister. During World War II the cannon was threatened with being melted down to help the war effort and was only saved after a Retford gentleman bought it and hid it until the war was over.

THE TIFFIN BAR

6 Cannon Square, Retford, Nottinghamshire DN22 6PJ
Tel: 01777 704771

Cannon Square in the heart of Retford takes its name from the Russian cannon captured during the Crimean War that stands here. Directly opposite the cannon is Bill and Irene Smith's **Tiffin Bar** which they opened way back in 1957 and is now the longest established eating place in Retford. Their regular menu, together with the specials board, offers a wide variety of dishes with the all day breakfast now one of the most popular dishes. Bill and Irene are assisted by their daughter Sarah and son-in-law Graham; together they make this a really delightful place to eat.

Not far from Cannon Square is, reputedly, the oldest chemist's shop in the country still on its original site. Opened in 1779, Norths Chemists first belonged to a local vet, Francis Clater, whose books on animal medicine and treatment were bestsellers for over 100 years.

One of Retford's most infamous visitors was the highwayman Dick Turpin and several historic inns still stand as a reminder of the romantic days of stage coach travel. Another man who stood and delivered here, though in a more respectable fashion, was John Wesley, who conducted many open air meetings in East Retford.

Whilst in Retford, it is well worth visiting the **Bassetlaw Museum** (free) in Amcott House, Grove Street. This imposing late 18th century town house was once the home of the Whartons, the woollen drapers; Sir Wharton Amcotts, MP for the Borough of East Retford; and the Peglers, the local industrialists. It was extensively restored and opened as a museum for the District of Bassetlaw in 1986. The house is noted for its finely executed internal plasterwork and elegant wrought iron staircase, which the restoration has returned to their full Georgian splendour. The museum has a distinct local emphasis, with displays of local archaeology, civic, social and industrial history, and fine and applied art. Occupying the former service wing of the house, the **Percy Laws Memorial Gallery** has a permanent display of historic Retford civic plate and also hosts short term exhibitions.

AROUND RETFORD

CLUMBER PARK
6 miles N of Edwinstowe off the A614

Clumber Park (NT) was created in 1707

when the 3rd Duke of Newcastle was granted permission to enclose part of the Forest of Sherwood as a hunting ground for Queen Anne. The building of Clumber House began in 1760 though it was much altered in the early 19th century. After a devastating fire in 1879, the house was rebuilt in an Italianate style but, due to the vast expense of its upkeep, Clumber House was demolished in 1938. All that remains today are the foundations.

However, any sense of disappointment is quickly dispelled by the charm of the buildings that remain in this lovely setting. The estate houses with their high pitched gables and massive chimneys are most picturesque. The red-brick stables are particularly fine as they are surmounted by a clocktower crowned by a domed cupola. The inset clock in the tower dates back to 1763 and the stables now house the café and visitor centre.

By far the most striking building on the estate, however, is the **Chapel of St Mary the Virgin,** built by G.F. Bodley in the 1880s. It was commissioned by the 7th Duke of Newcastle to commemorate his coming of age. A fervent Anglo-Catholic, he spent the then-colossal sum of £30,000 on its construction. The church has many elaborate features including some wonderful stone and woodwork.

The 4000-acre Clumber Park is owned by the National Trust and attracts more than a million visitors each year. The man-made lake is particularly lovely and is crossed by a fine classical bridge. Five different roads enter the park and each entrance is marked by an impressive gateway. Most imposing of them all is the Apleyhead Gate, off the A614, which leads into the glorious Duke's Drive. Stretching for a distance of two miles, the drive is the longest double avenue of limes in Europe and contains some 1296 trees.

EATON
2 miles S of Retford on the A638

This small hamlet is believed to be the site of a major Saxon battle in 617AD when King Edwin of Mercia defeated the Northumbrian army. Later it became part of the estate of the Dukes of Newcastle, vast holdings which also incorporated several other nearby villages.

The land now known as **Eaton Wood** and managed by the Nottinghamshire Wildlife Trust, was mentioned in the Domesday Book as an area of pasture woodland and some of the ancient ridges and furrows can still be seen. A wood of mainly ash, elm, and hazel with some oak, Eaton Wood is more important for the plant life it sustains such as moschatel, yellow archangel, and several orchids.

GAMSTON
3 miles S of Retford on the A638

In the time of the Normans, it was recorded that there were three mills and two manors in this small village beside the River Idle. Like Eaton, Gamston later became part of the estate the Dukes of Newcastle. In 1782, under the Duke's patronage, a candlewick factory opened in the village, the first of its kind in the world. Local men and women were employed round the clock. This venture however closed in the mid-19th century

and the ground-breaking factory buildings were demolished in 1854.

EAST DRAYTON
6 miles SE of Retford off the A57

In this small rural village overlooking the River Trent, the architect Nicholas Hawksmoor was born in 1661. He left the village at the age of 18, trained as an architect, and was for many years an assistant to Sir Christopher Wren. He worked on many projects, including the Royal Naval College at Greenwich, and later with Sir John Vanbrugh at Blenheim Palace. Hawksmoor's capabilities tended to be eclipsed by his more celebrated associates, but his outstanding solo achievement was the designing of six elegant London churches.

East Drayton has been designated as a conservation area and several of the older buildings in the village centre have undergone restoration work to bring them back to their former picturesque appearance.

NORTH LEVERTON
5 miles E of Retford off the A620

The correct name for this attractive village is 'North Leverton with Habblesthorpe', a mouthful which has been hailed in the *Guinness Book of Records* as the longest multiple place name in England.

THE QUEENS HOTEL
High Street, East Markham, Newark, Nottinghamshire NG22 0RE
Tel: 01777 870288

The Queens Hotel looks very inviting with its gleaming white walls and tables outside. Originally a farmhouse, it was also once an alehouse with a smithy at the back, before it became an inn. Inside this free house is very cosy and full of character and there's always a warm welcome from mine hosts, Barbara and Chris. Barbara is an accomplished cook and her appetising food is available all day up until 10pm (except Mondays unless it's a Bank Holiday). She serves an extensive menu of home made dishes, including Indian and Chinese, which can be eaten in or taken out. To accompany your meal there's a choice of 3 real ales and a wide range of other popular brews. The entertainment includes dominoes, darts and pool, with Sky sports and a golf society whilst outside is a large beer garden.

The 12th century village Church of St Martin is reached via a bridge over a stream and with its 18th century Dutch gables looks rather like an import from Holland. So too does the splendid **North Leverton Windmill**, the only one in Nottinghamshire still grinding corn. When the mill was built in 1813, it was known as the 'North Leverton Subscription Mill' in acknowledgement of the farmers from four surrounding parishes who subscribed to the cost. Three storeys high, the elegant structure has four sails, one of which was struck by lightning in 1958. Thanks to the efforts of local people, assisted by financial support from the County Council, the mill is now fully operational and visitors can follow the whole milling process in action. If they wish, they can also purchase some of the freshly ground flour.

About 3 miles south of the village, **Sundown Kiddies Adventureland** is a unique theme park designed especially for the under 10s. There's a pet shop where the animals join in and sing a musical chorus; a Witches' Kitchen where the kids are in charge of the gruesome cuisine; rides; an adventure play area; café and much more.

STURTON-LE-STEEPLE
5 miles NE of Retford off the A620

Sturton is a corruption of the word Stretton, meaning 'the town on the street': the street being the Roman road known as Till Bridge Lane which linked Lincoln to Doncaster. The origin of the other part of the name becomes immediately obvious as you approach the village. The splendid tower, with its 12 impressive pinnacles, rises high above the houses and is quite the highest point for miles around in this level landscape. The tower and steeple is all that remains of the village's medieval church which was

destroyed by fire in 1901: the adjoining nave and chancel are early-20th century, constructed using many of the old stones and containing some flame-scorched, but still impressive monuments, salvaged from the older church.

NORTH WHEATLEY
4 miles NE of Retford off the A620

This village is famous for its strawberries which are sought after for their delicious taste and excellent quality. North Wheatley is also home to a peculiar brick house, dated 1673 and with the Cartwright arms above its brick porch. Known as the Old Hall, all the external features, including the vase-like decorations, have been made from bricks and the building is a popular subject for local artists.

CLAYWORTH
4 miles N of Retford on the B1403

An attractive village set beside the Chesterfield Canal, Clayworth has a church that incorporates elements from many centuries: from Saxon foundations to Victorian stained glass windows. One of the church's 17th century Rectors, the Revd William Sampson, compiled a fascinating *Rector's Book,* written on parchment and detailing the day-to-day life of his rural parish in the quarter of a century between 1676 and 1701. His manuscript was published in 1910 but sadly is now out of print and copies are difficult to find.

The church where the Revd Sampson was minister is entered through a porch over which is a sundial inscribed with the words *Our days on earth are but a shadow.* This dispiriting message is re-inforced by one of the memorials inside. A member of the Hartshorne family who died in 1678 is commemorated by a brass depicting Father Time lying on his back with an hour-glass at his feet. All the sand in the glass has trickled into the lower globe. Another impressive monument honours the memory of Humphrey Fitzwilliam, a judge in Tudor times, with a huge stone tomb delicately carved with foliage and a shield of arms.

MATTERSEY
5 miles N of Retford off the B6045

Gringley on the Hill

From the eastern end of the village, a rubbly lane leads down to the sparse ruins of the romantically sited **Mattersey Priory**, founded in 1185 for the Gilbertine Order, the only monastic order to be established by an Englishman, Roger de Mattersey. When the Priory was founded, it had only six canons. Though the number of priests fluctuated over the years, Mattersey was never a wealthy institution: at the time of the Dissolution of the Monasteries only five canons had to be turned out onto the streets.

The original priory buildings at Mattersey were destroyed by fire in 1279 so the remains seen today are of the 14th century dormitory, refectory, and the walls of the Chapel of St Helen. The site is rarely visited by tourists but, with the River Idle flowing nearby, it is a peaceful and picturesque hidden place, well worth seeking out.

GRINGLEY ON THE HILL
6 miles NE of Retford on the A631

Even though the 'hill' it stands on is a mere 82 feet above sea level, Gringley commands some astonishingly wide views over Yorkshire, Lincolnshire, and Nottinghamshire. The best vantage point is Beacon Hill (235ft), on the east side of the village. As the name suggests, Beacon Hill was used as the site for beacon fires designed to warn of impending invasion.

The village Church of St Peter and St Paul dates from the 12th century and one of the church bells is, rather unusually, dated to the time of the Commonwealth. During this period, bells and other decorative items were considered frivolous and were generally dispensed with but, as the parish records show, the people of Gringley did not subscribe to such kill-joy ideas: they also celebrated Christmas in defiance of Puritan edicts forbidding the festival.

MISTERTON
9 miles NE of Retford on the A161

This village owes much of its early prosperity to Charles I. In the 17th century, he appointed the Dutch engineer, Sir Cornelius Vermuyden, to drain the marshes in the area. Famous for building the complex drainage system in East Anglia, Vermuyden and his Dutch workforce again worked to provide excellent arable fields on the reclaimed land which became known as the Isle of Axholme. As a consequence of this work, many of the farms date from this time.

Another improvement to the quality of life in Misterton came in 1777 with the opening of the Chesterfield Canal. It linked the village to other market towns and it was discovered that the clay cut to build the waterway was ideal for brick making - brickworks were opened along the banks of the canal.

Surrounded by old cottages and farm buildings, the village church has a rather stumpy spire, which rises from its tower without a parapet and is known as a broach spire. One notable feature inside the church can be found in the Lady Chapel - a stained glass window designed by John Piper depicting the Crucifixion using the symbols of hands and feet and the Sacred Heart.

BARNBY MOOR
4 miles NW of Retford on the A634

This is one of Nottinghamshire's smallest villages, but in the days of stage coach travel Barnby Moor profited greatly from its position on the Great North Road and

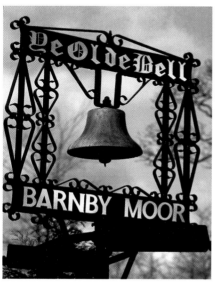

Coaching Inn Sign, Barnby Moor

boasted several fine coaching inns. One of the village inns, the Blue Bell, had 60 rooms and twice as many horses in its stables. Now renamed Ye Olde Bell Hotel, this grand old hostelry is still a huge, sprawling building but the only horses it sees nowadays are on Boxing Day when the local hunt meets here.

WORKSOP

Despite the unattractive modern houses that lead into the town, there are some fine Georgian buildings to be found in Bridge Street. One of the major attractions of Worksop is the **Priory Gatehouse** which is best approached from Potter Street, where the full glory of the 14th century building can be seen. Its great niches house large and beautifully carved statues and the immense entrance is rather reminiscent of a cave opening. Originally the portal to a large Augustinian monastery, the gatehouse together with the Church of St Mary and St Cuthbert is all that remains. There is also a wayside shrine, which makes it a unique ecclesiastical attraction. Today, the upper floor of the gatehouse houses an art gallery and exhibitions are put on here regularly.

The first canal to be built in Nottinghamshire was the **Chesterfield Canal** which runs from Chesterfield in Derbyshire to the River Trent. Some 46 miles long, work on the canal was begun in 1771 and it took 6 years to complete under the supervision of John Varley, the deputy of the great canal engineer, James Brindley. In the mid-1800s, the canal was taken over by the Sheffield and Lincoln Junction Railway, which in 1863 decided to cease maintaining the waterway and allowed it to run down. The collapse of one of the canal's two tunnels, at Norwood in 1908, hastened its decline by effectively cutting off Chesterfield from the rest of the waterway.

During the canal's heyday, in the early 1800s, it was indeed a busy waterway and many buildings lined its route, particularly through Worksop. Pickford's Depository, spanning the canal in the centre of the town, was typical of this time. The trap doors in the stone archway over the canal were used for the loading and unloading of the 'cuckoos', as the narrowboats on the Chesterfield Canal were called.

A recent acquisition by the National Trust, **Mr Straw's House** at 7 Blyth Grove, is quite unique and well worth visiting. The house, together with an endowment of one million pounds, was left to the Trust by William Straw in his will. The Trust's surveyors were surprised to find upon inspection of the Edwardian semi-

detached house that they were actually stepping back in time. Inside, everything had remained untouched since the death in 1932 of William Straw senior, a grocer and seed merchant in Worksop. His wife, who died seven years later, neither altered nor added anything. Nor did her two sons, William and Walter, who lived a bachelor existence at the house. Walter, who took on the family business, died in 1976; his brother, William, in 1990.

In all those years, virtually nothing had changed in the house. The parents' bedroom had been closed up and everything left as it was. A 1932 calendar was still hanging on the wall; William Senior's hats were still perched in the hall; his pipes and tobacco pouch were ready by the fireside.

Worksop Museum, found in Memorial Avenue, is housed in a large purpose-built

THE PARISH OVEN

Worksop Road, Thorpe Salvin, nr Worksop, Nottinghamshire S80 3JU
Tel: 01909 770685

A glance at the hanging baskets festooning the walls of **The Parish Oven** explains why this smart modern pub has won numerous county and national awards for its floral displays. The inn was built in 1972 on the site of an old farmhouse where the oven was used by all the residents of this small village. Hence the name. Recalling that period, there's a splendid old Victorian range in the bar, complete with earthenware hot water bottles! Lots of bygones, prints of the village and the surrounding area, all add to the charm.

The inn is a family run business with Andrew and Cathryn Gough, and Cathryn's father Alan all working together to ensure its smooth running. Good wholesome food is available every day from noon until 9pm and booking is strongly recommended at weekends. Andrew and Cathryn both cook: their specialities are a delicious mixed grill – and value for money. The dining room has no smoking areas and children are welcome up to 9pm. For fair weather days, there's a pleasant beer garden with a children's play area and also a patio. Inside, you'll find TV, pool and fruit machines, and if you're here on a Thursday evening you'll find a pub quiz under way from 8.15pm. A karaoke evening takes place every second Friday and the Gough's also arrange occasional themed evenings.

gallery within the library and museum provided by the Carnegie United Kingdom Trust which was opened in 1938. Within the museum are small exhibitions relating to the history of Worksop and the neighbouring area of landed estates known as the Dukeries, together with a larger display on the Pilgrim Fathers whose roots lay in north Nottinghamshire. Presiding over the Pilgrim Fathers Exhibition is a life-size model of the Pilgrim Elder William Brewster, one of the leaders of the movement.

The Museum is also the start of the **Mayflower Trail** which guides visitors around the local sites connected with the Pilgrim Fathers, including William Brewster's Manor House at Scooby and Gainsborough Old Hall, just across the Trent in Lincolnshire.

To the southeast of the town stretches the glorious expanse of Clumber Park, a former ducal estate which is described more fully in Chapter 10.

AROUND WORKSOP

CRESSWELL
3 miles SW of Worksop on the A616

Cresswell village is actually in Derbyshire but its most famous feature lies just inside the Nottinghamshire border. **Cresswell Crags** form a dramatic limestone gorge pitted with deep, dark and mysterious caves. Here the bones of prehistoric bison, bears, wolves, woolly rhinos and lions twice the size of their modern descendants have been found. Around 45,000BC, humans took over the caves. One of them was a gifted artist as a bone fragment engraved with a fine carving of a horse bears witness. The Vistors' Centre contains some fascinating archaeological

finds and there are some pleasant walks past the lakes to the crags.

SHIREOAKS
2 miles NW of Worksop off the A57

This former mining village takes its name from an ancient oak tree that once stood here overlooking the three shires of Yorkshire, Derbyshire, and Nottinghamshire. In the 1660s, the diarist John Evelyn measured the base of the trunk and recorded a girth of 94ft.

Once a forest village, Shireoaks, like so many others in the area, became a colliery village when a pit was sunk in the 1840s. It was formally opened by its owner, the 4th Duke of Newcastle, who also built the long row of miners' cottages near the church. The church itself, built in medieval style, was a gift of the 5th Duke who persuaded his friend, the Prince of Wales (later Edward VII), to lay the foundation stone in 1861. Also attending this glittering event was William Gladstone, at that time Chancellor of the Exchequer. Two years later, the Duke died. The prince and the politician together paid for the stained glass window honouring his memory.

OLDCOTES
5 miles N of Worksop on the A634

A pretty brook runs through the village and there is also an unusually styled farmhouse with Gothic windows. The Roman Catholic Church of St Helen, with its lovely interior, was built in 1869 by the owner of nearby Hermeston Hall. Whilst the excavations for the church's foundations were being made, the remains of a Roman villa were unearthed complete with a mosaic floor which is thought to have been laid at around the same time as Hadrian's Wall was being built.

THE RIDDELL ARMS

90 Doncaster Road, Carlton-in-Lindrick,
Nottinghamshire S81 9JU
Tel: 01909 730327

Located on the A60 about 4 miles north of Worksop,
The Riddell Arms takes its name from a local 18th
century Squire of that name. It's a substantial red
brick building which was comprehensively
refurbished early in 2000. Richard Marsden took over
when the inn re-opened for business in March and
his affable presence
has very quickly

made The Riddell Arms a popular venue. Children are welcome -
there's a play area for them in the large beer garden with even a
bouncy castle to enjoy during the summer, weather permitting.

Richard is a gifted cook and shares the cooking with his chef.
Their appetising dishes are available throughout the day, (except
Monday & Tuesday afternoons during school term time), and
customers can enjoy this wholesome fare throughout the inn or
outside. Specialities include a Giant Yorkshire Filled Pudding and
there are always special fish dishes on Fridays. The extensive range
of beverages includes a real ale. If you are visiting on a Tuesday, feel
free to join in the pub quiz that starts around 8.30pm. Richard is
currently applying for an entertainment licence so there may well
be live music at The Riddell Arms by the time you read this. The inn
has a large off road car park and accepts all major credit cards except
American Express and Diners.

CARLTON-IN-LINDRICK
3 miles N of Worksop on the A616

This village's name has a delightful
meaning - the "freedmen's enclosure in
the lime wood". In fact it is not one, but
two villages, North Carlton and South
Carlton, the latter of which is the more
ancient. Believed to have been a Saxon
settlement, South Carlton, or Carlton
Barron as it was also called, is home to
the village church. With its massive
Saxon tower, the church is quite awe-
inspiring as it soars above the village. In
Church Lane is the **Old Mill Museum**,
housed in a converted 18th century water
mill. On display are some unusual linen
pictures, used by the Victorians as
educational material, as well as farming
implements and mill machinery.

BLYTH
5 miles NE of Worksop on the A634

A village on the old Great North Road,

Blyth is distinguished by a fine church
and, until the 1970s, also boasted a
stately home, Blyth Hall. The latter was
demolished and the site is now covered
by "executive homes". But the
magnificent **Church of St Mary and St
Martin** still stands, its great tower
surmounted by eight lofty pinnacles
soaring high above the village.

The original church was built around
1100 and much of that Norman building
has survived in all its sturdy strength.
Pevsner thought that there was *"nothing
like Blyth to get a feeling for early Norman
grimness"*. Opinions differ on that, since
the now bare and rough-hewn walls were
originally brightly painted. However,
most agree that the medieval Gothic
additions to the church were eminently
successful. The most treasured possession
here is a 15th century wall painting of the
Last Judgment, one of the largest and
most complete medieval murals in

England. Restored in 1987, the mural has been described as 'unsophisticated', "probably done by a travelling artist", but it is still mightily impressive.

There are many other buildings of note in the village, including a handsome stable block and the former rectory, surmounted by a cupola. Among the redbrick Georgian houses there are also a number of coaching inns providing a reminder that Blyth was once an important staging post on the Great North Road.

At the far end of the village is **St John's Hospital**, originally founded as a leper hospital in the 12th century and later converted into a school. The former schoolhouse stands on a diamond shaped island of grass, obviously dating back to a time when these poor unfortunates (the lepers, not the pupils!) would have been kept isolated from the villagers.

Just to the southwest of the village lies Hodsock Priory (private) and its beautiful Gardens surrounded by parkland and meadows. Although this would seem to be the perfect setting for a medieval monastery, no priory ever stood here. The present house was built in 1829 in the Tudor style to complement the marvellous 16th century gatehouse. The gatehouse is approached across an ancient rectangular moat and, within this area, the gardens have been laid out. The southern arm of the moat was made into a small lake around 1880. **The Snowdrop Garden and Snowdrop Woodland Walk** are open to visitors for 4 weeks from early February

Between Blyth and the nearby village of Styrrup, to the north, lies the Tournament Field. Dating back to the Middle Ages, the field was one of only five in the country to be granted a royal licence by Richard I.

SCROOBY
8 miles NE of Worksop on the A638

'Scroppenthor' existed here before 958, the year that King Edgar granted the land rights to Oscytel, the Archbishop of York. But Scrooby's greatest claim to fame is through William Brewster, a founder member of the Pilgrim Fathers.

It was at Cambridge that Brewster's radical ideas on religion were formed and his spell in the Netherlands, with its toleration of religious views, gave him a new perspective. He returned to England, settling in Scrooby. In 1598 he was summoned before the ecclesiastical court for poor church attendance, but he continued to maintain his battle for religious belief to be free of State control. Because of his unorthodox and outspoken views, Brewster was eventually forced to resign his post. He was imprisoned for a short time in Boston, Lincolnshire, and then made his way back to Amsterdam. After some years he returned to England and became an Elder of the Separatist

Cottages, Scrooby

Church. It was a group of some 40 members of this church who in 1620 boarded the *Mayflower* for the famous voyage which eventually landed at what is now Plymouth, New England. Brewster died there in 1644, at about the age of 77.

Though Brewster is by far the most famous of the Pilgrim Fathers there are two other interesting gentlemen who played an equally important role. One of the youngest members of the movement, William Bradford, who was born into a prominent Yorkshire family in 1589, had to withstand his family's opposition to his beliefs. To escape their disapproval and the penalties for not attending his local church, Bradford joined the group at Scrooby. It was another gentleman, Richard Clyfton, who persuaded Bradford to travel to America on board the Mayflower and it is through his writings that the early days of the colony is known. Clyfton was the rector of Babworth Church (a few miles south of Scrooby) and it was his inspirational addresses which laid the foundations of the movement. He was forced out of his post and became their pastor. Scrooby's 15th century church was used by the

Pilgrim Fathers as their place of worship and is justly proud of its historic connections.

For such a small village, Scrooby has a wealth of other interesting features. There is a stone walled pinfold near the churchyard where straying cattle or sheep were rounded up and only released on payment of a fine. The **Pilgrim Fathers Inn** dates back to 1771, although it was originally called The Saracen's Head. The Monks Mill, which stands on the old course of the River Ryton, is now a private dwelling and despite the name it has never had any close associations with a monastery.

Scrooby was also the scene of a particularly grisly murder. In 1779, a shepherd from North Leverton called John Spencer murdered the local tollbar keeper, William Yealdon, and his mother Mary. Caught in the act of trying to dispose of the bodies in the river nearby, Spencer was later executed at Nottingham. His body was then taken back to Scrooby to hang in chains from a gibbet that had been specially erected near the scene of the crime.

List of Tourist Information Centres

BOSTON

Market Place, Boston,
Lincolnshire PE21 6NN
Tel/Fax: 01205 356656

BRIGG

The Buttercross, Market Place, Brigg,
Lincolnshire DN20 8ER
Tel/Fax: 01652 657053

CLEETHORPES

42-43 Alexandra Road, Cleethorpes,
Lincolnshire DN35 8LE
Tel: 01472 323111 Fax: 01472 323112

GRANTHAM

The Guildhall Centre, St Peter's Hill,
Grantham, Lincolnshire NG31 6PZ
Tel: 01476 566444

LINCOLN

9 Castle Square, Lincoln,
Lincolnshire LN1 3AA
Tel: 01522 529828

LOUTH

The New Market Hall, off Cornmarket,
Louth, Lincolnshire LN11 9PY
Tel/Fax: 01507 609289

MABLETHORPE

The Dunes Theatre, Central Promenade,
Mablethorpe, Lincolnshire LN12 1RG
Tel: 01507 472496 Fax: 01507 478765

NEWARK

The Gilstrap Centre, Castlegate, Newark,
Nottinghamshire NG24 1BG
Tel: 01636 678962 Fax: 01636 612274

NOTTINGHAM

1-4 Smithy Row, Nottingham,
Nottinghamshire NG1 2BY
Tel: 0115 915 5330 Fax: 0115 915 5323

OLLERTON

Sherwood Heath, Ollerton Roundabout,
Ollerton, Nottinghamshire NG22 9DR
Tel/Fax: 01623 824545

RETFORD

Amcott House, 40 Grove Street, Retford,
Nottinghamshire DN22 6LD
Tel/Fax: 01777 860780

SKEGNESS

Embassy Centre, Grand Parade, Skegness,
Lincolnshire PE25 2UG
Tel: 01754 764821

SLEAFORD

The Mill, Money's Yard, Carre Street,
Sleaford, Lincolnshire NG34 7TW
Tel/Fax: 01529 414294

SPALDING

Ayscoughfee Hall Museum, Churchgate,
Spalding, Lincolnshire PE11 2RA
Tel: 01775 725468 Fax: 01775 762715

STAMFORD

The Arts Centre, 27 St Mary's Street,
Stamford, Lincolnshire PE9 2DL
Tel: 01780 755611

WEST BRIDGFORD

County Hall, Loughborough Road, West
Bridgford, Nottinghamshire NG2 7QP
Tel: 0115 977 3558 Fax: 0115 977 3886

WORKSOP

Worksop Library, Memorial Avenue,
Worksop, Nottinghamshire S80 2BP
Tel/Fax: 01909 501148

Index of Towns, Villages and Places of Interest

List of Advertisers

Hidden Places Order Form

To order any of our publications just fill in the payment details below and complete the order form *overleaf*. For orders of less than 4 copies please add £1 per book for postage and packing. Orders over 4 copies are P & P free.

Please Complete Either:

I enclose a cheque for £ [   ] made payable to Travel Publishing Ltd

Or:

Card No: [   ]

Expiry Date: [   ]

Signature: [   ]

NAME: [   ]

ADDRESS: [   ]

POSTCODE: [   ]

TEL NO: [   ]

Please either send, telephone or e-mail your order to:

Travel Publishing Ltd, 7a Apollo House, Calleva Park, Aldermaston, Berkshire RG7 8TN

Tel : 0118 981 7777   Fax: 0118 982 0077

e-mail: karen@travelpublishing.co.uk

	PRICE	QUANTITY	VALUE
HIDDEN PLACES REGIONAL TITLES			
Cambs & Lincolnshire	£7.99	....	....
Chilterns	£8.99	....	....
Cornwall	£8.99	....	....
Derbyshire	£7.99	....	....
Devon	£8.99	....	....
Dorset, Hants & Isle of Wight	£8.99	....	....
East Anglia	£8.99	....	....
Gloucestershire & Wiltshire	£7.99	....	....
Heart of England	£7.99	....	....
Hereford, Worcs & Shropshire	£7.99	....	....
Highlands & Islands	£7.99	....	....
Kent	£8.99	....	....
Lake District & Cumbria	£8.99	....	....
Lancashire & Cheshire	£8.99	....	....
Lincolnshire & Nottinghamshire	£8.99	....	....
Northumberland & Durham	£8.99	....	....
Somerset	£7.99	....	....
Sussex	£7.99	....	....
Thames Valley	£7.99	....	....
Yorkshire	£7.99	....	....
HIDDEN PLACES NATIONAL TITLES			
England	£9.99	....	....
Ireland	£9.99	....	....
Scotland	£9.99	....	....
Wales	£9.99	....	....
HIDDEN INNS TITLES			
Heart of England	£5.99	....	....
Lancashire & Cheshire	£5.99	....	....
South	£5.99	....	....
South East	£5.99	....	....
South and Central Scotland	£5.99	....	....
Wales	£5.99	....	....
Welsh Borders	£5.99	....	....
West Country	£5.99	....	....

*For orders of less than 4 copies please
add £1 per book for postage & packing.
Orders over 4 copies P & P free.*

181

Hidden Places Order Form

To order any of our publications just fill in the payment details below and complete the order form *overleaf*. For orders of less than 4 copies please add £1 per book for postage and packing. Orders over 4 copies are P & P free.

Please Complete Either:

I enclose a cheque for £ [_____] made payable to Travel Publishing Ltd

Or:

Card No: [_____]

Expiry Date: [_____]

Signature: [_____]

NAME: [_____]

ADDRESS: [_____]

POSTCODE: [_____]

TEL NO: [_____]

Please either send, telephone or e-mail your order to:

Travel Publishing Ltd, 7a Apollo House, Calleva Park, Aldermaston, Berkshire RG7 8TN

Tel : 0118 981 7777   Fax: 0118 982 0077

e-mail: karen@travelpublishing.co.uk

	PRICE	QUANTITY	VALUE

HIDDEN PLACES REGIONAL TITLES

Cambs & Lincolnshire	£7.99
Chilterns	£8.99
Cornwall	£8.99
Derbyshire	£7.99
Devon	£8.99
Dorset, Hants & Isle of Wight	£8.99
East Anglia	£8.99
Gloucestershire & Wiltshire	£7.99
Heart of England	£7.99
Hereford, Worcs & Shropshire	£7.99
Highlands & Islands	£7.99
Kent	£8.99
Lake District & Cumbria	£8.99
Lancashire & Cheshire	£8.99
Lincolnshire & Nottinghamshire	£8.99
Northumberland & Durham	£8.99
Somerset	£7.99
Sussex	£7.99
Thames Valley	£7.99
Yorkshire	£7.99

HIDDEN PLACES NATIONAL TITLES

England	£9.99
Ireland	£9.99
Scotland	£9.99
Wales	£9.99

HIDDEN INNS TITLES

Heart of England	£5.99
Lancashire & Cheshire	£5.99
South	£5.99
South East	£5.99
South and Central Scotland	£5.99
Wales	£5.99
Welsh Borders	£5.99
West Country	£5.99

For orders of less than 4 copies please add £1 per book for postage & packing. Orders over 4 copies P & P free.

Hidden Places Reader Reaction

The *Hidden Places* research team would like to receive reader's comments on any visitor attractions or places reviewed in the book and also recommendations for suitable entries to be included in the next edition. This will help ensure that the *Hidden Places* series continues to provide its readers with useful information on the more interesting, unusual or unique features of each attraction or place ensuring that their stay in the local area is an enjoyable and stimulating experience. To provide your comments or recommendations would you please complete the forms below and overleaf as indicated and send to:

The Research Department, Travel Publishing Ltd,
7a Apollo House, Calleva Park, Aldermaston, Reading, RG7 8TN.

Your Name:

Your Address:

Your Telephone Number:

Please tick as appropriate: Comments ☐   Recommendation ☐

Name of *"Hidden Place"*:

Address:

Telephone Number:

Name of Contact:

Hidden Places Reader Reaction

Comment or Reason for Recommendation: